My Journey to Lhasa

MADAME ALEXANDRA DAVID-NEEL

My Journey to Lhasa

Alexandra David-Neel

With a New Foreword by
HIS HOLINESS THE DALAI LAMA

and a New Introduction by
DIANA N. ROWAN

BEACON PRESS
BOSTON

Beacon Press
25 Beacon Street
Boston, Massachusetts 02108-2892

Beacon Press books
are published under the auspices of
the Unitarian Universalist Association of Congregations.

99 98   8 7 6 5 4

Library of Congress Cataloging-in-Publication Data

David-Neel, Alexandra, 1868–1969.
[Voyage d'une Parisienne à Lhassa. English]
My journey to Lhasa / Alexandra David-Neel with a new foreword
by His Holiness the Dalai Lama and a new introduction
by Diana N. Rowan.
p. cm.
Includes bibliographical references.
ISBN 0-8070-5903-X
1. Lhasa (China)—Description and travel. 2. David-Neel,
Alexandra, 1868–1969—Journeys—China—Lhasa. I. Title.
DS785.D27813 1993
915.1'5—dc20   93-16631

*To all those
who knowingly or unconsciously
have in any way helped me
during my long tramps
with loving thankfulness
this account of my fifth journey
in Thibetan land
is dedicated*

FOREWORD

IT HAS never been easy to reach Tibet. The encircling high mountains, the vast extent of its sparsely populated open spaces, and the climatic extremes at such an altitude made it all but inaccessible. In addition, for too long Tibet cherished its isolation. Foreigners were actively discouraged from entering the country. A sense of material and spiritual self-sufficiency allowed conservative elements among Tibetan policymakers to overlook the importance of friendship with the outside world. We paid a heavy price for this aloofness later.

Of the few foreign travelers who managed to penetrate Tibet's cautious defenses in the early part of this century, the distinguished Frenchwoman Alexandra David-Neel was exceptional. Not only were independent women travelers like her unusual, but Europeans versed in Sanskrit and Buddhist philosophy, who also spoke Tibetan and could communicate with those they met, were extremely rare. What made her unique, however, is that she reached Lhasa.

Her book recounting her experiences, which began near my own birthplace in Amdo, continued for some years in Kham, and culminated in her attending the Great Prayer Festival in Lhasa, was first published more than sixty years ago. Its great merit is that it conveys the authentic flavor of Tibet as she found it, described with affectionate humor. Perhaps scholars and historians today would challenge many of the author's opinions, but this does not affect her work's intrinsic worth. Sadly, due to changes imposed on the Land of Snows and its people in recent years, much of what David-Neel describes is now lost forever, which only increases the value of her account.

FOREWORD

This new edition of *My Journey to Lhasa*, with its tale of adventure and vivid portrayal of Tibet, will surely delight a whole new generation of readers.

Tenzin Gyatso, The Fourteenth Dalai Lama
December 7, 1992

NEW INTRODUCTION

Learn Tibetan!
The Thirteenth Dalai Lama,
to Alexandra David-Neel
Sikkim, 1912

Repression will never crush the determination
of any people to live in freedom and dignity.
His Holiness Tenzin Gyatso
The Fourteenth Dalai Lama
Nobel Peace Prize Laureate, 1989

"Lha gyalo! De thamched pham!"[1] Conquering a treacherous
19,000-foot Himalayan pass in the dead of night, winter 1924,
Alexandra David-Neel paused in her final surge toward the forbidden city of Lhasa to echo the ancient Tibetan cry of victory—
"The gods have won! The demons are vanquished." But she did
so silently. It is the Tibetan custom to shout it loudly from the
mountain summits, celebrating the triumph of universal good—
but only in daylight. It doesn't do to tempt fate and the darker
forces after sundown. David-Neel complied with this custom,
and, as she recounts in her compelling narrative, she looked out
over the moonlit glaciers and peaks and called to the six directions
with the old Sanskrit mantra, *"Subham astu sarvajagatam."* May
all beings find happiness. In Tibetan, it is offered thus: *"Gé-o!*
Gé-o! Gé-o!"[2]

The myriad beings her solitary blessing might have touched in
this vast realm of Tibet could have included the nobles and no-

---

[1] The spelling of Tibetan words sometimes varies, especially over time.
David-Neel spells this phrase differently on two occasions in her memoir. Lodi
Gyari, a contemporary Tibetan leader and Special Envoy to His Holiness the
Dalai Lama, suggests this spelling as the most accurate.

[2] Conversation with a Tibetan lama, December 1992.

ix

mads alike, the merchants and tenant farmers, craftsmen and courtesans, and the legions of monks and nuns in Tibet's 6,254 monastery-universities. Many of these were great golden-roofed cities with massive libraries and temples full of ancient Buddhist texts and scriptures, priceless *thangkas* (sacred paintings on silk), and thousands of turquoise and jewel-studded sacred figures exquisitely crafted in gold and silver: Buddha, Avalokiteshvara (the male bodhisattva of infinite compassion), Chenrezig (who is held to be reincarnated in the Dalai lamas), and Tara, the primordial Tibetan Mother Protector, simultaneously tender and powerful, held to be the equal of Buddha in wisdom and compassion.

David-Neel's blessing in the thin, bitter cold air of that peak echoed the core of Buddhist belief, the concept of Bodhicitta—a respect for and active devotion to the welfare of all beings and forms of life, from the human animal to the smallest insect, as well as vegetation and the land itself. Tibet's land was 600,000 square miles in area, more than two-thirds the size of India and the same size as the entire European community. David-Neel's mantra included the thousands of square miles of virgin forest on the High Plateau, the massive 500- to 800-year-old cypress and cedar, the groves of rare 3,000-year-old trees and botanical wonders in the more temperate zones of the "Roof of the World." It included the elusive *sazik* (the snow leopard), the great herds of *drong* (Tibetan wild yaks), *kiang* (wild ass), and *gowa* (Tibetan gazelles). And her words reached out to the flocks of stately crane, the eagles, and other wild birds she had glimpsed in her years of traveling through Tibet.

Her prayer touched an ancient race. In the words of the present, the fourteenth, Dalai Lama, "Tibetan history goes back at least four thousand years. There were more than twenty kings before Buddhism came."[3] Buddhism came to Tibet from India around 600 A.D.

United for roughly a thousand years as an independent nation, Tibet's unique and complex culture was informed by the teach-

[3] His Holiness the Dalai Lama, *My Tibet*, photographs and introduction by Galen Rowell (Berkeley: University of California Press, 1990), p. 116.

ings of Shakyamuni Buddha, with its laity and clergy alike making Buddhist prayer and practice the core of daily life. Even the humblest farmers' houses had their own small altars, while noble families had ornate chapels rivaling those of monasteries.

The spiritual heart of the country, the Potala Palace in Lhasa, was another sacred city unto itself. The "Abode of Buddhas" and successive Dalai Lamas, the spiritual and temporal rulers of Tibet since the seventeenth century, the Potala had been built on a high promontory in the middle of Lhasa by the "Great Fifth" Dalai Lama, and still commands the city, an enormous complex of shrine rooms, temple sanctuaries, administrative offices, and living quarters. Indeed, David-Neel's exclamation could have touched even the Thirteenth Dalai Lama, then in residence in the Potala. She had had an audience with him in 1912 when he lived briefly in exile in Sikkim, while Tibet fought off yet another Chinese invasion. She was the first Western woman to have been received by *any* Dalai Lama, and he questioned her, at first suspiciously—how could she have become a Buddhist without a master? Then, convinced by her deep knowledge, her spirit, and her stated scholarly objective of correcting certain Western misconceptions about the religious doctrines of Tibet, he conversed with her at length, deciding that she must be an "emanation" of Dorje Phagmo, a powerful thunderbolt being, Tibet's only female incarnation.

Perhaps the Dalai Lama sensed, in this extraordinary European woman—a rational Buddhist, as she called herself, and a passionate scholar and explorer of Asia—her destiny as a pivotal figure between two monumentally different cultures. He left her with one command: "Learn Tibetan." It was a directive she followed with enthusiasm, and her interlocutor's successor, Tenzin Gyatso, the Fourteenth Dalai Lama, would eventually call David-Neel "an enthusiastic Buddhist, the first to introduce the real Tibet to the West."

What Alexandra David-Neel means to our generation, particularly in light of the tragedy that has befallen Tibet in the past four decades under the latest Chinese onslaught, can be sensed in that moment on the frozen peak as much as in her eventual historic triumph as the first Western woman to enter the holy city of Lhasa. By that point in her extraordinary life, David-Neel had lived in Tibetan monasteries, translating the sacred Sanskrit texts as yet unknown to the West, had debated esoteric spiritual matters with high lamas, and had begun writing serious philosophical studies of Tibetan Buddhism. Yet at that moment she was transmitting the same expression of Bodhicitta that now, almost seventy years later, millions of Western Buddhists of various lineages—Zen, Vipassana, Tibetan—strive to achieve in their own lives. (There are an estimated twelve million Buddhists in America alone, and their numbers are growing.)

As the Fourteenth Dalai Lama has said, "I preach a very simple religion, that of kindness and compassion," adding that one needs no ornate temple for this, only the daily work and relationships of our lives in which to practice.[4] It is an exquisitely simple religion; but one infinitely challenging to realize fully— as shown by the persistent way greed, hatred, and delusion (the "three poisons") afflict both one's own personal life and that of the entire human race.

"Learn Tibetan!" There is a phrase in Tibetan, *"Lha-khang gi kyi zahm-bu-ling gi kyi chik-ba ray,"* which means the center of the temple and the center of the world are the same. One might well find some solitary spot and ponder this riddle (possibly a "koan," to borrow a Japanese Zen term). Alexandra David-Neel offers us clues—in her transcendent moment upon the high pass as well as in the years spent studying and meditating in monasteries and in her solitary hermitage or traveling in caravan, content with her rough tent in the wilds.

Her life has also inspired thousands of modern women—and men—in the courage, determination, and sheer physical fortitude it took for this woman, delicately reared in Paris and Brussels, to tackle some of the roughest terrain and climate in the world—and survive. All too often, given the primitive travel conditions, disease, frequent outbreaks of war, and the ever-

---

[4] Sidney Pilburn, ed., *The Dalai Lama: A Policy of Kindness*, foreword by Senator Clairborne Pell (Ithaca: Snow Lion Publications, 1990).

present danger of border control and random banditry, survival was by a hairbreadth. And though her life was monumental in the perspective of history, her daily reality—some of which she records in her travelogues—was certainly more a matter of mud, vermin, intermittent illness, excruciating discomfort and cold, and a constant worry about finding money enough to continue her explorations.

Contemporary women have found in David-Neel a valuable role model, recalling her ringing declaration, "It is not in my nature to admit defeat!" (In Tibetan: "*Ngay rangshi la phamgoon khyerdo med!*") The American mountaineer and biochemist Arlene Blum is one example. She led the first women's expedition to conquer Annapurna in the Himalayas in the late 1970s, a riveting adventure which she recounts in her book *Annapurna: A Woman's Place* (Sierra Club Books, 1980), and held David-Neel's courage as exemplary. She later planned treks in the early 1980s to follow in David-Neel's footsteps.

David-Neel's physical determination and survival skills also impressed China Galland, one of the founders of Women in the Wilderness. Through camping, mountain climbing, white-water rafting, and other wilderness programs in the 1970s and 1980s, Galland helped women develop not only athletic prowess but a new sense of emotional stamina and independence. For many, it was their first real experience of testing their own leadership skills. Galland, a Tibetan Buddhist, went on to focus her spiritual practice on the powerful Tibetan mother deity, Tara, and wrote a fascinating study of her own spiritual journey, *Longing for Darkness: Tara and the Black Madonna* (Viking Penguin, 1990).

For countless other women and men, Alexandra David-Neel has been the first introduction, as the Fourteenth Dalai Lama said, to the "real Tibet." But what was the historical Tibet, as she knew it from study and exploration, and what is it now, as defined under the present harsh military rule of the People's Republic of China?

"*Ritse thamched ngatsoe sung mo yin!*" The peaks are our sentinels. So ran a proud old Tibetan adage, when foreign access to the "Roof of the World" still had minimal impact. The Jesuit and

NEW INTRODUCTION

Capuchin missionaries and the occasional layman tough enough to survive the grueling journey were tolerated until the mid-nineteenth century, when the borders were sealed against the burgeoning Russian and British empires. Tibet continued to deal with intermittent Chinese incursions from an increasingly vulnerable position of isolation from other world powers.

Tibet had developed into a great empire under the reign of King Song-tsen Gampo during the seventh century. With his nation strategically located between Tibet's ancestral enemy, China, to the north and east and India to the south, Song-tsen Gampo was quintessentially astute when he married a Chinese princess, an alliance much underlined by the present People's Republic of China. In fact, the Tibetan king also married two other princesses for good measure—one Tibetan and one Nepalese.

Song-tsen Gampo also promulgated the first comprehensive system of laws in Tibet, based on the Buddhist moral laws of India, with no relation to the Confucian canon of Chinese tradition. As Tibet scholar Robert Thurman points out, only a Western-educated Tibetan has ever even heard of Confucius. The Tibetan national sense of history draws from the wellspring of Buddhist spiritual and ethical values, and every Tibetan government since the Yarlung dynasty in the seventh century has received its legitimacy through its active connection to the "Buddha dharma."[5]

Still warlike, however, the early Tibetan empire was viewed as a great threat to the Chinese and a major reason for building the Great Wall. Tibet conquered the T'ang capital at Chang-an (Sian) in 763 A.D. and was considered a formidable presence by Mongol emperors, Kublai Khan among them, and by Manchu emperors, who regarded good relations with the Tibetans as beneficial in dealing with the ferocious Mongols. Numerous wars and stone-carved treaties between Tibet and China attest to the distinctness of the empires. Both fell under the Mongol yoke in the thirteenth century. Though proudly denying being conquered, Tibet submitted in 1207 to the famous "priest-patron"

[5] Robert Thurman, "An Outline of Tibetan Culture," *Cultural Survival Quarterly*, vol. 12, no. 1 (1988).

NEW INTRODUCTION

relationship between its Sakyapa lamas and the Mongol emperors. China was overrun about 1280. Tibetans regained their freedom almost a century later, establishing a new lineage in 1358, while the Chinese drove out the Mongols a decade after that, establishing the native Ming dynasty.

Present Chinese claims to Tibet stem from this era, prompting acerbic scholarly retorts that under similar argument, India could claim Burma as its own, since both were once part of the British Empire! Ming and Ching dynasty claims that Tibet was a "vassal state" should be examined, advises the Tibetologist H. E. Richardson, in light of similar assertions by the Chinese that Holland, Portugal, Russia, Britain, and the Papacy were also tributaries![6]

As summarized in a report to the United Nations Commission on Human Rights, Tibet suffered further intervention by a Central Asian (not Chinese) emperor, K'ang Hsi, in the early eighteenth century.[7] At that time it lost control of the eastern and northern provinces of Kham and Amdo, inhabited almost entirely by ethnic Tibetans, thus establishing some two centuries of what the Chinese see as their suzerainty over Tibet. Largely recaptured by the Tibetans in 1865, the territories were again briefly lost to Chinese control during 1911–12 (the year David-Neel met the Thirteenth Dalai Lama in Sikkim). But the bitter fighting that year led to yet another expulsion of the Chinese, whose military strength had been weakened by the fall of the Manchu dynasty in 1911.

Tibet, meanwhile, also had to deal with interference by the British, whose colonial influence was increasingly felt along the Himalayan border in the latter half of the eighteenth century. Though border relations were generally peaceful, the expedition of Captain Younghusband, whose British troops shot their way into Lhasa in 1904, was aimed primarily at blocking any potential Russian influence; unfortunately, it also had a severe desta-

[6] H. E. Richardson, *A Short History of Tibet* (New York: E. P. Dutton & Co., 1962).

[7] Scientific Buddhist Association, *Tibet: The Facts*, a report to the United Nations Commission on Human Rights, ed. Paul Ingram (Dharamsala: Tibetan Young Buddhist Association, 1990).

bilizing impact and severely increased hostilities between Tibet and China. Eastern Tibet had to fight off Chinese forces again in 1918 and in the 1930s, although Tibet's independence was confirmed at the Treaty of Simla (1914). Though China repudiated the treaty, the U.N. human rights report notes, "the two remaining signatories [Tibet and British India] . . . then abrogated the rights and privileges claimed by the Chinese in Tibet. For the next thirty-eight years Tibet was entirely independent of China."

This, then, was the volatile political climate of the country that had drawn Alexandra David-Neel "since infancy," according to her. Her infancy and upbringing were scarcely designed to produce a world-class scholar and wilderness explorer. David-Neel was born in 1868, in Paris, to a family whose background was the very model of bourgeois respectability. Though her father, Louis David, was an intellectual engaged in politics and journalism, he had married stability itself—a complacent Belgian from a wealthy and socially prominent Brussels family. The young Alexandra David was raised by a succession of governesses and formally educated in a Calvinist boarding school and a Catholic convent. Swathed in Belgian lace and steeped in etiquette, she would most likely have been destined to a life of dance cards, formal dinner parties, and of course an equally suitable marriage. Instead, she seems to have shown a fierce rebellious instinct from the earliest time she could run away from her nurses, "to find her very own tree," she said, to when she left to explore the open road.

Ruth Middleton notes in her biography *Alexandra David-Neel: Portrait of an Adventurer* (Shambhala, 1989) that David-Neel's interest in comparative religion had been established by the age of six, possibly through her awareness of her father's Protestantism and her mother's devout Catholicism. At the convent school of Bois Fleuri in Brussels, where she herself records that she first studied "Buddhist mythology" at age thirteen, her bedroom held both a figure of Christ and a Chinese porcelain Buddha. Thanks to the vigorous nineteenth-century commercial trade between British colonialists and the Orient, Buddhist objects of art were already filling museums and private collections in Europe—and a growing number of Buddhist texts became available in translation as Alexandra's interest deepened and matured.

Investigating a host of spiritual enclaves and disciplines, including the Theosophical Society in Paris, she delved further into Buddhism and other oriental philosophies and steeped herself particularly in the rich offering of texts and sacred art she found in the Musée Guimet. Making her first journey in search of Buddhist Asia, she traveled to India in 1891. She then spent some years, surprisingly, as a light-opera singer and journalist, finally marrying dapper Philip Neel, an affluent, but quite conventional, French engineer in Tunis. It instantly seemed a mistake, given David-Neel's passion for independence, but in retrospect a mutually inspired one. Though she struggled with her aversion to domesticity for seven years (not days, as detractors have claimed) before she finally left again for Asia, suffering physical ailments and nervous depression in the interim, her childhood drive finally prevailed. As she said of herself even as a five-year-old, "I craved to go beyond the garden gate, to follow the road that passed it by, and to set out for the Unknown."

Philip and Alexandra's story could have ended there; yet he continued to support her explorations, though sporadically, and to act more or less as her literary agent as her body of firsthand research of the Orient grew. She wrote almost daily to Philip, whose last name she bore for the rest of her life, sending great packets of letters and manuscripts from Asia; it took months for them to reach him in Paris or Tunis, where they had established a home. Her voluminous journals and notes would eventually provide material for scores of articles and major book-length studies of Tibetan Buddhism and culture. (Among those available in English are *Buddhism: Its Doctrines and Methods*, *Initiations and Initiates in Tibet*, *Magic and Mystery in Tibet*, *The Power of Nothingness*, as well as this book, her most famous, *My Journey to Lhasa*.)

Though separated for years by geography and by her avowed allergic reaction to confinement, Philip and Alexandra remained closest friends, he her "*bien cher Mouchy*" and an emotional anchor to the country and culture of her birth. As she told him in one characteristically frank letter, "I believe you are the only person in the world for whom I have a feeling of attachment but I am not made for married life." Philip Neel could have repudiated her at any time for abandonment of her expected marital duties, another fact her detractors ignored as they persisted in heaping cynical pity on the poor fellow; but his phenomenon of a wife clearly fascinated him. Whatever the dynamics, this extraordinary relationship persisted for four decades until Philip Neel's death in 1941.

Alexandra David-Neel had her first taste of "Thibet" in 1912, just a brief glimpse over the Sikkimese border toward the massive trans-Himalayan tableland beyond—but she was awed by the "calm solitudes" that told her she "had come home after a tiring, cheerless pilgrimage." She made more forays a few miles over the border, and in the winter of 1914, while world-war clouds brewed in the West, she stayed with nuns who lived a rugged reclusive life in their small monastery of Chorten Nyima, or "Sun Shrine," high in the Himalayas.

Barred by the British from travel into Bhutan, much less Tibet during these years, she found spiritual companionship and a political patron in the Sikkimese crown prince Sidkeong. Together they discussed Buddhist philosophy and sketched plans for reforming and refining Buddhism as practiced in his country. In 1914, David-Neel was presented by the monks of Sikkim with the consecrated robes of a "lamina," a female lama, making her in their eyes an ordained Buddhist clergywoman. Making the rounds of monasteries, she expounded on esoteric doctrine to the young monks. Her growing renown, meanwhile, added to British officials' unease.

After Prince Sidkeong's sudden death under suspicious political circumstances, she took solace in a mountain hermitage she built herself high in the Himalayas of Sikkim, where she meditated and studied for a year and a half under the tutelage of a respected lama, the Gomchen (Great Hermit) of Lachen. Though she would later spend productive years studying and pursuing scholarly research in Tibetan monasteries, she felt the deepest regard for hermit-lamas like the Gomchen, who had renounced the mundane world and even the complex political establishments most monasteries represented. As she wrote, "I esteen unreservedly . . . those yogis who have broken with all nursery games and who live alone with their audacious thoughts."

In 1916 she finally forged into southeastern Tibet at the invitation of the Panchen Lama, second in spiritual rank only to the Dalai Lama in Lhasa; he was also Abbot of Tashilhunpo, the great monastic university-city near the thriving Tibetan market center of Shigatse. The Panchen Lama evidently gave the orientalist-lamina a cordial reception and held her in high regard. He made Tashilhunpo's immense libraries accessible to her and showed her every corner of its temples, great halls, and palaces, where gold, turquoise, and silver decorated the altars, tombs, and even doors, and intricate frescoes depicted the myriad deities and protectors of Tibet. She was entertained by the Panchen Lama and his mother, with whom she remained longtime friends, in the lavish style of high lamas and officials, using jewel-encrusted household items every day. David-Neel preferred, however, the sacred texts of Tashilhunpo, works of art in themselves, and challenging philosophical conversation with the monks to this lavish lifestyle. "The special psychic atmosphere of the place enchanted me," she later wrote. "I have seldom enjoyed such blissful hours."

In 1916, when David-Neel visited Tashilhunpo, it had 3,800 monks, half of whom were scholars—a point to remember when one considers the devastation of Tibet's 6,254 monasteries and of its culture in general a scant few decades later. Barbara and Michael Foster, in their comprehensive and deeply perceptive biography *Forbidden Journey: The Life of Alexandra David-Neel* (Harper & Row, 1987), cite both her joy during this visit and the demanding high standards she set for herself. "My journey to Shigatse has also revealed to me the scholastic Tibet, its monastic universities, its immense libraries," she wrote. "How many things are left for me to learn!"

Declining the Panchen Lama's offer to remain indefinitely under his patronage (her astute political sense told her that he did not have the power to countermand Lhasa's veto on foreigners), she returned to Sikkim with honorary lama's robes and the equivalent of a Doctor of Philosophy from Tashilhunpo. She also found herself slapped with a deportation notice from the British colonial authorities, who were infuriated by her insouciant disregard of their no-entry edict. Jealousy from local Western missionary groups may also have fanned the flames; angry at being barred from "the mission field of Tibet, rife with infidels," the Fosters note that they probably "burned the ears" of local British officials. David-Neel later wrote of the British, "What right had they to erect barriers around a country which was not even lawfully theirs?" She held her successful entry into Lhasa as much a "witty Parisian joke" upon them as a personal triumph of her own.

Thrown out of Sikkim, parted from her lama-teacher, as well as her beloved mountain hermitage which was demolished behind her, she left in low spirits to travel in Japan and Korea, convinced she would never see Tibet again. "I have a homesickness for a country that isn't mine," she declared soon after. "The steppes, the solitude, the eternal snows and the big skies up there haunt me. . . . One remains permanently engulfed in the silence where only the wind sings, in the solitudes almost naked of greenery, the chaos of fantastic rocks, dizzying peaks and horizons of blinding light."

But she had taken with her a young Sikkimese monk, Aphur Yongden, who would become her adopted son and travel with her the rest of his life. Years later, he would be with her at the famous iron bridge in Kham poised on their final push toward Lhasa where she took an oath not to be turned back again and vowed to show "what the will of a woman can do!"

Ironically, when they finally reached Lhasa, there was no reception by the Dalai Lama and his pontiffs, no tour of scholarly treasures, no honorary lama's robes. The only way David-Neel and Yongden succeeded was to travel disguised as *najorpas*, as two of the countless beggar-pilgrims who journeyed toward Lhasa and the other holy places of Tibet. So with her face blackened by cooking-pot soot, yak-hair pigtails, and a traditional fur hat topping her ragged attire, she and Yongden trekked onward with the lightest backpacks possible.

David-Neel's account of the journey is short on statistics, exact dates, and geographical detail; she dared take no surveying equipment, camera, or anything else that might have marked her, possibly fatally, as a *philing*, a foreigner. Even her small compass could have betrayed her, and she kept it hidden under her rags—along with a pistol and a prince's ransom in heavy gold jewelry, a gift from Sidkeong. Though she and Yongden nearly starved several times on their mid-winter trek over the mountains, she refused then and in years that followed ever to part with a single piece of the jewelry. When they finally slipped into Lhasa, they were able to lose themselves in the great swarm of pilgrims celebrating the joyous Tibetan New Year and religious festival of Monlam. Although because of historical circumstances she was denied the opportunity to speak again with the Thirteenth Dalai Lama and other scholar-monks, she was still able to mingle with the Tibetan people—since she had indeed learned Tibetan—and experience the phenomenal pageantry of their culture.

It is said that the hardship of a journey invests the pilgrim path with its power and that each step is an offering. In this light, David-Neel's whole life and her work at each step are offerings to all of us—every sentient being without exception. Her story is as much the chronicle of an inner journey as it is the most tantalizing travelogue about a terrain that is largely unknown to us.

The tragedy of the story is that the Tibet Alexandra David-Neel experienced has been virtually destroyed. Since the military invasion by the People's Republic of China in 1949 (euphemistically termed by the Chinese as "the peaceful liberation" or as reuniting Tibet with the Motherland), more than 1.2 million Tibetans have died in wartime violence, by execution, the effects of long imprisonment, torture, starvation, or suicide. Forced abortions and sterilizations were once a policy. There are vast areas now, particularly in Kham and Amdo, where most Tibetan families lack any male members over the age of thirty-five.[8]

This overwhelming loss of life has been termed the Buddhist Holocaust. The Fourteenth Dalai Lama escaped it in 1959, and since then tens of thousands of refugees have followed him into exile. Due to the massive population influx of Han Chinese, more than seven million—Tibet's population is about six million—the Tibetans are now a minority in their own country and treated as a distinctly inferior one. The destruction of their social infrastructure and the systematic denial of medical care, education, and job training, despite Chinese claims to the contrary, have seriously jeopardized future generations of young Tibetans.[9]

Just as significantly, the whole system of values on which Tibetan culture has been based is changing. All but a handful of the country's thousands of monastery-universities, which formed the intellectual, spiritual, and indeed the political heart of the nation, were bombed or battered literally by hand into rubble, 80 percent of the destruction taking place *before* the Cultural Revolution. Out of the 600,000 monks and nuns in those monasteries, scholars estimate only 7,000 survived. Many of them were executed or died in prison. The townspeople were forced to destroy and desecrate what was left behind. Sacred mani stones with scriptures carved into them were used as paving blocks and Tibetans were forced to walk on them; centuries-old sacred texts were plowed in with manure; and holy places such as the Jokhang Temple in Lhasa were used as stables, pigsties, and slaughterhouses.[10]

The Dalai Lama has written, "In my library in the Potala I had more than fifty irreplaceable Indian manuscripts that were

[8] The Dalai Lama, *My Tibet*, p. 14.

[9] "Tibetans Shortchanged by China's Economic Aid," *Action for Cultural Survival: A Bulletin of Peoples and Nations* (July/August 1992).

[10] China Galland, *Longing for Darkness: Tara and the Black Madonna* (New York: Viking Penguin, 1990), p. 88. See also, John F. Avedon, *In Exile from the Land of Snows: The First Full Account of the Dalai Lama and Tibet since the Chinese Conquest* (New York: Vintage, 1986), passim.

NEW INTRODUCTION

more than one thousand years old. When I left suddenly in 1959, they disappeared. No copies, no hope."[11] Most of the exquisite, centuries-old painted *thangkas* and the jeweled, golden figures of Buddha, White Tara, and countless other deities are gone from Tibet, taken by the Chinese to be sold on the international art market or to be stripped of their precious gems and melted down for making gold coins. Some remaining monasteries kept open as tourist attractions for foreigners are being renovated—according to the monks inside—by Chinese workers and by methods inimical to the Tibetan aesthetic.

While the visitor pays a government agency for admission to one monastery near Lhasa, Chinese police stand guard at the front gates with submachine guns. A Tibetan explains to the foreigner in a whisper that the guns are necessary to keep the monks from walking to Lhasa to protest in the Barkhor, the public marketplace. Another historic fifteenth-century monastic city, which once housed more than 4,000 monks, is doubly tragic. Once an imposing city on a high mountain ridge, it was dynamited into little more than a heap of broken stone. A few buildings have risen from the ruins, the frescoes have been repainted, and modern sacred images brought in. The handful of monks there do a brisk business selling incense and religious items to Tibetan pilgrims as well as to visitors. But the atmosphere is tense. An elderly monk, who with a beaming smile on his wizened face ushers foreign visitors through the myriad chapels and shrines, encouraging donations, is allegedly a notorious informer. If a young monk expresses the wrong political views, it could mean a two- to three-year prison sentence, possibly torture and death. Recent reports by Amnesty International and Asia Watch, as well as the International Campaign for Tibet, confirm the ongoing human rights violations.[12]

And what about Tibet's teeming wildlife? A mesmerizing tale is told by the present Dalai Lama's elder brother, Khalon (Min-

[11] The Dalai Lama, *My Tibet*, p. 113.

[12] Amnesty International and Asia Watch reports of torture and other human rights violations over the past few years comprise a voluminous file. See also, Scientific Buddhist Association, *Tibet: The Facts*, passim.

ister) Gyalo Thondup, now Chairman of the Kashag, or the Cabinet of the Tibetan Government in Exile based in Dharamsala, India.[13] When the high Tibetan lamas came to his native home in Amdo province to take the newly recognized, three-year-old, Fourteenth Dalai Lama and his family back to the holy city of Lhasa, Khalon Thondup recalls a moving phenomenon. Their substantial horseback entourage was accompanied for weeks by great herds of curious wild deer and other animals, and glorious flocks of migrating birds, all utterly unafraid since they had never been hunted by human predators.

The herds and flocks have since been killed, often by machine-gun, for food by the Chinese, bringing many species to the brink of extinction. Environmentalists state that a documented 75 percent of the old-growth timberlands have been clear-cut, causing massive flooding in southern China. Despite governmental claims that China is reforesting areas, severe deforestation has also caused a disruption of the monsoon patterns in India. According to worried environmentalists worldwide, *including* Chinese experts, there will be serious global consequences for disrupting the earth's atmospheric conditions. Further erosion and serious environmental degradation are the result of strip-mining, making a terrible irony of China's name for Tibet: "Store House of the West"—obviously a storehouse to be plundered at will.[14]

Recent visitors traveled through the eastern Tibetan highlands of Kham, one of three former provinces, unfrequented by most Westerners and requiring a military permit. It is now separated from the so-called Tibetan Autonomous Region (T.A.R.) and incorporated as a prefecture in China's Szechuan province, as Amdo province to the north was claimed as part of the Chinese province of Quinghai. The visitors counted, in one three-hour

[13] Diana Rowan, "The Kalachakra for World Peace," *Turning Wheel: Journal of the Buddhist Peace Fellowship* (Winter 1992).

[14] International Campaign for Tibet, *Tibetan Environment and Development News* (November 1992). See also, Lodi Gyari, "Report to the Permanent Peoples' Tribunal," session on Tibet, November 1992, Strasbourg, France; EcoTibet reports, passim.

period of an average working afternoon, about 150 logging trucks, streaming down the narrow highway in Kham through the highlands and peaks toward Szechuan, all loaded with old-growth timber. On a subsequent day, there were 300 logging trucks, interspersed with trucks bearing coal and minerals. A Western scientist also reported recently that he had discovered a grove of 3,000-year-old trees, cut down and left to rot "for no apparent reason."

What has this to do with Alexandra David-Neel and her personal vision of Tibet? Many of the logs the visitors saw were majestic centuries-old trunks from the forests she likely walked or rode through on her 8,000-mile, four-year circuitous journey toward Lhasa. If she had seen these massive trees, still oozing sap, destined to be hacked apart for furniture and housing material in China, her eyes would have held the same intense sadness as the gray-haired, leonine Khalon Thondup's.

Could she have known that there would be open hunting season offered by the Chinese on the rare snow leopard and game such as the wild yak, the red deer, and the argali, an increasingly rare Mongolian big-horned sheep prized by big game hunters, her eyes might have flashed fire. The $23,000 government-issued hunting license to kill argali in Tibet finds many trophy-hunting clients, while severe poaching by Tibetans and Chinese alike has decimated many species, the antelope, for example, whose wool brings $120 a pound on the black market. Blue sheep and Mongolian gazelle are killed illegally and shipped to Chinese meat-processing plants (*China Daily*, March 1990). Other species on the endangered list include the giant panda, the Asian black bear, the red panda, and the snow leopard—its pelt is sold openly in Tibet and its bones prized for Asian medicine.[15]

The Fourteenth Dalai Lama, Tenzin Gyatso, when asked if he hates the Chinese for what their government has done to his people and his country, answers simply, "No, I do not." But, he

---

[15] Laura Ten Eyck, "Shangri-la Lost: What Has the Chinese Rule Done to the Wildlife of Tibet?" *Animals* (May/June 1992), reported in *Tibet Press Watch* (September 1992). See also, "Wild Yaks Slaughtered in Amdo," *Tibetan Environment and Development News* (November 1992).

NEW INTRODUCTION

adds, when there is wrongdoing, then it is our *responsibility* to confront it—never in hatred or anger, but in compassion for the person committing it so that the wrongdoing does not continue to harm the perpetrator as well as those who suffer the wrong.[16]

Tibetan refugees continue to stream across the Indian border to Dharamsala (which means "shelter for pilgrims"), the Dalai Lama's home in exile in India, now a city full to bursting. Though he travels widely, teaching and speaking out for peace, the Dalai Lama personally receives each new refugee when he is in Dharamsala, listening to their stories of torture and imprisonment and lost relatives. Parents deliver their small children and newborns to Dharamsala, hoping that they will grow up in freedom. Consequently, orphanages are overflowing and medical and educational facilities are strained. Western-based Tibetan relief organizations such as the Tibet Fund seek to help, raising funds for job training, education, and medical facilities.

There is a passage in the "Prayer of Request to the Lady Tara" which runs: "Thinking that all the living beings extensive as space are mothers, and remembering their kindness again and again, bestow your blessings so that I may proceed on the stages of the path, training in love, compassion, and Bodhicitta." Exploitation of the environment and its inhabitants is anathema to those imbued with Tibet's Buddhist philosophy. Under the law of Karma, or cause and effect, what goes around comes around, in that homely saying. Treat all living beings with respect and compassion, and not only will others benefit but, the belief has it, you will find favorable rebirth and eventual enlightenment, or Buddhahood. Act cruelly or irresponsibly toward others, and suffering will come to those mistreated *and* to you; rebirth as a lower being, a "hell being," or "hungry ghost" is inevitable. Though expressed differently, active compassion is a universal theme in the world's spiritual traditions: in the Christian Saint Francis's protection of the smallest bird or bug, in the Australian Aborigines' sense of sacred and intimate connection with the earth and

---

[16] Kalachakra teachings by His Holiness the Dalai Lama, New York, October 1991, and personal conversation afterward.

its creatures, and in the Lakota Sioux phrase "All my relations—of earth, sea, and sky."

To appreciate the enormous change in values from the Tibetan culture of David-Neel's time, consider Heinrich Harrer's anecdote in *Seven Years in Tibet*, which describes Tibetans' attitudes before the Chinese invasion. Working on a construction project with Tibetans in Lhasa, he noted with mingled admiration and exasperation that "there were many interruptions and pauses. There was an outcry if anyone discovered a worm on a spade. The earth was thrown aside, work suspended and the creature put in a safe place." Killing wildlife was strictly prohibited, and domestic animals could be killed for food only on certain days. But with the Chinese "liberation" of Tibet came a systematic effort to break this value system. Along with the wholesale killing of wildlife for food, all dogs and cats were shot, as a useless burden on the food supply. The citizens were even forced to join in the killing. Zong Rinpoche, a Tibetan Buddhist monk, recalls, "The Chinese forced monks and children to kill small animals such as birds and insects on their way to work in the fields. They were given a quota and had to show evidence of the number killed such as legs or wings. Failure to fulfill the quota would invite severe punishment" (*News Tibet*, a publication of the Office of Tibet, and quoted in Laura Ten Eyck, "Shangri-La Lost," *Tibet Press Watch* [September 1992]).

In the infamous "struggle sessions" during the Cultural Revolution (1966–76), Tibetans were forced to commit violence against one another, just as Chinese citizens were in their own country. Although the Chinese blame much of the destruction on the Cultural Revolution, most of it actually occurred before those years, when eighty percent of the monasteries were systematically bombed, sometimes even while full of unarmed citizens on pilgrimage. (Lithiang Monastery, for instance, was bombed on June 1, 1956, in retaliation for a major rebellion that had originated in that area.) Streams of refugees were attacked or reportedly strafed from the air.[17] The fierce horsemen of Kham

---

[17] Scientific Buddhist Association, *Tibet: The Facts*, pp. 15–16.

NEW INTRODUCTION

fought the Chinese for another very bloody twenty years before their resistance was crushed.[18] And still, the People's Republic of China speaks of "returning Tibet to the rightful embrace of the Motherland." One's Chinese guide through shattered ruins of a once magnificent culture can speak benignly of the backward era "Before Liberation"—and believe it.

Contemporary visitors aware of Tibet's troubled history are moved to find evidence of its people's unquenchable warmth, humor, and generosity of spirit and to witness their spiritual faith despite decades of repression. Communities help to rebuild what they can of monasteries and temples, contributing labor and the little money they have. Monks struggle to continue studying and teaching, though the few hours they are allowed by Chinese officials are often followed by lectures on the evils of the West. Visitors can choose to accept the Chinese claim that Tibet was always a satellite and that its ignorant and superstitious people's reluctance to accept progress and "reunification" necessitated such a wrenching "modernization." Or they can recall and respond to the Thirteenth Dalai Lama's exhortation to Alexandra David-Neel: "Learn Tibetan!"

One can listen to the young monk in a dilapidated shrine room when the Chinese guide's back is turned: *"Bot mie semshoog namyang michag!"* The spirit of the Tibetan people will never break! One can go deeper and listen to the meaning of each word: *Botmie* means "of Tibet," *semshoog* "spirit," *namyang* "never," and *michag* "break."

One can walk with him over the monastery paths Alexandra David-Neel visited and stand on the heap of stone and broken glass that was once a great temple assembly hall and one of the glories of Tibetan monastic architecture. One can gaze out over the jagged broken walls, past the skinny dog nosing in litter where the high altar used to be. One can look at the unbroken Himalayan range beyond and state firmly, in defiance of fate and

---

[18] Jamyang Norbu, *Warriors of Tibet: The Story of Aten and the Khampas' Fight for the Freedom of Their Country* (Boston: Wisdom Publications, 1986).

NEW INTRODUCTION

the powers of darkness: "*Sacha tsachenpo ray.*" This is a sacred place.

"*Dhey shap-den che-gi-yo-ray-peh?*" Do you have ceremonies here? "*La yo-ray, tse-ba chu-ngah law.*" Yes, on the full moon. One may remember that Tara—the beloved Tibetan mother, goddess of compassion, and the "essential nature of wisdom" (*prajna*)—is also revered as a moon goddess, her light "dispelling shadows and defilements," as one eighth-century prayer in Sanskrit says. A Tibetan prayer to her runs: "*Jigten gi lhasung thamched chigdui thutob denpai dolma la tod chag pgul.*" Praises to Tara who has the power to summon together the entire assembly of earthly protectors.[19]

One may recall Alexandra David-Neel, standing on a 19,000-foot Tibetan pass in snowy moonlight, a single, determined human being offering an age-old prayer of blessing to all human beings without exception. One might also look down at whatever bit of earth or brick or asphalt one stands on anywhere in the world, holding in one's heart the center of that great ruined temple or grove of 3,000-year-old trees cut and left to rot, and repeat, "Sacha tsachenpo ray," *this* is a sacred place—vowing to find one's own particular place in that vast "assembly of protectors."

One can learn Tibetan,[20] if just to call to the six directions, "*Lha Gyalo!*" The gods have won. May the good prevail. And "*Gé-o! Gé-o! Gé-o!*" May all beings find happiness!

Diana N. Rowan
March 1993

---

[19] Martin Wilson, *In Praise of Tara: Songs of the Savioress* (Boston: Wisdom Publications, 1986). See also, standard prayer books. Spelling suggested by Lodi Gyari.

[20] Suggestions for studying Tibetan: *A Tibetan Phrasebook* (Ithaca: Snow Lion Publications, 1987); for more literary and textual study: Stephen Hodge, *An Introduction to Classical Tibetan* (Warminster, England: Aris and Phillips, 1990) and Joe B. Wilson, *Translating Buddhism from Tibetan* (Ithaca: Snow Lion Publications, 1992).

INTRODUCTION

MY travels in remote parts of Asia, including my fifth expedition, a journey to Thibet, of which I give a short account in the present book, were undertaken as the result of certain peculiar circumstances, and a brief résumé of these may not be uninteresting to the reader.

Ever since I was five years old, a tiny precocious child of Paris, I wished to move out of the narrow limits in which, like all children of my age, I was then kept. I craved to go beyond the garden gate, to follow the road that passed it by, and to set out for the Unknown. But, strangely enough, this "Unknown" fancied by my baby mind always turned out to be a solitary spot where I could sit alone, with no one near, and as the road toward it was closed to me I sought solitude behind any bush, any mound of sand, that I could find in the garden, or wherever else my nurse took me.

Later on, I never asked my parents for any gifts except books on travel, maps, and the privilege of being taken abroad during my school holidays. When a girl, I could remain for hours near a railway line, fascinated by the glittering rails and fancying the many lands toward which they led. But, again, my imagination did not evoke towns, buildings, gay crowds, or stately pageants; I dreamed of wild hills, immense deserted steppes and impassable landscapes of glaciers!

When grown up, although I was in no sense a sedentary scholar, my love of Oriental philosophy and of comparative religion won me a position as a writer and a lecturer in a Belgian university.

I had already travelled in the East when, in 1910, I was commissioned by the French Ministry of Education to proceed to India and Burma to make some Oriental researches.

At that time the ruler of Thibet, the Dalai lama, had fled

from his capital, because of political troubles with China, and had taken refuge in an Himalayan village in British Bhutan, called Kalimpong.

Thibet was not altogether unfamiliar to me. I had been a pupil of the Sanskrit and Thibetan scholar, Professor Edouard Foucaux, of the College de France, and knew something of Thibetan literature. Naturally, I wanted to see the Thibetan Pope-king and his court.

I was informed by the British Resident that this was not easy. For up to that time this exalted lama had obstinately refused to receive foreign ladies. But I had managed to secure pressing letters of introduction from high Buddhist personages, and the result was that the desire of the Dalai lama to see me grew even stronger than mine to see him!

Around the monk-sovereign, I found a strange royal household of clerical personages, clad in shining yellow satin, dark-red cloth, and gold brocade, who related fantastic stories and spoke of a wonderland. Although when listening to them I wisely made a liberal allowance for legend and exaggeration, I instinctively felt that behind those dark wooded hills which I saw before me, and the huge snowy peaks which pointed their lofty heads beyond them, there was, truly, a land different from all others. Needless to say, my heart leaped with the desire to enter it! It was in June of the year 1912 that I had my first glimpse of Thibet. The path which I had preferred to the road most usually taken starts from a low point in Sikkim, amid tropical vegetation, wild orchids, and the living fireworks of fireflies. Gradually, as one climbs, the scenery changes, nature becomes severe, the singing of birds and the noisy buzzing of insects subside. The huge trees, in their turn, are unable to struggle in the rarefied air of the summits. With each mile the forest becomes more stunted, till the shrubs are reduced to the size of dwarfs creeping on the ground, while still higher up they cannot even continue to exist. The traveller is left amidst rocks richly embroidered with brightly coloured lichens, cold water falls, half frozen lakes and giant glaciers. Then from the Sepo pass [1] one suddenly discovers the immensity of the trans-Himalayan tableland of Thibet, with its distant horizon of peaks bathed in strange mauve and orange hues, and carrying queerly shaped caps of snow upon their mighty heads.

What an unforgettable vision! I was at last in the calm solitudes of which I had dreamed since my infancy. I felt as if I had come home after a tiring, cheerless pilgrimage.

However, the very peculiar natural aspect of Thibet is not the only reason for the attraction which that country has exercised over me. Like many Oriental scholars, of whom I am but an humble colleague, I deeply regret the loss, in their Sanskrit original, of a number of Mahâyânist Buddhist Scriptures. These are more or less available in Chinese translations, but what is the extent of the Thibetan translation and what original philosophic and mystic works have been written by Thibetan authors, either in accordance with Mahâyânist doctrines or contrary to them, is as much *terra incognita* as the land of Thibet itself. Thus, hunting after books and old manuscripts and seeking meetings with the *literati* of the country became my self-assigned task. Anyhow, things could not end there. The unsuspected is the daily fare of the traveller in Thibet, and my researches led me face to face with a world still more amazing than the landscapes I had beheld from the high passes through which one enters Thibet. I refer to the mystic anchorites, the dwellers on the frozen summits. But this is a subject to be treated elsewhere.

Strange as the fact may appear, I must confess that, unlike most travellers who have attempted to reach Lhasa, and have failed to reach their goal, I never entertained a strong desire to visit the sacred lamaist city. I had, as I have said, met the Dalai lama, and as for researches regarding the literature, philosophy, and secret lore of Thibet, these things could be pursued more profitably amongst the *literati* and mystics

[1] Where the Himalayan range ends. Not to be confused with the Sepo Khang la in eastern Thibet, mentioned in Chapter III.

INTRODUCTION

in the freely accessible and more intellectual parts of north-eastern Thibet, than in the capital.

What decided me to go to Lhasa was, above all, the absurd prohibition which closes Thibet. A prohibition—one could hardly think it possible—that extends over a gradually increasing area is now placed on foreigners who wish to cross territories over which they could travel at will a few years ago, and where, in a still more ancient period, missionaries have even owned properties.[1]

[1] As an instance, the French traveller, M. Bacot, crossed the Tsarong province and visited Menkong in 1909. Captain F. Kingdon Ward visited the same region in 1911 and again in 1914. (In 1924 he went to Pemakoichen, being at that time commissioned by the British Government or, at least, allowed by it to travel in Thibet.)

In 1860 the French Roman Catholic missionaries had established several quarters in the Tsarong province.

Bouvalot, with Prince Henri d'Orléans, Dutreuil de Rheims, with M. Fernand Grenard, Sven Hedin and others, who failed in their attempts to reach Lhasa, had nevertheless crossed part of the northern Thibetan solitudes before being stopped. No one, nowadays, could openly proceed so far in the country.

But, in more remote periods, Lhasa itself has been open to those who did not shrink from the hardships of such a journey. Several missionaries and lay travellers not only entered the sacred lamaist city but made prolonged stays there. To support my statement, I quote here what has been written on the subject by Edmund Candler, who accompanied the British military expedition to Lhasa in 1904:

"It must be remembered that Thibet has not always been closed to strangers. . . . Until the end of the 18th century, only physical obstacles stood in the way of an entry to the capital. Jesuits and Capuchins reached Lhasa, made long stays there and were even encouraged by the Thibetan Government. The first Europeans to visit the city and leave an authentic record of their journey were the Fathers Grueber and d'Orville, who penetrated Thibet from China in 1661 by the Sining road and stayed in Lhasa two months—Friar Oderic of Portone is supposed to have visited Lhasa in 1325, but the authenticity of this record is open to doubt. In 1715 the Jesuits Desideri and Freyre reached Lhasa; Desideri stayed there thirteen years. In 1719, arrived Horace de la Penna and the Capuchin Mission, who built a chapel and a hospice, made several converts and were not finally expelled till 1740. The Dutchman Van der Putte, first lay man to penetrate to the capital, arrived in 1720, and stayed there some years. After this we have no record of a European reaching Lhasa until the journey in 1811 of Thomas Manning, the first and only Englishman to reach the city before this year. Manning arrived in the retinue of a Chinese general whom he had met at Phari Jong and whose gratitude he had won for medical services. He remained four

INTRODUCTION

My wanderings in Thibet began with a few excursions across the tableland which extends immediately to the north of the Himalayas. A few years later I paid a visit to the Penchen lama, better known to foreigners under the name of Tashi lama. I was most cordially welcomed. The high lama wished me to stay with him for a long time, if not forever. He offered me free access to all libraries, and a lodging either in a nunnery or in a hermitage or in a house in the town of Shigatze itself. I knew, alas! that he was not in a position to carry out his kind intentions, and that I could not, therefore, take advantage of the wonderful opportunity he wanted to give me for Oriental research.

The Tashi lama is a learned, enlightened, and liberal-minded man. People who are not in the least acquainted with him have said that he is a backward and superstitious monk, the enemy of foreigners and all that pertains to Western civilization. This is completely wrong. It may be that the great lama of Tashilhumpo does not like one particular nation, that he resents the servitude in which the British government keeps his country. No one can blame him for being a patriot, and it is still more difficult to find fault with him because, as a Buddhist, he is a pacifist and does not encourage those who increase each year the taxes paid by the poorest villagers in order to support the ridiculous army they have been led to organize to serve the interests of the very people who seize their land.

A Westerner may have ideas about the necessity or usefulness of colonization, the subjection of less civilized people, and be somewhat justified in his views. But the Asiatic who sees his country enslaved is still more justified in lacking friendly

---

months in the capital . . . in 1846 the Lazarist missionaries Huc and Gabet reached Lhasa." (*The Unveiling of Lhasa.*)

These two French priests were the last travellers to enter Lhasa freely. After the British expedition, apart from political officers and their doctors, no foreigner has been allowed to go to Lhasa.

Amongst Europeans who went to Thibet, may also be named Bogle in 1774 and Turner in 1783. These two did not visit Lhasa. They were sent from India to Shigatze as emissaries of Warren Hastings to the Tashi lama.

feelings toward the people who have robbed him of his possessions, whatever methods, diplomatic ruses or sheer violence they may have used.

As for myself, I profoundly despise everything which is connected with politics, and carefully avoid mixing in such matters. In writing this I only wish to do justice to my kind host. If he had been the ruler of Thibet, instead of being compelled to fly from Tashilhumpo to save his life, he would have gladly opened the country to explorers, savants and all honest and well-meaning travellers.

As a result of my visit to Shigatze, the inhabitants of a village situated about twelve miles down the hill from the hermitage where I lived had to pay immediately a fine amounting to two hundred rupees for having failed to inform the British authorities of my departure. The Resident who sentenced them did not take the trouble to consider that these men had no knowledge whatever of my move, since I started from a monastery situated in Thibetan territory, three or four days' march away from their village. The latter revenged themselves, according to their primitive mentality of savages, in partly looting my cottage. I complained in vain. No justice was accorded me and I was given fourteen days to leave the country.

These uncivilized proceedings made me wish to retaliate, but in a witty way, befitting the spirit of the great city in which I had the privilege of being born.

A few years later, while travelling in Kham, I fell ill and wished to proceed to Bhatang to be nursed there by the foreign doctors at the Mission hospital. Bhatang is an important Thibetan town under Chinese control, as is also Kanze, in which neighbourhood I happened to be at that time. But since the Lhasa troops had conquered the region between these two places, it had been declared forbidden to foreigners.

The officer in charge of the frontier post enquired if I carried a permit from the British consul at Tachienlu.[1] The

---

[1] A Thibetan town at the extremity of the Kham province, being included in Szetchuan.

INTRODUCTION

"Great Man of Tachienlu," he called him. With this permit, he added, I could go wherever I liked in Thibet, but he could not let me proceed without it.

However, I continued on my way, only to be stopped a few days later and to be told again about the "Great Man of Tachienlu," holder of the keys of the "Forbidden Land." In the meantime my health grew worse. I explained my case quite freely to the Thibetan officials with all the realistic details necessary to describe a severe attack of enteric, in which the language of Thibet is indeed rich. But it was of no use. The fear of the "Great Man of Tachienlu" overpowered the natural kindness of the terrorized officers with whom I had to deal. But although I had to give up all hope of being attended by the doctors at Bhatang, I refused energetically to retrace my steps, as I was ordered to do. I decided to go to Jakyendo, a market town situated on the Lhasa road, beyond the conquered area, still in the hands of the Chinese. Jakyendo lies at the extreme southeast of the "Desert of Grass"; I knew that I could find there—if I lived to reach it—the pure milk and curd which might cure me. Moreover, I suspected that a trip through the territory newly brought under the Lhasa rule might prove interesting. I therefore kept firm to my resolve. A full account of the days spent in argument would sound like an epic poem of olden days, half comic, half sad. At last, when each and all had clearly understood that unless they shot me they could not prevent me from going to Jakyendo, I went on my way through the newly forbidden enclave. My hopes were not disappointed; that trip was interesting in all respects, and became the starting point of a new period of wanderings truly wonderful.

While at Jakyendo I met an unfortunate Danish traveller who, like a number of others, had been stopped near Chang Nachuka, the frontier post on the trade-route from Mongolia to Lhasa. That gentleman, as his journey had been cut short against his will, wished to return quickly to Shanghai. The road he should have followed crosses the very tract of land on which I had fought my battle with the authorities. Before he had even reached it, soldiers who had been posted to watch the passage prevented him from going forward. The poor traveller turned out to be another "Wandering Jew" and was compelled to recross the "Desert of Grass."

He had to organize a caravan to carry food and baggage for a journey lasting at least one month, through a wild region which has a particularly bad name for being haunted by large gangs of armed robbers. And even then he reached the extreme northwest of the Chinese border, while he had wanted to come through to the coast. This meant another journey of about two months!

This meaningless tour could have been avoided by following the direct road, which can be travelled in a sedan chair, without any caravan, food and inns being found on every day's march. Thus half the total time would have been saved.

Such stories as this were not without their effect upon me. More than ever I decided to enter once more this land so jealously guarded. I therefore planned to reach the banks of the Salween, and to visit the "hot valleys" of Tsawa rong and Tsa rong. Would I have gone from there to Lhasa? Perhaps, but more likely I would have followed some track toward Lutzekiang or Zayul and travelled, in an opposite direction, a part of the much longer journey which I was to complete successfully eighteen months later.

I started from Jakyendo at the end of the winter, travelling on foot and accompanied by only one servant. Most passes were blocked by the snow, and we experienced dreadful hardships in negotiating some of them. We had happily surmounted material obstacles, crossed the frontier post under the very windows of the official who guarded it, and were nearing the Salween, when we were stopped. I myself had not been detected, but my luggage, containing some instruments and various requisites for botanical research, betrayed me. This small caravan was in charge of Mr. Yongden, a young Thibetan, the faithful companion of many of my journeys, and my adopted son. Though he travelled several days' march behind me and trusted to be taken as a trader, the contents of the

INTRODUCTION

boxes he carried revealed his connection with me. He was stopped; men were despatched to look for me through the country, and thus my trip was brought to an end.

It was then that the idea of visiting Lhasa really became implanted in my mind. Before the frontier post to which I had been escorted I took an oath that in spite of all obstacles I would reach Lhasa and show what the will of a woman could achieve! But I did not think only of avenging my own defeats. I wanted the right to exhort others to pull down the antiquated barriers which surround, in the center of Asia, a vast area extending approximately from 79° to 99° longitude.

Had I spoken after my attempts had failed, some might have thought that I did it out of vexation. Now that success has been mine, I can calmly expose the obscure situation of Thibet to-day. Perhaps some of those who read of it, will remember that if "heaven is the Lord's," the earth is the inheritance of man, and that consequently any honest traveller has the right to walk as he chooses, all over that globe which is his.

Before ending, I wish to assure my many English friends that my criticism of the part their government has played in this situation is not the outcome of bad feelings against the English nation as a whole. Quite the opposite. I have, from my early youth, when I spent my school holidays on the Kentish coast, liked the company of English people, as well as their ways. My long stay in the East has greatly increased that feeling, to which I now add a sincere gratitude for so many hearty welcomes in so many houses where kind ladies have endeavoured to make me feel as if I were in my real home. In their country, just as in mine or in any other one, the policy of the government does not always represent the best side of the nation's mind. I suppose that the citizens of Great Britain and the Dominions are as little acquainted with the devious proceedings of political offices regarding far-off colonies or protectorates, as is the rest of the world. It follows that they cannot resent criticisms which are not addressed to them.

INTRODUCTION

What I have said may even astonish many of them, especially Christian missionaries, who may rightly ask why a self-styled Christian nation should forbid the entrance of the Bible and its preachers into a land where she is at liberty to send her troops and to sell her guns.

I must add a word regarding the spelling of the Thibetan names in this book. I have merely given them phonetically, without trying to follow the Thibetan spelling, which is very misleading for those who are not acquainted with that language and capable of reading it in its own peculiar characters. As an instance I will say that the word pronounced *naljor* is written *rnal byor*, the name of *dölma* is written *sgrolma*, and so on. As for the name *Thibet*, it may be interesting to know that it is a word unknown in the Thibetan language. Its origin is not quite clearly traced, but Thibetans ignore it completely. They call their country *Pöd yul* and themselves *Pöd pas.*[1]

[1] To be pronounced Pö.

My Journey to Lhasa

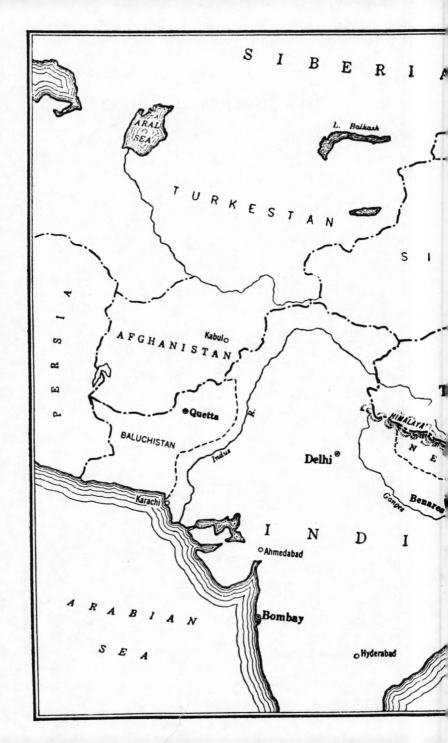

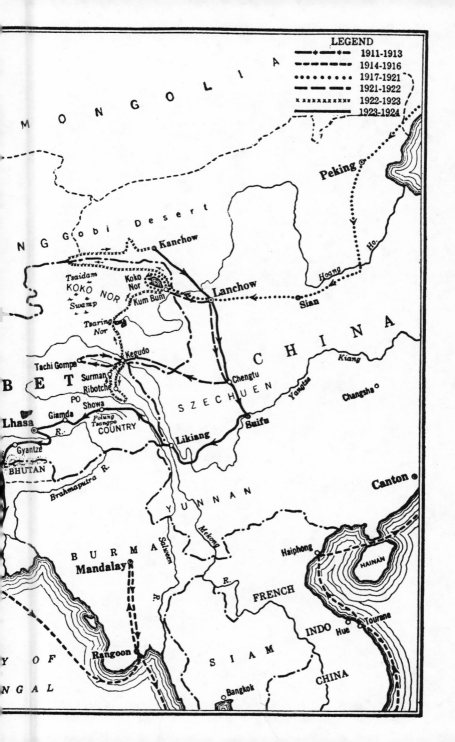

MY JOURNEY TO LHASA

CHAPTER I

FAREWELL! . . . Farewell! . . . We are off! At the bend of the path I look back once more, one last time. Standing at the gate of his residence I see the foreign missionary who welcomed Yongden and me a few days ago when, without being in the least acquainted with him, we begged his hospitality. Some anxiety may be detected in his kind smile and his intent gaze. To what extent have we succeeded in deceiving that most excellent man? I cannot tell. He does not know the object of our journey, there is no doubt about that. But the programme we laid before him was vague enough to awaken the suspicion that we were trying to conceal the fact that we were to undertake a dangerous expedition! Where would we be going, alone, on foot and without luggage, he wonders. He cannot guess, and I am certain that the names of the mysterious wayfarers who slept for a few nights under his roof will be remembered in his prayers. May his own wishes be ever fulfilled! May he be blessed for the warmth that his cordiality adds to the glorious sunshine that lights my fifth departure for the forbidden "Land of Snow!"

Farewell! . . . We have turned the corner of the road, the Mission House is out of sight. The adventure begins.

This is, as I have said, my fifth journey into Thibet, and very different, indeed, have been the circumstances and manner of these successive departures. Some have been joyful, enlivened by the babbling and broad laughter of the servants and country folk, the jingling of the bells hung on the mules' necks,

1

and that rough yet gay fuss that the people of Central Asia so love. Others were touching, grave, almost solemn, when, dressed in the full lamaist garb of dark purple and golden brocade, I blessed the villagers or the *dokpas* [1] who had congregated to pay for the last time their respects to the *Kandhoma* [2] of foreign land. I have also known tragic departures, when blizzards raged in the solitudes, sweeping across awe-inspiring white landscapes of impassable snow and ice, soon to be wrapped again in dead silence. But this time the bright sun of the Chinese autumn shines in a deep blue sky, and the green wooded hills seem to beckon us, promising pleasant walks and happy days. With our two coolies carrying a small tent and an ample supply of food, we look as if we were starting for a mere tour of a week or two. In fact, this is precisely what we have told the good villagers whom we have just left, namely, that we are going for a botanical excursion in the neighbouring mountains.

What would be the end of this new attempt? I was full of hope. A previous experience had proved to me that in the disguise of a poor traveller I could escape notice. But although we had already succeeded in leaving quietly behind the baggage brought with us to cross China, we had yet to assume our full disguise and (most difficult task) to get rid of the two coolies whom we were compelled to take with us to avoid the gossip which would certainly have spread in the Mission House amongst the servants and neighbours, had they seen a European lady setting out with a load upon her back.

I had, however, already thought of a way of freeing myself from the coolies. My plan depended, it is true, upon certain circumstances over which I had no control, and any little unforeseen incident might wreck it; but I could not think of a better one, and so relied upon my good luck.

We had started late, and our first stage was rather short. We encamped on a small and sheltered tableland near which

---

[1] *Dokpas:* literally, inhabitants of the solitudes, the cowmen who do not practice husbandry.
[2] A kind of incarnated fairy.

one could get a beautiful view of the highest peak of the Kha Karpo range. The place is called "the Vultures' Cemetery," because once a year the Chinese slaughter hundreds of these birds there to procure their feathers, with which they do a big trade. They attract the birds with the carcass of a horse or a mule as bait, capture them with nets, and when the poor creatures are caught in the meshes they beat them to death. The plucked bodies are then used as bait to snare other vultures, which in turn share the fate of the first comers. This plucking of vultures' feathers lasts for a whole month amidst putrefaction and pestilence. Happily, when I reached that spot it was not the vulture-killing season, and I saw only heaps of bleached bones amongst the short and thorny vegetation which covers the ground.

Nature has a language of its own, or maybe those who have lived long in solitude read in it their own unconscious inner feelings and mysterious foreknowledge. The majestic Kha Karpo, towering in a clear sky lit by a full moon, did not appear to me that evening as the menacing guardian of an impassable frontier. It looked more like a worshipful but affable Deity, standing at the threshold of a mystic land, ready to welcome and protect the adventurous lover of Thibet.

The next morning I saw again the huge peak of Kha Karpo shining at sunrise, and it seemed to smile encouragement to me with all its glittering snows. I saluted it and accepted the omen.

That night I slept at the entrance of a gorge in which a tributary of the Mekong roared loudly—a wild, picturesque spot inclosed between dark reddish rocks. The morrow was to be a decisive day. It would see me at the foot of the track that leads to the Dokar Pass which has become the frontier of the self-styled "Independent Thibet." My scheme was to be tested there. Would it work as I hoped? . . . Would the coolies leave me without suspecting anything of my designs? . . . Would the situation of that village of Londre, about which I had but little information, favour an escape by night over a small path leading, higher up on the hills, to the pilgrimage road round the Kha Karpo, which crosses the Dokar Pass?

3

... A number of questions arose in my mind, each with its own anxiety. However, as I lay on the ground, in the small tent that Yongden had made himself in the Lolos' country, that particular happy feeling of ease and freedom which the stay in solitary places always brings to me wrapped my mind in bliss and I went to sleep calm as a child lulled by fairy tales.

Next morning, leaving my old friend, the Mekong, we turned westward through the rocky gorge at the entrance of which we had slept. Soon it opened out into a narrow, densely wooded valley. The weather was sunny and walking easier. We passed two mounted Tibetan traders, who gave us scarcely a glance. Perhaps they thought we were Chinamen, for Yongden and I both wore Chinese dresses. Nevertheless this first meeting, precursor of the many which were to follow, gave us a little shock. Although we were yet in that part of Thibet, still under Chinese rule, wherein foreigners can travel freely, though at their own risk, it was most important that rumours of my wanderings in the neighbourhood of the border should not spread. For the Thibetan officials, once warned and on the alert, would have the road carefully watched, which would greatly increase the difficulties of our entering the forbidden area.

A little before noon we came in sight of Londre. Had we been alone, Yongden and I, we could have easily avoided passing through the village by hiding ourselves in the wood until evening. It would have saved us much trouble and fatigue, for between the steep slopes of the Kha Karpo range which we were about to climb, there was but the width of this torrential river which we had followed upwards and crossed several times in the narrow gorge. But such a thing was out of the question, for I had expressly told the coolies that I intended to go into the country of the Loutze tribes to collect plants, and the road to Lutze-Kiang went through Londre and there turned in a direction exactly opposite to the Kha Karpo.

Very disturbed, and reflecting that each step added a difficulty to my approaching flight, I followed the two Thibetans who meant to take me to a wooded tableland about ten miles higher, where they knew of a good camping-ground. As far as they could see, Yongden and I scarcely cast a glance at the country in the direction of the Dokar Pass; but in reality we did our best to impress on our memory the shape and peculiarities of the landscape which would help us when we had to cross it on the next night.

Our passage in Londre was as inconspicuous as we could have wished. Not one of the villagers whom we met appeared to take any particular notice of us. This most happy circumstance was perhaps due to the fact that an American naturalist worked in the vicinity and employed a large number of people. No doubt the villagers thought that we were on our way to join him as assistants.

After having proceeded for a few miles on the Lutze-Kiang path, turning my back to my real goal, I thought it imprudent to proceed farther. Safety required that plenty of time be allowed for the long tramp on the opposite side of Londre, so that dawn should find us far away from the village, having, if possible, reached the pilgrimage road. Once there, we could easily pretend to have come from any northern Thibetan part we cared to name, in order to get round the Sacred Mountain.

I had hesitated a long time in choosing the road I would take in order to enter independent Thibet. The one I preferred, or perhaps I should say the one which circumstances seemed to be thrusting upon me, is followed every autumn by many travellers. By taking it I foresaw that I should run the danger of frequent meetings. Not that this inconvenience was without its favourable aspect, since our tracks could be more easily lost amongst those of pilgrims from various Thibetan regions, each of whom spoke in different dialect, and whose womenfolk had a variety of different dress and coiffures. The little peculiarities of my accent, my features, or my clothes would more easily be overlooked on such a road, and if enquiries were to be made, they would have to embrace so many people that confusion might very likely follow to my advantage. But of course I sincerely hoped that no enquiry would be made, and that we should meet as few people as possible during the first few weeks of our trek.

We had reached a point where the road commanded the view of the valley at the entrance of which Londre was built. It was covered with a dense jungle in the middle of which flowed a clear stream. A trail descended to it from the road, and it was here that I paused for a few minutes, wondering once more how I should get rid of my two unwanted followers. I soon made up my mind.

"My feet are swollen and sore," I said to the men. "I cannot walk any longer. Let us go down near the stream, and we will make tea and camp."

They were not astonished. Truly my feet had been hurt by my Chinese rope sandals, and the coolies had seen them bleeding when I had washed them in a stream.

We went down, and I chose a small clearing surrounded by thick bushes and there pitched my tent. The presence of the water, and the protection afforded against the wind by the thickets would certainly have justified my choice of the spot had the two peasants or any other persons questioned me about the selection of this rather gloomy place.

A fire was lighted, and I gave the coolies a good meal. Yongden and I endeavoured to swallow a little *tsampa*,[1] although the imminence of our departure, the fear of seeing our plans upset at the last minute, had left us little appetite. However, when the meal was finished, I ordered one of the men to go up the hill to cut some dry logs, since only twigs could be found near us. When he had gone I explained to his companion that I had no need of him because I meant to stay there about a week collecting plants on the neighbouring mountains, before I went to Lutze-Kiang. When necessary, I added, I would hire a man from the villagers of Londre to carry my luggage. He understood and, well pleased with good wages, he started immediately for home, convinced, of course, that the man who had gone to cut the wood would remain to attend on me.

[1] Flour made of roasted barley, the staple food of Thibetans.

The latter was told exactly the same thing, when he came back with the wood, but as I did not want him to meet his companion for some time, lest they should discuss my strange plan of camping alone, I added that, as I could not proceed at once to Lutze-Kiang, he was to carry there a letter and a parcel. From there, he could return to his village by a direct road, without coming back to Londre.

The parcel contained a few clothes, a gift to the poor. Must I relate that, shut in the small tent, Yongden and I had again examined our baggage and, finding it still too heavy, we had given up the waterproof ground-sheet that was meant to keep us, when sleeping, from direct contact with the damp or frozen ground? Yongdon and I discarded also the only pieces of spare clothing we had kept. Nothing was now left us except the clothes we were wearing. We had not even a blanket, although we knew that, during the winter, we should have to cross high, snowy ranges, passes of over 18,000 feet; and as much food as possible had to be carried, since we did not wish to show ourselves in the villages for at least a fortnight. Later on, when crossing desert regions, a full load of provisions would again be indispensable; success and even life might depend upon it.

The small package was addressed to a missionary whom I had never seen and who had probably never heard of me. Such was my plan of ridding myself of my last coolie. He went away, as satisfied as his comrade, with a few dollars in his pocket, believing that the other peasant had been sent on some errand in the neighbourhood from which he would return before evening.

What these two said, a few days later, when they met after having rounded the same range, one on the northern and his friend on the southern side, must have been amusing, but I never heard it!

All necessary arrangements had been made. We stood, Yongden and I, in the thick jungle, alone and free. The novelty of our situation bewildered us a little. For months, dur-

7

ing the long journey from the sands of Gobi to Yunnan, we had been discussing the way in which we could "disappear," as we used to say, and assume other personalities. Now, the hour had come and we were to start that very night for the Dokar Pass,[1] which now forms the border of independent Thibet.

"Let us drink a cup of tea," I said to the young lama, "and then you will start on a scouting tour. At any rate, we should reach the foot of the Kha Karpo track without meeting anybody, and be out of sight from the village before daybreak."

Hastily I revived the fire. Yongden brought water from the stream, and we prepared the Thibetan tea, with butter and salt, in the simple manner of poor travellers who cannot enjoy the luxury of a churn to mix it.

I may as well explain immediately the composition of our cantine. We had only one aluminum pot, which was our kettle, teapot, and saucepan all in one. There was also one lama wooden bowl for Yongden, an aluminum bowl for myself, two spoons, and a Chinese travelling case containing one long knife and chopsticks, which could be hung from the belt. That was all. We did not intend to indulge in refined cooking. Our meals were to be those of the common Thibetan travellers; that is to say, *tsampa*, mixed with buttered tea, or eaten nearly dry, kneaded with butter. When circumstances would allow, we would make a soup. Forks were useless with such a diet, and even our two cheap spoons could not be produced freely, as they were of a foreign pattern such as only affluent Thibetans possess. *Arjopas* (pilgrims travelling on foot and often begging their food), as we pretended to be, have none. In fact, these spoons became, later on, the occasion of a short drama in which I nearly killed a man. I shall tell the story in due course.

The tea drunk, Yongden started. Hours passed; night had fallen. I remained seated near the fire which I did not dare to let blaze, fearing that it might be seen from afar and betray our presence. The remains of the tea, kept as a last cordial to cheer our departure, were simmering on the embers; the ris-

[1] Eighteen thousand four hundred feet above sea level.

8

ing moon tinged with bluish and russet hues the melancholy depths of the valley. All was silence and solitude.

What had I dared to dream? . . . Into what mad adventure was I about to throw myself? I remembered previous journeys in Thibet, hardships endured, dangers that I had confronted. . . . It was that again, or even worse, which lay before me. . . . And what would be the end? Would I triumph, reach Lhasa, laughing at those who close the roads of Thibet? Would I be stopped on my way, or would I fail, this time forever, meeting death at the bottom of a precipice, hit by the bullet of a robber, or dying miserably of fever beneath a tree, or in a cave, like some wild beast? Who knew?

But I did not allow gloomy thoughts to overpower my mind. Whatever might be the future, I would not shrink from it.

"Stop here! Go no farther!" Such were the commands of a few Western politicians, to explorers, savants, missionaries, scholars, to all, in fact, except their agents, who travelled freely, wherever they were sent, in this so-called "Forbidden Land." What right had they to erect barriers around a country which was not even lawfully theirs? Many travellers had been stopped on their way to Lhasa, and had accepted failure. I would not. I had taken the challenge by my oath on the "iron bridge" [1] and was now ready to show what a woman can do!

As I was thus musing, Yongden emerged suddenly from the bushes. Strangely lit by the moon, he looked a little like a legendary mountain spirit.

Briefly he reported the result of his scouting: To avoid the village we should have to cross a rickety footbridge higher up the valley, and follow the stream downward on the opposite bank. Perhaps it was possible to make a direct descent by wading in the river itself past any village house that might be perched upon the bank. This would certainly be a short cut,

[1] In a previous attempt, which was stopped after a few weeks' journey and led me through a very interesting part of the province of Kham. I had then every opportunity of studying at first hand the conditions of the inhabitants, as the Lhasa government had succeeded in establishing complete ascendency there after its victory over the Chinese.

but, as people were in the fields nearby, he had not been able to test the depth of the water.

Whichever road we might choose, we could not avoid passing in front of a few houses between the small bridge on the stream flowing out of the valley where we pitched our camp, and the large one on the tributary of the Mekong, which we had seen on our arrival.

When we had crossed that second bridge, we could look for the bypath which was to lead us to the pilgrimage road. Yongden had seen it clearly, winding up the steep slope, but he had failed to discover the exact point from which it branched from the bank of the river.

With these vague ideas, I hurriedly set out. It was already late and we could not guess how many miles we should have to tramp that night until we could reach a spot which afforded some degree of safety.

Was my load heavy on my shoulders? Were its rough straps cutting my flesh? Indeed they were! I felt it later, but at that moment I was not aware of it. I was aware of nothing. I knocked myself against sharp rocks, I tore my hands and my face in the thorny bushes. I was dead to all sensation, stiffened, hypnotized by the will to succeed.

For several hours we trudged in the valley. We had first climbed up to the main road, and then, skirting isolated farms, tried the passage in the stream. It proved impossible at night-time. The water was rather high, the current swift and breaking against boulders. We should have fallen in two minutes. And so we again directed our steps in search of the foot-bridge. Several times we lost our road. The trails that my young friend had marked in the day were difficult to find by the dim light of the moon, veiled in mist. At last we found ourselves on an easy but very winding track on the opposite bank. It led tortuously beside the stream, and we were exasperated by the precious moments lost in following it. When at last we caught sight of the village, we put our loads down, drank a draught of the clear water that flowed past us, swallowed a granule of strychnine to rouse fresh energy in our tired bodies, and took the dreaded passage on the run.

A bridge, the houses, the second and larger bridge . . . safely passed. We stood at the foot of the wild and solitary hill on which a narrow, twisting trail led to other tracks and paths and roads leading into the very heart of Thibet, the Forbidden Capital of the Lamas. . . .

A dog had given a low, suppressed bark when we were near the river—a single dog, in that village where a dozen or more of these rather fierce animals wandered to and fro all night! It reminded me of the Indian tales relating the nightly flight of those sons of good family, who, in quest of the "Supreme Deliverance," abandon their home to take to the religious life of the sannyasin. In order, we read, to make their flight easier, "the gods lulled the men to sleep and silenced the dogs." So had it been with me, and smilingly I returned thanks to the invisible friends who protected my departure.

In our haste to be off we overlooked a small landslide just in front of us, which was in reality the beginning of the bypath leading upward that had fallen in. We searched for the road along the river bank until we neared a steep gorge which afforded no means of ascent and we were thus forced to return to the bridge. Another half-hour was wasted here; we were in full sight of the village and trembled for fear of being noticed! Moreover, the right track, which we found a little after midnight, happened to be extremely steep and sandy. Heavily loaded as we were, we could only make slow progress, in spite of our strenuous efforts, being compelled to stop frequently, out of breath. It was terrible, and my feelings could well be compared to those of a nightmare in which the dreamer imagines himself to be pursued by murderers and tries his utmost to run away, but cannot move his feet!

Toward the end of the night we reached a gloomy spot sheltered by large trees. Our steps awakened a number of big birds perched on the branches, which flew away noisily. A streamlet flowed nearby and Yongden, who had not enjoyed a minute's rest since the morning of the previous day, craved a refreshing bowl of tea.

Thirst parched my mouth and I shared the desire of my companion, but nevertheless I was most reluctant to stop. This dark place, the only one where water was obtainable, did not appear to me very safe. It might possibly be haunted by leopards and panthers, of which there are many on these hills. Above all, I wished to put as great a distance as possible between us and Londre. Had I been alone, I would have suffered no matter what agony, and would have crept on my knees if I could no longer stand, rather than delay a single minute. But the exhausted lama's fatigue overcame prudence. Nothing could be done; he fell rather than sat upon the wet ground, and I went in search of fuel.

The hot drink was most comforting. Unfortunately, his new sense of well-being lulled my companion to sleep. I could have cried. Each minute wasted on that path diminished our chances of success. However, in such cases nothing is to be done; sleep is a necessity that cannot be resisted. Nevertheless, Yongden was not allowed a long rest and we continued on our way.

The solitude reassured us. The sun had long since risen and we were still climbing when we heard a voice above us. Then, without exchanging a single word, panic-stricken, Yongden and I threw ourselves out of the path and rushed like scared game, through the thick jungle, our only idea being to escape from sight.

I found myself, without being able to remember how I had come there, on an old stony landslide surrounded by thorny bushes. Of my companion there was no trace.

However, he had not gone far and we soon found each other. But we did not dare to walk again in broad daylight. Woodcutters, cattle drovers, or others might be going down to Londre and talk about us there. Pilgrims might perhaps follow that path, overtake us, notice something peculiar in our appearance, and repeat it in gossip on the other side of the border. We expected the worst, anxious to give bad luck as little chance as possible. We therefore spent the first day of our journey squatting under the trees. From our resting-place we could hear, higher up, invisible folk driving equally invisible cattle. A wood-cutter appeared on an opposite slope. I watched him for some time; he sang prettily as he piled his logs and doubtless was not in the least aware of the agony he was causing a foreign woman. The autumn foliage probably screened us completely from the gaze of distant observers, and the villagers did not suspect our presence. Nevertheless, in my fear of having been seen, I was filled with the most pessimistic ideas. I almost believed that failure was awaiting me and that I had come here in vain from far away Turkestan, across the whole of China.

Soon after sunset we began our nocturnal tramp. When darkness came we saw several fires higher up on the hill. We could not be sure that the winding path which we followed would not lead us to them, and we were very much worried. Coal men or, perhaps, pilgrims were camped there and the prospect of arriving at night amongst Thibetans by the Londre track did not please us in the least; for such a meeting would have been the occasion for many embarrassing questions from inquisitive people.

We remained for a long time seated on the grass in a clearing, waiting for the moon to rise. We could not see the trail, yet all the time we *could* see these alarming, glowing fires! They gave a peculiarly disquieting and demoniacal aspect to the black, indistinct landscape of pines and huge rocks jutting around them in the dark starlit sky. How thankful we were when we saw them far behind us and were certain that we could not meet the people near them.

Soon afterwards we arrived at a small *chörten* [1] marking the junction of our track and the pilgrims' road. The latter was a rather large mule path, and walking became easy and pleasant. To have reached this spot without meeting anybody was indeed fortunate. If my luck held out, I might, with equal

[1] Thibetan monument erected to hold religious objects or the remains of great departed lamas.

13

fortune, cross the Dokar Pass and reach the district of Menkong. I could then congratulate myself on having made the most important step toward final success, for in that country many roads cross, bringing together travellers from various directions. Our tracks would be easily lost, and with a little cleverness we could lose ourselves in the anonymous mass of poor Thibetan pilgrims whom the officials do not condescend to honour with so much as a single glance.

Thirst was torturing us still more than upon the previous night when we reached a large roaring mountain torrent which cut across the road. A small bridge spanned it rather high above the water which rushed, white with foam, amidst a chaos of boulders. Yongden thought only of his thirst, and wished to go down the road immediately to drink. This was dangerous, since, in the darkness, he could not see the obstacles which might cause him to stumble and roll into the torrent, which would have immediately carried him away. I remonstrated with the obstinate fellow, but he argued that as water was so scarce, seeing that we had found none since the previous night, it was indeed possible it would be hours before we struck water again. I could not contradict him, but thirst was preferable to being drowned. I therefore ordered him to cross the footbridge. On the other side, the bank was less steep and an easy way down could be seen. Although time was precious, and I did not like to light a fire so close to the road, I was thinking of halting, when, to our dismay, we heard a voice calling us. It was that of a man who offered us red embers to kindle a fire, and even a cup of ready-made tea to begin with!

We remained motionless, speechless. We had talked in English a few minutes before. Had that man heard us?

"Who are you?" asked another voice. "Why are you walking at night?"

We still could see nobody, but the sound came from a huge tree. I thought that it might be hollow and that travellers had taken it as hostelry for the night.

"We are pilgrims," answered Yongden. "*Dokpas* from

Amdo. We cannot bear the heat of this country. When we walk in the sunshine, we get fever. So we tramp around the Holy Hill at night."

That was quite a plausible reason. The man who had asked the question asked nothing more, but Yongden continued:

"And you, who are you?"

"We, too, are pilgrims."

"Well, good-bye," I said, to cut the talk short. "We will still walk a little, and camp the next time we find water."

So ended the first chance meeting on our way to Lhasa. We congratulated each other that it did not happen while we were still on the track climbing from Londre, but at the same time we learned that even night marches were not absolutely secure, and that we had to be prepared at any hour and at any place to explain, in a way that awoke no suspicion whatever, the reason of our doings.

We continued our way for several hours without finding further traces of water. I felt exhausted and walked mechanically, half asleep. Once I thought that we were approaching a hut built on the road and turned over in my mind what I would say and do if I met Thibetans. But the "hut" turned out to be a passage between two great rocks. At last utter exhaustion compelled us to rest. The site was not in the least fit for camping; the exceedingly narrow trail skirted a stony, natural wall, and, on the other side, ended perpendicularly. We lay down on a rocky mattress whose roughness we unpleasantly felt through our clothes and endeavoured to remember even in our sleep that we were perched on the edge of a precipice whose depth was unfathomable in the night.

In such wise we spent the second happy night of our wonderful adventure. Day had not yet broken when Yongden and I loaded our burdens on our backs and continued the tramp through the forest. More than twenty-four hours had now elapsed since we had eaten and drunk. We had not yet become accustomed to prolonged fasts, and this first one was hard to bear.

We proceeded as fast as we could in order to reach some

stream before hiding ourselves for the day. It was a race with the sun, which was now rising rapidly. It appeared somewhere above a summit hidden in the thick foliage, and its heat soon began to light and warm the underwood. The time had come for us to take shelter in the forest. The men whom we had met during the night might overtake us, and that would mean a long talk, a lot of explanations, and, what was still worse, our showing ourselves in broad daylight.

We crept between the thickets that extended beyond some *do-chöd* [1] until we were completely invisible from the path. Looking down, I discerned some blue smoke floating far below between the trees. A distant noise of running water could also be heard. Travellers or wood-cutters were enjoying their morning meal, an idea which so increased our hunger that Yongden decided to risk himself on the road with our kettle in search of water.

While alone, I hid our baggage under some branches, and lay down flat on the dry leaves and threw others over me. Any wanderer through the wood could have passed very near without detecting my presence. Indeed, this happened to Yongden when he came back with his kettle full of water. I had fallen asleep and he roamed a long time in the jungle looking for the place where he had left me. He did not dare to call aloud, and had I not been awakened by the noise he made in wading through the dry leaves and got up, he would have wandered still longer.

We had discussed, during the previous night, the question of our disguise. Till then we had worn our Chinese robes, which would not have compromised us even if I were recognized as a white woman, for, as a rule, all foreigners in these remote parts of Thibetan China dress in this way. But we now hoped that no one who could detect us would come along our road. Our fellow-travellers would probably be pilgrims from various regions of Thibet, and our best plan was to merge at once in their number, like inconspicuous, common *arjopas*.

---

[1] Literally, offerings of stones—*i.e.*, cairns placed on the top of the hills and many other places as offerings to the gods.

MY JOURNEY TO LHASA

The *arjopas* are those mendicant pilgrims who, all through the year, ramble in thousands across Thibet, going from one to another of its sacred places. The *arjopa*, not necessarily, but for the most part, belongs to the religious order—either as a monk or as a nun. He or she may be a true pauper or even a professional beggar, but the mass of them have homes and means of subsistence in their own countries, although they cannot afford to ride on horseback during their pious journeys.

Some *arjopas* start without any money and rely entirely upon charity during their pilgrimages; others are not entirely penniless, but keep carefully the few coins they possess for the unlucky days when alms-givers are few or none. A third category is rich enough to purchase the simple food of the ordinary Thibetan diet. However, for the most part, the pilgrim passes easily from one to another of these different classes. A lama capable of reading the Scriptures, who can perform the different lamaist ceremonies, and can, above all, act as exorcist and fortune-teller, may at any time find himself so well provided with food, clothing, and even money, that he may dispense with begging for several months. On the other hand, the owner of a heavy purse may fall ill, be delayed on his way by other circumstances, or be robbed—a thing which happens frequently—and have to take his place, in the same day, amongst the poorest of his colleagues.

I had chosen to travel as an *arjopa* because it is the best disguise to pass without attracting notice. Yongden, who is an authentic and well-read lama, looked his part perfectly, and I, his aged mother, who had undertaken a long pilgrimage for devotional reasons, constituted a rather touching and sympathetic figure. These considerations had their full weight when I decided upon our disguises, but—and why should I not confess it?—the absolute freedom of the *arjopa*, who, like Diogenes, carries all his possessions with him, and who is free from the care of servants, horses, luggage, sleeping each night where he pleases, attracted me greatly. I had had a taste of it during a previous short trip in Kham, and wished to enjoy it more fully and longer. And now that I have thoroughly experienced the joys and the hardship of the *arjopa's* life in Thibet, I deem it to be the most blessed existence one can dream of, and I consider as the happiest in my life those days when, with a load upon my back, I wandered as one of the countless tribe of Thibetan beggar pilgrims.

After a copious meal of *tsampa*, dried meat and buttered tea, we began to disguise ourselves. After all, was it really a disguise? Yongden clad himself as a lama, as he did when residing in a monastery. As for me, I had for years accustomed myself to wearing Thibetan clothes, the only novelty being in the coarseness of the plain white lay dress I put on for the journey.

The headgear caused me some little annoyance. I had brought no hat from Amdo, thinking that I would purchase one at Atunze. But I did not pass that town, and I could not find a hat in any of the villages on our way. For the time being, an old red belt would suffice, twisted around my head in the fashion of the Lutzchiang. The boots which I had brought from Kham showed, as well as the peculiar material of my dress, that we hailed from that province and provided me with a certificate of Thibetan nationality.

Two years previously, in another attempt of the same kind, I had cut my plaits; now, in the part of a lay woman, I required long ones. I therefore lengthened mine, which had not yet grown long enough, with jet-black yak's[1] hair, and in order to match that colour I rubbed a wet stick of Chinese ink on my own brown hair. I hung large earrings on my ears, and they altered my appearance. Finally I powdered my face with a mixture of cocoa and crushed charcoal, to obtain a dark complexion. The "make-up" was rather strange, but suppliers to the theatrical trade, from whom I could have obtained better ingredients, have not yet opened branches in the Thibetan wilds!

At sunset, we gathered our baggage and emerged from the jungle full-fledged Thibetan wayfarers.

[1] Yak, the long-haired ox of Thibet.

The next morning we found as a camping ground, after our long tramp, only a most unhealthy place nearly level with a stream, and which was certainly part of its summer water-bed. We could not see the ground beneath us, it being hidden by reeds which had been burned in a forest fire and which had fallen in an inextricable entanglement now covered by a thick layer of green moss. We ate, but owing to the nearness of the road, we did not dare to light a fire, and drank the icy water that had an unpleasant taste.

How long had I slept? I could not say. When I opened my eyes I saw a man clad in Thibetan dress, wearing a soft felt hat of foreign shape, as Thibetan soldiers outside of Lhasa do.

In less than a second many thoughts dashed through my still slumbering mind: A Thibetan soldier—we are still on Chinese territory—what is he doing here? . . . Has he been sent across the border to watch us? . . . Have the Thibetan officials been informed that we are proceeding toward the Dokar Pass? . . . At any rate, I must convince him that I am a true Thibetan; and, as the best means of convincing him, I pretended to blow my nose with my fingers.

That gesture thoroughly awakened me, and what I had taken to be the soldier turned out to be nothing more than a rock and a few branches.

But I had not the heart to laugh at myself. I had been too much frightened, and to make things worse, I began to shiver in a way which left no doubt in my mind that I was in for an attack of fever as the result of our prolonged stay in that damp spot.

I looked at my watch. It was only three o'clock, but days were short at this time of the year, and the waning moon did not rise until the middle of the night. During the next fortnight we should have to chance our luck and proceed partly during the day, or we would linger too long in the country, which would indeed be dangerous.

Late in the evening we arrived at a peculiarly beautiful spot, a kind of wide, natural clearing surrounded by ramparts of thickets. Shadowed by giant trees which veiled an intense darkness, it looked like a temple meant for some solemn occult rites and made me think of the Druids.

Pilgrims used to camp there; one knew it from the large number of *mi deussa*[1] to be seen scattered about. Some sybaritic devotees had gone so far in their search for comfort as to spread a double thickness of fir-tree branches around the primitive hearths, in order to provide themselves with a carpet, and these dark-green patches on the golden brown leaves which autumn had strewn over the ground still further increased the impression one had of being in a mysterious sanctuary.

Big logs lay scattered around, and without taking much trouble we soon enjoyed a most glorious fire. Invisible animals were roaming in the jungles; we could hear the noise of the small branches they broke as they stalked through the bushes. Sometimes, we heard steps quite near us; maybe one of the four-footed wanderers was watching us, but we could not see it in the circle of darkness that surrounded the clearing and veiled its farthest corners. I trusted, nevertheless, that no beast would venture near the heap of glowing coal from which, at times, flames leaped high and clear.

With flaming branches in his hands, Yongden went twice to fetch water from the river. I told him to chant some Thibetan liturgy all along his way, so that, together with the bright light, the noise would frighten away any leopards or panthers which might be prowling around. That grave psalmody in the depths of the forest matched perfectly the peculiar atmosphere of the place and aroused in me the desire to perform there the fearful rite which Thibetan hermits hold in high esteem as a way of liberating one's mind from all attachment. It is poetic in spite of its stern symbolism, and Thibetans fully

[1] Literally, men's resting place—*i.e.*, few stones that have been arranged by travellers to place a cauldron on the fire, which one sees, blackened among ashes, along the trodden tracks at the spots where water can be got and wayfarers use to camp.

initiated into its meaning smile at the terror of the novices, who train themselves in its practice amongst dread and inspiring surroundings.

I ignored the danger of being overheard by travellers, if any such should happen on the road, as had been my experience the night when I had imprudently spoken English near a torrent. If anyone saw me forming the figures of the mystic dance and calling upon the gods and the demons, he could but be convinced that I was a Thibetan *naljorma*[1] and, being struck with terror, would certainly not remain in the vicinity to ask idle questions.

After a short rest, we did our best to start before daybreak, but the waning moon's light could not penetrate the thick foliage. We were not able to find our way, and had to return to our camp and wait.

As we ascended the sacred mountain the forest changed its character. It became darker and wilder than in the neighbourhood of Londre. Our night tramp was wonderful; we felt as if we had entered another world. Born of the moon's rays, filtering through clouds and branches, or perhaps of other and unknown causes, strange shapes rose before us. Often we saw the glimmer of fires hidden in the recess of the mountains. Moving shadows were silhouetted indistinctly in the dim light; peculiar notes were heard.

Once, while walking ahead, I saw two tall figures coming toward us. Retracing my steps, nearly crawling on the ground to avoid giving ourselves away, I dragged Yongden along the dry bed of a high-banked stream, and there we stayed, crouching amongst the stones and the fallen leaves, watching the intermittent glare of a fire at the foot of a distant huge perpendicular rock.

Early in the morning, at the time when Thibetan travellers start for the day's march, we listened attentively, trying to detect sounds of human voices or the noise of animals. But the forest remained silent. I was more puzzled than ever

[1] One who has embraced the religious life and follows the mystic path. *Naljorpa* is the masculine.

and, to gratify my curiosity, we went a long way off the trail to the big rock.

It was surrounded by thorny bushes and a few dead trees. No suitable place for a camp could be found near by. The rock itself had been decorated long ago—as are many in Thibet—with the image of Padmasambhava, and some mystic formulæ, but these had nearly disappeared beneath the moss. Of fire, embers, ashes, or charred wood, there was no trace.

I noticed a long, narrow crevice between the ground and the rock, and here the stone seemed blackened with smoke. I thought, however, it was rather its natural colouring. Yongden and I roamed more than an hour in an attempt to discover the entrance of a cave beneath the rock. We found none.

While we were busy a few blackbirds alighted on some branches and appeared to follow our doings with a mocking interest, moving their heads and uttering chirps like laughter. Their noise was unpleasant and Yongden grew angry.

"These little black fellows," he told me, "do not seem to be natural birds. They must be the same mischievous *mi ma yin* [1] who play tricks at night with fire and music to delay us on the road, and have now taken another shape."

I smiled at his imagination, but he was quite in earnest. His great-grandfather had been a somewhat famous magician-lama, and I believe the blood of that ancestor was now alive in him. He recited a *zung* (magic formula) with the necessary ritualistic gesture and, strangely enough, the birds flew away, shrieking loudly.

"You see," triumphed the young lama, "I knew it! It is unwise of us to stay here."

I smiled again; but as to the necessity of pushing on I could not argue. That very night we meant to cross the border of "the Forbidden Land."

The approach to the pass was most beautiful. Early morning found us in a large valley white with frost. On our left, strangely shaped rocky hills seemed crowned with turreted

---

[1] *Mi ma yin*—literally, *not man*. One of the six classes of beings, according to Thibetans.

castles. At first sight I thought that a monastery had been erected there for the use of contemplative lamas, as there are a large number in Thibet, but I soon realized that Nature was the only responsible architect, and had herself built these dignified yet graceful edifices.

I very much regretted that the nearness of the border and the extreme care I had to take in order to avoid being seen, prevented me from camping a few days on this site. I would have liked to find a way by which I might climb into these fairy dwellings. Knowing Thibet and its people as I did, it would have been no surprise to me to have found a hermit in this eyrie.

Proceeding toward a ridge which seemed to be the summit of the pass, we crossed several abundant springs. Water was flowing everywhere on natural terraces supported by rocky walls. In summer, *dokpas* bring their cattle to these heights. We had seen signs of them in the valley, but at this time of the year silence reigned supreme.

The belief that we had only a short distance to cover to be at the end of our climb infused fresh strength in us. We walked fast and soon arrived at a bend of the track, nearing the spot which we had taken for the pass. Here we saw that we had only reached another broad valley which, far away, was fringed by slopes which doubtless led to the Dokar Pass, but the pass itself could not yet be seen. This was an unpleasant surprise. We were tired, for the troubles of the previous night had not allowed us much rest. Moreover, we did not deem it prudent to proceed during the middle of the day in that open place, in which we could be observed from every side. A chaos of huge rocks, very likely the product of some landslide that happened centuries ago, could, fortunately, be used as a refuge. Stunted fir trees were still thriving there, in spite of the high level, and served us as a shelter.

From that place I could still see the tops of the fairy palaces that I had admired from the valley beneath, but I was now above them and thus could see that the other side of the hill was much less steep.

I have myself lived for several years, in caves or rough cabins, in the grassy desert and at the foot of the everlasting snows, the strange and wonderful life of the Thibetan mystics. I feel deeply its particular attraction, and all that is connected with it immediately awakens my interest. Now it appeared to me that those natural edifices were inhabited. A mysterious message seemed to be conveyed to my mind, as I sat gazing intently at them, a kind of silent talk between speakers invisible to each other. What did it matter, after all, if on that hill there lived a human being like myself? What I heard was the thousand-year-old echo of thoughts which are re-thought over and over again in the East, and which, nowadays, appear to have fixed their stronghold in the majestic heights of Thibet.

We set out again in the middle of the afternoon. We felt confident that no one would be on the road at that time. Thibetans always manage to cross these high passes at noon, to allow time to go far enough down on the other side to avoid excessive cold and lack of fuel during the night.

We were not ordinary travellers, and the usual rules dictated by prudence could not be part of our own code, which consisted in one single article: *to avoid detection.* For the rest, we relied on our robust constitutions and the strength of our will.

During the short halt that we made at the foot of the final climb we noticed a man leading a horse, who had reached the beginning of the upper valley, near the place where we had camped, and from which I had gazed at the rocky castles and allowed my mind to dwell on their imaginary inhabitant. The man sat down when we moved on, and we lost sight of him. I may say at once that the following day he should have caught up with us, for there was only the one pilgrims' road and circumstances had delayed us long on our way. But he never appeared. We asked some pilgrims who overtook us about him, and they answered that they had met nobody. This fact somewhat confirmed my intuition as to the presence of a hermit in the vicinity. The man with the horse was probably his *jinda* (supporter), who brought him a supply of food. He had left the track and would perhaps remain a few days with the lama. That the majesty of that solitary site had been appreciated by an ascetic was not astonishing, for one who knew the "Land of Snows" and its religious folk.

The Dokar Pass now stood before us, most impressive against a gray evening sky. It is a depression in a gigantic barren range whose Cyclopean slopes sag like cables outstretched across rivers to serve as bridges. The knowledge that it marks the threshold of the guarded region added to the sternness of its aspect.

The ground around the pass is most sacred to the gods, and the Thibetan pilgrims who walk along the track have built countless tiny altars, made of three standing stones, and a fourth one as a roof, under which offerings are made to spirits.

On the pass itself and following the neighbouring ridges, the mystic flags which can be seen on all the heights of Thibet were planted in exceptionally large numbers. In the falling light they looked alive, belligerent, and threatening, like so many soldiers scaling the crests, ready to fight the presumptuous traveller who would venture on the road to the Holy City.

As we reached the cairn marking the top, a gust of wind welcomed us—the violent, icy kiss of the austere country whose severe charm has held me so long bewitched and to which I always return. Turning successively toward the four quarters, the zenith and the nadir, we uttered the Buddhist wish, "May all beings be happy!" and began to climb down.

A blizzard descended upon the peaks. Black clouds rolled hither and thither, turning into sleet. We hurried in our effort to reach the base of this steep and inhospitable slope before nightfall.

But darkness came early. We missed the path winding between the landslides, and found ourselves slipping helplessly with crumbling stones under our feet. It became dangerous to proceed in that way, with a speed that we could not control.

So, having succeeded in pulling up, we fixed our pilgrim staffs before us in the ground as a point of support. Clinging to each other for safety, our loads still on our backs, we remained squatting upon the snow, which fell from eight o'clock in the evening till two the next morning. Then a last melancholy quarter of the moon rose between the clouds and we descended to the wooded zone.

We were resting, seated at the edge of a glade where a forest fire had destroyed the big trees and which was now covered with short shrubs, when I noticed the forms of two long animals with phosphorescent eyes, which crossed the track several times and finally disappeared in the direction of the river. They were quite distinctly visible in the moonlight and I pointed them out to Yongden. He saw them well, but persisted in saying that they were deer, though their shape and the peculiar glimmer of their eyes indicated carnivorous wild beasts. I delayed a little, to avoid an undesirable encounter, and then we continued our descent to the river.

We were exhausted and there was no certainty that we could soon find water again, as the stream entered a gorge and our trail climbed up on the hill. So, in the hope that the animals would let us alone if they were still in the vicinity, we lit a fire to make tea.

While we were drinking, we heard some noise behind the bushes, but we were beginning to be accustomed to the prowling of wild beasts around our camps. Yongden fell asleep. I decided to watch, but my eyes were heavy, and closed in spite of my efforts.

I was dozing, when the sound of a low sniff awakened me. A few feet from the place where we were lying, one of the animals with glimmering eyes was looking at us, and I could see its spotted coat!

I did not awaken Yongden. It was not the first time that I had seen creatures of that kind at such close range. They seldom attack men unless provoked or wounded, and I was convinced that they would never harm me or those who were near me.

That nocturnal meeting reminded me of another one which I had had, in broad daylight, several years before, with a superb tiger.

"Little thing," I murmured, looking at the graceful animal, "I have seen, near to, a much bigger prince of the jungle than you. Go to sleep and be happy." I doubt whether the "little thing" understood me. However, after a few minutes, it went leisurely away, its curiosity satisfied.

We could not allow ourselves a longer rest. The day had broken and it was time for us to retire to a hiding-place, away from the trail. I awakened Yongden and we went. A few minutes after we started the young man pointed out with his stick something under the trees.

"There they are," he said.

The pair of spotted fellows were indeed there. They turned their heads toward us, looked for a little while, and then went their way along the stream, while we climbed the path.

As we went up, the aspect of the forest changed once more. It was now much less dense. The sun that had risen lit the undergrowth, and through the openings in the foliage we could see the opposite bank of the river beneath us. We noticed with astonishment that it seemed to be cultivated, but cultivated in a fanciful way, more in the fashion of gardens and parks than of common fields.

It was a glorious morning, and we enjoyed our walk so much that we continued it long after the hour at which we usually sought shelter. The river bent suddenly and we confronted a village built on a slope at the foot of which our path turned along the stream. A few isolated houses could even be seen quite near us on the sides of the path itself.

What village was this? It was not charted on any map and none of the people of the country from whom we had cleverly got information, before our departure, had ever told us a word about it. Its architecture was peculiar. We did not see cottages and farms, but villas and miniature palaces surrounded by small yet stately looking parks!

The strange town was bathed in a pale golden light. No

sound of human voices, no noises of animals, were heard in it. But, now and then, a faint silvery jingling struck our ears. We were amazed. Were we in Thibet or had we reached fairyland?

We could not, however, remain standing in the path. People might come along, and to be seen so near the frontier posts was imprudent. It was imperative, for safety's sake, that we should delay our investigations until the evening. Once more we retreated amongst the bushes and the rocks. There, over-tired, I sank on the moss and fell asleep, feverish and raving a little.

Our impatience to see again the fantastic village, our fear of having to cross an inhabited place, and the desire to look for ways to avoid it, brought us on the trail before sunset at the spot on which we had stood in the morning.

Where were the graceful villas, the stately little palaces and the sunny gardens?

The forest was empty. A severe landscape of dark trees extended before us, and a cold breeze, wailing among the branches, took the place of the harmonious jingling.

"We have dreamed," I said to Yongden. "We did not see anything this morning. All that happened while we were asleep."

"Dreamed!" exclaimed the lama. "I will show you how we have dreamed. This morning, while you were looking at the miraculous town, I drew a *sungpo* [magic sign] on a rock with the spike of my staff, so that neither gods nor demons could oppose our progress. I shall find it again." And he looked on a flat stone at the foot of a fir tree. "There it is!" he triumphed. "Look!"

I saw the roughly drawn *sungpo*. It silenced me for a moment.

"My son," I said, proceeding forward, "this world itself is but a dream, and so . . ."

"I know," interrupted my companion. "Nevertheless, the *sungpo* and the *ngags* [magic words] that I uttered while drawing it, have dispelled the mirage. It was certainly the work of some who wished to delay us!"

"Yes, like the blackbirds," I continued, laughing, "and maybe the small leopards, too."

"Like the birds, yes!" affirmed my son, decidedly vexed. "As for the leopards, I do not know. They looked honest beasts. Anyhow, we will soon be out of these Kha Karpo forests and confront true villages instead of dreamland ones, and true men, officials, soldiers, and others, instead of *mi ma yin*. Let us see, then, if we can manage our business with them as cleverly as I have done with the folks of other worlds."

"Have no fear about it," I replied, seriously, "I will look after that."

"How will you do it?" he asked.

"I will make them dream and see illusions, just as the *mi ma yins* did to us."

And I really did so when, a few days later, circumstances brought us before Thibetan officials.

The miracle which had allowed us to proceed for a whole week on a road followed by many pilgrims, without meeting a single soul, could not last forever. Arrived at one of the minor passes on the Kha Karpo range on our way down to the Salween, we suddenly heard a jingling of bells behind us. It was a party of pilgrims, men and women, with two horses, who had overtaken us. We exchanged a few words, and each of us walked devoutly around a *latza* [1] in which flags bearing printed mystic formulæ were stuck. The pilgrims, who were not impeded by loads on their backs, went down the trail more quickly than we did and, when we arrived at the bottom of a pretty, narrow valley in which several clear streams met, we found them already seated, drinking tea.

We had now to begin the apprenticeship of the career we had momentarily embraced. It would have been contrary to the custom to pass the place without taking our meal, for the

[1] A cairn placed on the summits as offerings to the gods.

time had come for *tshaphog*—that is to say, the halt in the middle of the day.

I looked round, ready to go collecting wood to make a fire, but the kind pilgrims, seeing a lama, invited us to join them. I felt delighted to be free to remain quietly seated, enjoying the scenery, which was grand.

In a frame made of several ridges of forest-covered mountains, one above and behind another, a gigantic peak of the Kha Karpo towered, dazzling white, its summit pointing straight into the dark-blue sky. Before it, our group seemed a gathering of tiny animals crawling on the ground. The sight was really crushing, and did indeed remind us of our nothingness. Yet the good pilgrims gave their whole attention to their food and some gossip, and turned their backs on the exalted abode of the gods they had come from afar to worship. As for myself, I was lost in a trance of admiration, forgetting that my attitude might look strange to the Thibetans. As a matter of fact, it did, and they enquired why I did not eat.

"Mother is with the gods," answered Yongden, who put a warm bowl of tea before me to bring me down to the world of men.

A woman, misunderstanding his answer, put a new question about me.

"Is the mother a *pamo?*" [1] she asked.

I was afraid that my companion would not be able to suppress his laughter at this funny idea, but he replied, gravely: "My father was a *nagspa;* [2] she was initiated his *sang yum.*" [3]

All looked at me with due consideration, and the chief of the party sent me a piece of dried meat. Until then he had offered us only *tsampa,* but the new personality that we revealed to them inspired respect in these benighted Thibetans.

[1] A female medium who is said to be possessed by gods or demons who speak through her mouth. When the medium is a male he is called *pawo.*

[2] A most dreaded kind of sorcerer, expert in magic formulæ, who is believed to command demons, and able to kill any being from afar.

[3] Literally, "secret mother." The respectful title given to the spouse of a tantrik lama.

Nagspa are dreaded for the occult powers they are supposed to possess, and to incur their displeasure or that of their kindred, even for involuntary offences, is a serious matter.

So, having suddenly become grave, they made us a little present of butter and *tsampa* and hastily went their way, desirous to escape our honourable but dangerous company. This was just what we wished.

The following day brought us to the limit of the Kha Karpo forests. From the top of a hill, we saw Aben on the bank of the Lhakang-ra river. This place, where the Chinese used to keep a small garrison, had become, we had been told, a Thibetan frontier post. Our difficulty was now no more a question of wandering through solitary forests, but of crossing a populated village which, with its outlying cultivation and isolated farms, stretched for several miles.

Our old trick of tramping by night was no longer of any use here. No doubt dogs frequented the road and were likely to be fierce at night, and in any case noisy. One cannot expect a miracle to happen at every turn. Until then we had enjoyed such wonderful luck that prudence naturally prompted us to make allowances for it and not count too much upon its protection. To be caught roving at night would have got us into trouble. Enquiries might follow and we feared nothing more than these. Our best plan, we thought, was to cross Aben before daybreak. By so doing we should get the benefit of darkness, and as Thibetan travellers are in the habit of starting at these early hours on their day's march, anyone who might hear us passing by or see us, would find in it nothing extraordinary.

We studied the aspect of the valley from the top of a woody hill in order to be able to proceed quickly in the dark. Fearing to arrive too early in the vicinity of the village, we remained a long time seated there, with the result that, since the road wound, in its descent, more than we had suspected, night fell long before we had reached the bottom of the valley.

For the first time since we had left Londre, the weather was really unpleasant, a cold wind pierced our clothes, and low

clouds foretold snow. We no longer knew the exact where-
abouts of the village. Bushes conspired with the darkness to
mislead us. Several times we sat on the ground with our loads
on our backs, overpowered by sleepiness. But we could not
allow ourselves even the poor comfort of a nap. Before taking
whatever rest we might enjoy that night, we needed to ascertain
that we had reached the Lhakang-ra road and that, hurrying
through the village a few hours later, we would have only to
walk straight before us. Unfortunately, we failed to find the
road amongst the intersections of the bypaths. At length we
found ourselves near some houses and were compelled to stop.
Snow began to fall. To spread our small tent over us like a
blanket was out of the question. Once untied, we could not
have repacked our loads properly in the dark, and might have
left behind us some compromising article. Nothing, therefore,
remained for us but to sleep uncovered for a while, with our
packs as pillows.

Long before daybreak we awoke and started. At a first
attempt we luckily reached the centre of the village. Hearing
voices inside a house and being panic-stricken, we hurriedly
turned a corner, ran straight before us, and found ourselves
again amongst the fields. In our haste we had mistaken the
direction. The early light of dawn revealed the river and we
saw that we were going up instead of down the stream as
we should. We now had to abandon our carefully considered
scheme. We should have to go through Aben in daylight.
Country folk were already to be seen going to their work.
There was nowhere to hide ourselves, and the longer we
waited, the worse our chances would be.

People whose hearts are not strong and who cannot sufficiently master their nerves are wiser to avoid journeys of this
kind. Such things might easily bring on heart failure or
madness.

We retraced our steps, passed once more under the windows
of the house where we had heard the voices which had frightened us. People were still talking, the blinds were open, and
I could see the flame of a fire. These blessed villagers would

drink hot tea, whereas our last meal had been taken early in the morning of the previous day, and we did not feel sure that we should be able to stop to eat during the day which was dawning.

All was well. We were on the right road! We went at a good pace and soon passed through the village. But all our troubles were not over, for another cluster of houses appeared on a hill overlooking the valley, which narrowed to the size of a gorge, giving passage to the river which entirely filled the bottom of it. A small path had been cut high up on its right bank, and this was our road. Looking up, I discovered from the foot of its sandy cliff a kind of loggia that commanded the view of the gorge from afar, and immediately jumped to the conclusion that sentries might well be posted there to observe travellers.

Perhaps it was an old Chinese building. It might indeed have been used by them as a watch tower, but most probably it was now put to another use. I did not, one can well understand, remain there to ascertain the history of that painted balcony. It left me perfectly indifferent. I did not even dare to stop to drink at the rivulet which crossed the path below, although I knew that I might not come across any more water for some miles. I ran and ran, as if flying. Contrary to my custom, which was to let Yongden march first, so that passers-by could see his face, while I remained more or less hidden behind him and his load, I told him to follow me because the possible danger was now behind us. Thus, if we walked close to each other, the watchmen from Aben, if there were any, could discern only the familiar sight of a load surmounted by the red cap of a lama, under which hung a raggy *shamtabs*.[1]

Nevertheless, we endeavoured to reach the end of that interminable gorge as quickly as possible. The path, following the windings of the cliff, alternately hid us from the spur on which the upper part of Aben fort or monastery was situated, and brought us again within sight of it. We took advantage

[1] The pleated large skirt worn by the lamas.

of this circumstance to rest a few minutes when we were sheltered. It seemed like a game, but a tiring, nerve-racking, meaningless game.

The walk without the preoccupations that spoiled it would have been charming. In this country autumn has the youthful charm of spring. The sun enveloped the scenery in a rosy light that spread joy from the river of opalescent green, flowing swiftly in the depths of the gorge, to the top of the cliffs, on which a few hardy fir trees pointed to the sky. Each pebble on the path seemed to enjoy the warmth of day, and chatted with suppressed laughter under our feet. A lilliputian shrub that grew on the side of the road perfumed the air with a strong aromatic scent.

It was one of those mornings when Nature bewitches us with her deceitful magic, when one sinks deep into the bliss of sensation and the joy of living.

It is but a short distance between Aben and Lhakang-ra. We did not want to be seen in the latter place and had again planned to cross it at night. We had, therefore, plenty of time—and as soon as we met a stream in a gorge that crossed our path, we halted to take a meal behind some big rocks a little below. Many groups of pilgrims and several lonely travellers passed near us without suspecting our presence. Strangely enough, now that we had crossed the Dokar Pass and entered Thibet, the stream of devotees which appeared to have been stopped during the first week of our journey began to flow as usual in that season. We saw, from behind our hiding-place, a most picturesque procession of men and women from different parts of eastern and northern Thibet, all making haste to reach Lhakang-ra early and to find room in the primitive inns there. Still, a few stopped as we did, and began to cook bread. We had no wheat flour and hoped they might be willing to sell us a small quantity of their own. Yongden went to propose this to them, but they had only a very little, and wanted to keep it. A talk followed in which my companion tried to get as much information as possible about the country. As the pilgrimage is usually performed thrice, at intervals of several years, some of the travellers we met were able to supply us with very useful information.

My companion returned, and we drank a bowl of tea. I was washing my handkerchief in the stream when one of the travellers came over to us and asked the lama to foretell the result of some litigation he had at home. That was the first time during our journey that Yongden acted in the capacity of a "Red Cap" lama, an adept in the art of *mo*.[1]

Years before, when we travelled in the northern country and I wore my beautiful lama robes, it was I who was requested to bless the people, blow on the sick to cure them, and prophesy about countless things. I performed a few miracles, chance, the faith and the robust constitution of those who were benefited making it difficult to abstain from working wonders, and I had some gratifying success as an oracle. That glorious time was gone! Now I humbly washed our pot in the stream, while Yongden solemnly revealed to his attentive listeners the secrets of the future concerning a disputed land many hundred miles away.

We passed to the left bank of the Lhakang-ra river, and the scenery changed entirely. The gorge had become very narrow and wild. On both sides there were dark cliffs of rock, which might in places have reached seven or eight hundred feet in height, leaving only a narrow ribbon of sky visible overhead. Yet the view was far from being gloomy or depressing. Perhaps the pictures painted and carved in large numbers on the rocks modified the character of the place itself. Hundreds of Buddhas, Bodhisatvas, famous lamas of yore and deities appeared there, all in the attitude of meditation, their eyes half closed in some inward gaze. That silent, motionless, saintly crowd had created in the dark defile a very peculiar mental atmosphere. Between the images were engraved large

[1] The art of telling fortunes, predicting the future, revealing the unknown, disclosing the cause of illness and other misfortunes as well as the remedy therefor, etc., etc., by means of various methods of divination. As there is no general equivalent for the word in English, fitting all cases, I shall be obliged to leave it in Thibetan throughout this book.

portions of philosophical treatises, as well as short mystic sentences or praises of the wisdom of Buddha. I remained for a long time reading here and there, enjoying the serenity conveyed by these old Scriptures.

I was indeed privileged to experience in a single day the intoxication arising from the beauty of nature and the peaceful delight of the mind brought to the threshold of the supreme Deliverance, and thrice blessed verily is the country that can offer both these things to those who tread its ground.

A *mendong*[1] covered by a roof, which we saw at dusk, might have provided us with shelter for the night, but we thought that we were still far from Lhakang-ra, and therefore continued our way. We crossed a bridge once more. The gorge bent suddenly, and the large Salween spread its green waters in front of us. We were in Lhakang-ra.

Although it was nearly dark, we did not dare to turn back. We could have been seen, and it would have seemed strange that pilgrims such as we were supposed to be avoided the village. The best way, as our plans were once more upset, was to spend the night bravely somewhere in a corner like other travellers.

We met several people who were camping near a fire, exchanged a few words with them and decided to stay in a small cave situated on the road we were to follow the next day. There we should be somewhat sheltered if snow fell. I gathered some twigs and dry cow dung on the road. I stole a few branches from the fences of the neighbouring fields, but *arjopas* must be cautious in their ways. Unless they halt in the forest, they are taken for thieves if they are seen burning big logs. Thibetan farmers do not like people to pillage the fences that protect the cultivated land from the intrusion of cattle, and in doing so one risks serious thrashings.

As we were in a hamlet and night protected us, Yongden thought that he might well take the opportunity to purchase food. We had lived until then on the supply that we had

[1] A low wall made of stones on which are engraved texts of the sacred Scriptures, or mystic sentences.

36

carried when leaving the Mission House. Ten days had elapsed since then, and our bags were nearly empty. I wrapped myself in my thick dress according to the manner of the poor Thibetans, and made a pretence of sleeping to avoid useless talk if, by any chance, some one passed near me, while my companion went toward the houses.

The first one he entered happened to be that of the lama in charge of the Lhakang-ra shrine. He was welcomed on his two-fold title of colleague and buyer, for the lama added to his profits as a shrinekeeper those he derived from a small shop where pilgrims could revictual and purchase sundry articles of devotion such as incense sticks, small flags bearing mystic drawings or words, etc. . . . They both, by chance, belonged to the same religious sect and sub-sect. Moreover, the lama was not a native of the country, his birthplace being in far northern Kham, where Yongden had long lived with me, and whose dialect he spoke rather well. That coincidence of circumstances made them friends in no time, but the affair was not to end there.

Looking round the room, Yongden saw books on a shelf and asked his permission to have a look at them. This being granted, he read *aloud* a few lines of the first one he opened.

"How beautifully you read!" admired the lama. "Are you able to read any book in that way?"

"Indeed!" answered my companion.

Then, passing suddenly to another topic, the lama shopkeeper pressed Yongden to spend the night in his house, offering to go himself to fetch and carry his luggage. Yongden refused but, as the lama insisted, he confessed that he was travelling with his aged mother. This did not in the least cool the good intentions of the kind host. There was room for the mother as well, and it was hard to convince him that, by this time, I was sleeping soundly and was best left alone.

Then the *keugner* (sacristan) being at a loss to manage the success of the scheme he had in mind, without making it known, was forced to disclose the fact that his hospitable feelings were not altogether disinterested.

"Lama," he said to Yongden, "some villagers have come here from the opposite side of the Giamo nu chu (Salween) and have asked me to perform the rites for the dead on behalf of one of their relatives who passed away recently. They are wealthy people and would have gone to the lama of their own country monastery had he not been away in Lhasa. I have been chosen in his place, and it would be very profitable for me . . . but I am not well read and I am so afraid of making mistakes in placing the ritual offerings and reciting the liturgy in the proper way. I see that you are learned. Perhaps you know these ceremonies?"

"I do know them," declared Yongden.

"Then I beg you to do me the service of staying here three days. I shall feed you both and give you some provisions for the road when you set out. The mother might recite *mani* [the well-known *Aum mani padme hum hri!*] at the door, and no doubt the villagers will give her some *tsampa.*"

Yongden declined the proposal on the ground that we belonged to a party of pilgrims who were already ahead. We could not linger behind, but were, on the contrary, compelled to proceed quickly in order to join them and return together to our own country.

When my companion returned with a few provisions, he told me of his talk with the lama, and I rather regretted that the vicinity of the border commanded a hasty progress. I would have enjoyed the fun of reciting *mani* "at the door." However, the near future was to give me more opportunities to enjoy that kind of fun than I could have ever dreamed of. I should find it hard to recount the number of times I have chanted *mani*, outdoors and indoors during my journey. I became rather expert at it, and was complimented twice for the nice way I had of chanting it. Perhaps, after all, Thibet helped me to discover the "jewel" which dwells in the heart of the "lotus." [1]

The cunning lama came in the early morning to talk again with Yongden. In order to avoid being seen by him I went down and walked around the shrine for about an hour, putting

[1] *Mani padme* means a jewel in a lotus.

into motion, as I walked, each of the many reels which contain tightly rolled bands of the paper on which is printed a thousand times the mystic sentence, *"Aum mani padme hum hri!"*

I deemed that morning's walk to be rather superfluous for one who would have to tramp a good number of miles during the day, but I found no better means of getting away, and even so, I did not escape a talk with the lama, who stopped for a little chat with me on his way back home.

CHAPTER II

ALONG the majestic Giamo nu chu (Salween) the road goes alternately through deep gorges and broad, widening valleys. The scenery in either case remains at once majestic and enchanting.

Truly, fear is still there, crouched in a corner of my heart, ready to spring up. Our stay at Lhakang-ra has been too long. Has the shrinekeeper begun to wonder who we are? I observe those who come behind me. Are we not followed, spied upon? That horseman yonder, riding in our direction, is he not a soldier sent to bring us back?

Eve, when she was banished from Eden, had explored all its pleasures, and except for these it could afford her no cause for regret. Even if Eve's mind were of a similar cast to mine, she might have found interest in the adventure which opened to her the wide unknown world beyond the inclosure of Paradise. But I, her little great-granddaughter, although I had wandered for years in my fairyland, I was far from having exhausted its interests. Had I been compelled to turn back now, I would never have known the new landscape hidden behind the woody hill that shut off my horizon, nor penetrated the mystery beyond that other rosy-coloured one which stood behind it, nor climbed the pass which, still farther, traced a mauve soft line on the sky between snow-white peaks. Forebodings still arose in my mind only to fade in their powerlessness to disturb the joy of those wonderful hours.

A few days after leaving Lhakang-ra, a tragic meeting saddened us. Near the road, in front of the Giamo nu chu, whose icy emerald water appeared in the bright sunlight like a glittering moving mirror, lay an old man, his head resting on a leather bag. When we approached, he gazed at us with vacant eyes, already dull, and with an effort he lifted himself a little on his elbow. I could see the poor fellow was near his end. Yongden asked him how he got there alone. The story was simple. The old peasant had left his village with a group of friends to travel round the Kha Karpo on a pilgrimage. An illness, whose cause he could not understand, had suddenly deprived him of his strength. He was unable to walk and had to fall behind. His companions had slackened their pace; they had even stopped for a whole day, and then they had gone on their way. Such is the Thibetan custom, even in the desert, where an abandoned sick man, if he cannot reach a *dokpas'* encampment, will die of starvation when once his provisions are exhausted. Nor must one forget the wolves and the bears who roam about.

"Shall I die?" the old man asked Yongden. "Lama, cast lots to know."

"No, you will not die," answered the latter, after having quickly performed the usual rites, in an attempt to cheer up the forlorn traveller.

He meant well, but I thought that the glimmer of hope he lighted would soon vanish if, the next morning, the man himself felt still weaker, or if in the darkness of the next night, he realized the approach of death. Then in spite of the promptings of prudence, it became impossible for me to continue my part of the aged, feeble-minded, and beggarly mother. In a few words I reminded him of the simple beliefs of the religion he had followed since his childhood, and promised him, not only this life, but a happy rebirth in the abode of Chenrezigs [1] which awaits those who die while on a pilgrimage, and, after thousands of years spent there in rest and delights, other lives again and again, till he reached the supreme enlightenment that liberates one from the bondage of life as well as of death.

He listened to me attentively and piously. He bent low and touched the bottom of my dress with his forehead, as Thibetans do to the lamas whom they worship. Maybe he

[1] The abode of Chenrezigs: Nub-dewa-chen, the western land of bliss, better known by its Sanskrit name, Sukhavati, by those acquainted with Mahayanist Buddhism.

believed that a *khandoma*[1] or a goddess had seen his distress and assumed the shape of a pilgrim to console him. What mattered, if the illusion enchanted his last hour?

"Can we help you in any way?" I asked him.

"No," he answered, "I have food and money in my bag. I am well here, with the gods. *Kale pheb*."[2]

"*Kale ju*,"[3] we both answered, and we went on our way.

I felt that *Nub-dewa-chen*—the land of bliss—shone now before his eyes that began to see but dimly the things of this world. The dying man was carried away by the vision I had evoked and had lost all desire for this life, for which, at first, he had begged my companion so anxiously.

We enjoyed a few days of relative tranquillity, loitering leisurely along the beautiful valley. We were no longer in a solitary region, as we had been during our tramps in the Kha Karpo forests. Villages were rather close together, and deeming it still wise to avoid staying over night amongst Thibetans or even being seen during the daytime by many people, we managed to pass these villages at daybreak or a little earlier. This mode of travelling compelled us to remain long in out-of-the-way and out-of-sight spots, waiting for the proper time to venture to pass the houses.

There was nothing unpleasant in such lazy vagrancy amidst beautiful scenery, favoured as we were with fine weather. The only drawback was that it made our progress dreadfully slow. Anyhow, we felt the benefit of these long rests in the jungle after the painful strain to which our nerves had been subjected. But perfect peace was far from our present reach. One morning, when we were imprudently taking our meal in a small cave near the road, a woman aroused the fear latent in our minds.

She was a well-dressed lady of rank, covered with jewels;

---

[1] A khandoma, one who walks through the sky—a kind of fairy—the Dâkini of the Sanskrit text.

[2] "Go slowly"—polite farewell to those who go away.

[3] "Stay (or sit) slowly"—polite farewell to those who remain.

MY JOURNEY TO LHASA

three maid servants followed her. She stopped before us and asked from what country we had come. At that time we styled ourselves Mongolian *dokpas* of the northern Koko-Nor [1] solitudes. Yongden, therefore, answered: "We are people from beyond the Blue Lake [*tso ñönpo po parcho la*]." She replied: "Are you *philings* [foreigners]?" I made a pretence of laughing at such an idea, and Yongden stood up to attract the attention of the lady to himself, so that she might, by scanning his regular Mongolian features, be convinced that he had nothing of a Westerner about him. "She is my mother," he declared, pointing to me. Then, after a few other questions, the woman went on her way.

A little later her husband passed us, riding a superb horse with a silver-and-gold-inlaid saddle. A dozen attendants followed, leading the horses of the lady and her maids.

The gentleman did not honour us with even a single glance. Yongden learned from a servant that they all came from a place situated beyond Menkong, and that circumstance added some strength to my resolution to avoid that small town, capital of the Tsarong province and seat of a governor.

The question asked by the woman had made us most unhappy. So, in spite of the trouble I had taken to powder myself with cocoa and charcoal, in spite of my pretty yak-hair hair-dressing, I did not look Thibetan enough in that Kham country where most women have a dark complexion! What more was to be done? It might be also that rumours had been spread about us, after our passage at Lhakang-ra. We did not know what to believe.

The jungle had ceased to be charming. I again began to see a spy behind every bush, and the water of the Salween muttered threatening or mocking words.

Then we bethought us that perchance we were alone responsible for the question that the Thibetan lady had asked us. We could not guess the extent of her geographical knowledge.

---

[1] The lake which appears on the maps under its Mongolian name, Koko-Nor—the Blue Lake—in Thibetan, Tso Nönpo. It is an immense salt lake in the Desert of Grass near the country of Amdo.

Perhaps she was learned enough to have thought of the Asiatic Russians when Yongden had mentioned "beyond the Blue Lake." But more likely she had confused *tso* (lake with *gya tso* (ocean) and had understood that we had come from the other side of the "blue ocean," which was tantamount to saying that we were not Asiatics. That idea reassured us, but we struck out forever from our travelling vocabulary the words "*tso parcho la,*" and transported our mother-country a good deal southward. We became natives of Amdo!

We were nearing the end of the last gorge before the wide broadening of the valley at the point where our path deserted the Giamo nu chu and turned toward the passes that led to the river Nu. Yongden walked ahead. He had already turned the corner of a rocky headland and was out of my sight, when a well-dressed man coming toward me appeared at the point of the small promontory. The path was exceedingly narrow and when two people met there one of them had to stand aside against the rock to allow the other to pass.

With a humility suitable to my part of an Oriental woman and beggar, I had already begun to make room for the traveller, but he stopped suddenly, quickly removing the gun he carried over his shoulder and the sword that was passed through his belt, according to the Thibetan fashion.[1] He first silently bowed down three times, then, with clasped hands and head bent, as when asking the benediction of a lama, he approached me.

Astonishment paralyzed thought. I mechanically obeyed an old habit acquired when I lived in lamaist monasteries, and laid my hands on the man's head. Before I had sufficiently recovered from my surprise to think of asking him who he was, he had again put on his gun and sword and was gone. I turned to look at him; he strode rapidly along the gorge, and after a few minutes was but a small moving black speck in the gigantic corridor.

[1] Thibetans do not enter monasteries or salute lamas with arms on them.

44

"Did you see that man?" I enquired of Yongden as soon as I rejoined him.

"Yes," he said.

"Did he speak to you?"

"No. He only greeted me with the usual '*Ogyay! ogyay!*' " [1]

"Do you know him?"

"Not in the least."

I related to my companion what had just happened, and he concluded that the man had seen that I was a *naljorma*.

As for me I suspected that the stranger had formerly met us both somewhere. He had recognized Yongden and had guessed the identity of the lay woman who followed him clad in plain white clothes. I was very sorry to have let him go without speaking with him. And now, although he had shown me respect by asking my blessing and, therefore, could have no bad intentions toward me, he might tell some one about his meeting and, as he was proceeding in the direction of Aben, such talks might prove dangerous.

But Yongden persisted in saying that he had never seen the man before, that he did not know us in the least, and that he had been prompted by some occult influences. Then he began to tell me several Thibetan stories about similar instances, and soon landed me in the phantasmagoric yet fascinating realm of thought-forms, previous lives, and many other kindred topics. But my modest wishes were confined to the desire that, whatever might have been the motive which he had obeyed, my safety might not be endangered by my unknown worshipper.

We were now approaching Thana, where we had been told that there existed a frontier station. Trusting the maps and some travel books that I had read, I believed that the pilgrims' road turned east toward a twin pass of the Dokar-la, leading to the Chinese territory on the watershed of the river Mekong. In reality the path to Menkong, the capital of Tsarong, is

[1] "You are taking trouble." A common polite expression that travellers exchange on the road, especially in eastern Thibet.

the only one to branch off at that place along the Giamo nu chu. The one which we were to follow northward forks only at Wabo. I did not know these details and was most preoccupied with the invention of a new story concerning the aim of our journey, as we should be leaving behind the sacred mountain which had until then supplied us with the plausible and respectable motive of performing a religious pilgrimage. I felt almost convinced that, if we kept to the circuitous road, nobody would take any notice of us, for was not that station at Thana probably established precisely in order to observe those who left it to set out for Thibet? I already had visions of barriers, of officials before whom travellers were led to be interrogated. What would that Thana village be like? I was puzzled and anxious.

As we were walking toward our fate—good or bad we could not know—we saw a few snowy peaks and a great part of the Kha Karpo itself, shining marvellously white, which, it pleased me to imagine, bid us a cordial farewell. At that time of year only dry, thorny shrubs were to be seen in the wide valley. The hills were barren and of a light-yellow colour. On the opposite bank of the river, which flows between high banks, we saw a monastery.

We managed to reach Thana at night. We arranged it even too well that time, it seems, for we were not able to find our way in the dark and arrived near a temple where there were a number of watch-dogs, who barked dreadfully at our approach. Happily, they were well shut in and could not escape to attack us; but I feared that people would look out to see who were causing the noise and make certain that they were not thieves. Furthermore, the passage of mysterious strangers in the night held the danger of enquiries about us and the risk of being reported at the station. To avoid this, Yongden called aloud to the shrinekeeper, asking shelter for the night for a tired *arjopa* who had hardly been able to struggle through the last lap of his journey on account of a bad leg. My companion's request was full of pathos and loud enough to be heard all over the temple buildings. During his performance I had

46

hidden myself out of sight. We were practically convinced that the shrinekeeper would not get up to receive a beggar at night. We knew our Thibet and Thibetans well enough to risk the trick, being certain of its result. When he had waited long enough, Yongden went away, lamenting aloud: "Oh, how unkind to leave a poor sick pilgrim out in the cold! How pitiless!" and so on. His plaintive voice faded gradually away, as at the opera in songs of supposed passers-by behind the scenes. It was rather a pretty effect amidst natural scenery of standing rocks, along a path that led downward to a stream. I nearly applauded.

We had passed the shrine all right. Whoever might have been staying in it would not, on the morrow, give a single thought to the crying beggar of the previous night. But where was the village? In the pitch dark we could not see it and, had we caught sight of houses, we should not have dared to venture in their direction, lest we fall in with dogs of the same species as those who watched over the temple.

Yongden insisted on lying down on the road itself. I preferred to go farther from the temple and find a more comfortable place. Discerning, in the shallow water, some stepping-stones which crossed the stream, I went scouting on the other side, where I discovered two caves. We had a house for the rest of the night! What a blessing! We should sleep as if really at home. I ran to fetch my companion, and we installed ourselves in one of the caves, where we ate our supper with the clear, fresh water of the stream as beverage (cool, perhaps, even too cool), and slept the sound sleep of the tired yet happy Thibetan *neskorpas* (pilgrims).

In the morning, when putting on my upper dress, which I used at night as a blanket, I discovered that I had lost my small compass. This was a most distressing event! First, the compass was useful to me, and, although I had another, I should miss it. But the worst danger was in leaving a foreign object behind us. If it was found, that compass might be talked about all over the country and officials would quickly realize that a foreigner had been staying in that locality. I spent some really unpleasant minutes searching in the dark for the lost article, which, fortunately, I found before long.

Anyhow, we had lost some extremely precious time. At daybreak a servant of the shrine came to fetch water at the stream, and we started in haste. We could now see the village quite near the place where we had slept. The country folk were already awake and busy with their early work, reciting, as they moved to and fro, those various mystic formulæ which, in lamaist lands, take the place which prayers occupy in other countries. Kindling the fire, giving fodder to the cattle, leading horses to drink at the stream, they went on with their muttering. A humming, like that from a hundred beehives, enveloped the village.

People looked at us from the top of their windows or from their flat roofs. We went along with our heads bent, humming like everybody else. Yongden enquired about the road from a man near the stream. A few minutes later we were out in the fields.

Some peasants, carrying ploughs, followed us on the way to their work; others were already occupied in distributing water in the irrigation canals. Although it was November, the temperature was mild. A winter crop grows in these valleys, so different in every respect from the bleak and icy trans-Himalayan Thibet. Here is a country where life is pleasant and easy, and nothing would interfere with the joviality of its inhabitants, if the taxes levied by the authorities did not increase every year.

We chatted with several people on our way till we reached the forest. Going through it, we ascended a pass called Tondo-la, the height of which is approximately 11,200 feet. Here, for the first time since leaving Yunnan, we pitched our tent. We had climbed down from the pass without finding any water on the road. At last I discovered a small spring in a narrow ravine and decided to stop there. It was extremely damp; I feared that we would both get sore eyes if we slept unsheltered, and thought that the tent might also afford us protection against wild animals who might carry off a part of our food supply during the night. However, we pitched it only long after nightfall and took it down before daybreak.

In the morning, we saw for the first time the river Nu, which flowed swiftly in a deep gorge to join the Giamo nu chu. We crossed it on a good bridge. At that time a large party of pilgrims overtook us and begged my companion to tell their fortunes. It is regarded as an unpardonable sin for a lama to refuse such a request. "Red Hat" sect lamas, in particular, who are credited with a profound knowledge of occult lore, can only with difficulty avoid acting as fortune-tellers, astrologers, exorcists, and the like. My companion endeavoured to combine each of his consultations with some simple words about the true Buddhist doctrine which might lead his hearers away from their deep-rooted superstition. He also added, according to circumstances, some advice about cleanliness—as far as hygiene can be understood by Thibetans.

On this occasion I had to remain for more than half an hour seated beneath a scorching sun which struck the yellowish barren cliff behind me. Yongden could not get rid of the exacting devotees. One consulted him about the way his cattle were prospering during his absence; another, desirous of adding a few carved stones in remembrance of his pilgrimage to the *mendong* which stood in his village, wished to know what would be the most meritorious and lucky sentence to inscribe on them. An overtired girl suffered from sore feet and feared to be left behind. She anxiously wanted to know if she would be able to walk in a few days' time, and her mother insisted upon knowing the name of the demon who had caused the swelling of the girl's feet and had stiffened her legs! That it could be the natural effect of long tramps neither she nor her daughter nor their companions would ever have admitted.

Faithful to a method which, for some years, had allowed us to relieve and cure many suffering Thibetans, Yongden, with impressive gravity, counted the beads of his rosary, threw some pebbles in the air, caught them again in his hand before they touched the ground, and performed a few other ceremonies accompanied by an unintelligible muttering in broken Sanskrit. My adopted son is really gifted for such ritualistic work and, had he continued his life in a lamasery, he might have become quite famous as an oracle or exorcist. But he had preferred an orthodox form of Buddhism which prohibits all superstitions.

"I see," he said, after some time, "there is a way to get rid of that demon, who is of a wicked kind. Listen well, all of you, so as to remember what I am about to tell you." The pilgrims immediately surrounded the lama, some squatting at his feet, some standing motionless with their backs against the cliff, straining their minds in a mighty effort to understand what the *ñönshes* [1] would order—a picturesque group, of which I felt sorry not to be able to take a snapshot.

"You will find a *chörten* on your way," declared Yongden— a prophecy that could not but be fulfilled, for *chörten* are numerous in Thibet. "You will stop at that place, and the sick girl will lie down next the *chörten* for three days, well sheltered, so that the sun's rays do not touch her head. Thrice each day, at sunrise, noon, and sunset, you will all assemble and chant *Dölma*.[2] Those who do not know *Dölma*, will recite *Mani*. The girl will go round the *chörten* three times while you are chanting, and, save for that short walk, she shall not move during the three days. After having walked round the *chörten*, the girl shall be each time well fed. Her feet and legs shall then be massaged in hot water, wherein you will put a pinch of the holy sand of the most sacred Samye monastery, which I will give you. After this has been done, the earth that has been wetted by the water shall be removed, thrown far away in a hole, and carefully covered with stones or earth, for the power of the demon will be washed away with that holy water and fall on the ground next the *chörten*. Should the demon fail to depart, this will show that you have made

---

[1] *Ñönshes:* a seer, a clairvoyant; literally, one who knows beforehand, who foresees.

[2] Praises of the Universal Mother. A mystic figure of the Tantrik pantheon, called in Sanskrit *Tara*.

some mistake in performing the rite and you must do it again at the second *chörten* you see on your way.

"Now, listen again. None of you must leave his companions until you have all reached your country together, for I see that the demon would immediately follow those who part from the girl, since he was not allowed to have his way with her, and would torment them in her stead. I will teach her mother a *zung* [1] and it will be a protection for her daughter and all of you, as long as you remain together.

The poor fellows felt as if in Heaven. The lama had spoken long, and what he had said they could neither well understand nor remember, which meant that he was exceedingly learned. Then Yongden commanded them to go on their way, and kept only the old mother, to impart to her the secret spell.

"*Bhhah!*" he thundered in her ear with terrific eyes.

Trembling, yet overjoyed at the thought that she had now nothing to fear from the evil spirits, the old woman bowed down with the utmost gratitude and went up the path, trying *sotto voce* to imitate the intonation of her initiator.

"Bhhah! . . . bhhah! bhaaa!" she muttered, and soon *a* turned into *ea*, into *e*, and finally seemed to stabilize itself in a sort of bleating: "Beaaa! beaaa!" I pretended to tie my garters, which had become loose, so as to remain behind and laugh at leisure, my head hidden in my large thick sleeves.

"What does it matter?" said Yongden, smiling. "The girl will get three days' rest, a little massage, and good food, and as the mother has the precious *zung* and will not leave her daughter, the other people will not abandon her, either. That is good honest work, and, moreover, I learned such tricks from you."

I could not reply. He was right, and I, too, thought that we had done a kind service to the afflicted and suffering maid.

When we reached the top of the cliff, we saw fields in all directions and a village before us, which we subsequently learned was called Ke. Most of the *neskorpas* had already reached it, and some were running back toward us.

[1] Zung, in Sanskrit *Dhārani*, a spell.

51

"Oh, Lama!" they said, "what a learned *ñönshes chen* you are! You told us rightly that we would quickly see a *chörten*. There it is, and the girl is already lying down. Please accept tea from us."

A *chörten* was indeed there, and also a small monastery whose few inmates, before long, heard about their wonderful colleague. The pilgrims, who were not beggars, but villagers of some means, had already bought several pots of spirit and drunk them, and they were now telling about strange miracles performed by my innocent companion. Each had contemplated a greater wonder than his friends. One asserted that, when crossing the river Nu, he had clearly perceived that the lama had not walked on the bridge, but alongside it, in midair!

Although he had not drunk any spirit, being a strict teetotaler, Yongden felt somewhat infected by their excitement. He told stories of far-off countries where he had been on pilgrimages—Riwo tse nga, the Chinese Hill of Five Peaks, near the great Pekin—the seat of the God of Wisdom, the *Changchub semspa Jampeion*,[1] and the most sacred mountain of *Kuntu Zungpo*,[2] where pure-minded pilgrims may see *Sangyais* [3] himself in a round *jalus*.[4]

I began to think that the fun was going too far. The whole village and the local *trapas* [5] had congregated round him, and he went on making *mo*, telling fortunes and the like. People brought presents, which he graciously accepted. I did not like such a compromising fame, but perhaps I was wrong, for who could have supposed that the mother of such a brilliant sorcerer was a foreign lady?

I managed, nevertheless, to attract the attention of my son, and with perhaps somewhat stern fervour I ejaculated, "*Karma*

[1] Better known by Orientalists under his Sanskrit name, Bodhisatva Manjushri.

[2] Samantabhadra, the all-good one.

[3] Buddha.

[4] Rainbow.

[5] *Trapas:* the real name of the lamaist monks, lama being the title of the ecclesiastic dignitaries, or incarnations of dead lamas. However, out of politeness, the title "Lama" is given to all members of the clergy when addressing them.

pa kien no!" which is a pious expression used by the followers of the Kargyud-Karma to call on their spiritual father, the head of the sect, but which in practice is now often no more than a mere exclamation. In the secret code which, as in a previous journey, I had devised, these holy words mean simply "Let us be off quickly!"

Perhaps a trifle vexed at giving up his triumph, Yongden declared that he would now ask leave to go on his way. People exclaimed that it was not possible, for the next village was far, we could not reach it before night, and not a drop of water was to be found on the way. Better, they added, it was to spend the night amongst them; they would give us a good room. My companion felt tempted—I understood it—but to the shy imploring glance he cast in my direction I replied with a still more fervid *"Karma pa kien no,"* which moved some of the people around me, who repeated devoutly, *"Karma pa kien no. . . . Karma pa kien no. . . ."*

Thus we went, and happy I felt to find myself again in silence and solitude. I scolded Yongden for the way in which he made himself conspicuous and told him a lot of things which made him sulky.

We climbed a pass which was about 7,500 feet high, and from there descended a dusty path cut into a range of white hills that reminded me of Kansu in northern China. Of water, truly, there was none, and the prospect of getting nothing to drink, either that evening or the next morning, added to the bad humour of the lama. The new moon lighted our way, and if we had not been tired we could easily have walked a part of the night. But at the sight of a small cave perched high above the road the desire to sleep overpowered us and we yielded to it all the more easily, since we had left behind two passes and a river, the dreaded Thana, and feared nothing from the next village. How wrong we were!

Picturesque indeed was our hostelry, with a small platform in front, but room and terrace were both so diminutive in size that we were fearful of rolling out of them in our sleep and breaking our necks on the rocks below.

The morrow was to be the first of a series of eventful days, well qualified to prostrate with nervous breakdown one less strong than myself.

We arrived at the village, which is called Wabo, in the middle of the morning, hungry and more especially thirsty. This was quite natural, as we had taken no refreshment whatsoever since our midday stay with the pilgrims near the *chörten*.

We had laughed so much at the demons the day before, that maybe a little one amongst them wished to play us a trick and suggested to us the idea (which we ought never to have conceived of) of stopping to make tea near a place where water had been brought through a rustic wooden aqueduct for the villagers.

A little snow had fallen during the night. I collected what twigs and dry cow dung I could find around the spot, while Yongden began to light the fire. The water was very long in boiling, my companion very slow in eating and drinking, and, as a result, a number of villagers—first two or three, then a dozen, and finally perhaps twice that number—gathered round us. A good woman, seeing how little wood I was able to pick up on the road, brought me some from her house. All would have gone smoothly had Yongden only spoken the tenth part of the "winged words" by means of which, like the divine Ulysses, he had delighted and bewitched the natives of Ke on the previous day. But an image could not have been more silent than the orator of yesterday. He did not utter a word or make a gesture. He only ate and drank and drank and ate alternately and endlessly. People looked at us with deep astonishment. Thibetans are a talkative lot, and Yongden's attitude upset all their notions concerning *arjopas*.

"Who are these people?" asked a woman, doubtless in the hope that we would answer the question. But the lama preserved the same stern silence.

What a pity! In my carefully devised secret code of formulæ for all emergencies I had not provided for the order, "Talk!" And now I was powerless, drinking my tea humbly behind the lama, who was seated on an old sack I had spread for him. I thought it prudent to accentuate my respect and to serve Yongden in all ways to avoid any suspicion about my personality. Alas! that, too, nearly turned to my loss.

I had taken away the empty kettle, at present used as a teapot, and proceeded to wash it, but the contact of the water with my hands had the natural result of cleaning them, and with that beginning of cleanliness appeared the whiteness of ny skin. I had not noticed this, so distressed was I by the strange danger-fraught behaviour of Yongden, when a woman, in a low voice, said to another near her:

"Her hands are like those of *philings!*"

Had she ever seen foreigners? That was doubtful, unless she had been at Bhatang, or elsewhere in Chinese Thibet, or again in Gyantze, in the extreme south of the country. But every Thibetan is imbued with a strong conviction about the cast of the foreigner's features. He or she is tall, fair-haired, with white skin, rosy cheeks, and *white* eyes, which may be understood to be the colour of any iris that is not black or dark brown. *"Mig kar"* (white eyes) is a common epithet of abuse for foreigners, all over Thibet. Nothing looks more horrid, according to Thibetan taste, than blue or gray eyes, and what they call *gray* hair, which is to say fair hair.

So the colour of my skin betrayed my nationality. I did not show in any way that I had heard the remark, and quickly rubbed my hands on the bottom of the greasy, smoked kitchen utensil.

Amongst the villagers there were now three soldiers. Good Heavens! There was a "post" in that village, and very likely there was none in Thana, which we had passed with such precautions. What would become of us! I heard a rumour spreading, "Are they *philings?*" And that petrified lama still continued to masticate some *tsampo!* I did not dare even to pronounce the *"Karma pa kieno,"* translated by "Let us be quickly off," lest my voice, in that awkward silence, should attract more attention to me.

At last Yongden rose and a villager ventured to ask him where he was going. What a terror! It was here, before all

55

these prying eyes, that we were to leave the pilgrims' road, since we were exactly at the junction of the road entering the Nu chu Valley and of the one going to China by way of the Kha Karpo range. That is, we had to confess openly that we intended to proceed toward the centre of Thibet!

Yongden calmly told them that we had made the pilgrimage, circumambulating the Kha Karpo, that it was now over, and that we were going back to our own country.

He did not add anything more. He put his load on his back. I imitated him, and we started off among the people, on the very road they all take when going to Lhasa.

And then the miracle happened—the little mischievous spirit who had enjoyed himself at our expense gave up the joke and began another one to our advantage.

The strain that was felt by everyone relaxed. I heard some men saying, jestingly:

"*Philings* going on a pilgrimage!"

This idea seemed extremely funny, and they all laughed.

"They are *Sokpos* [Mongolians]," said another, seriously, and this was what the whole village believed when, still silent, and walking as if in dream, we left the Kha Karpo pilgrims' road, and set out upon the greater pilgrimage to Lhasa.

We climbed toward a pass known as the Tong la. Travelling in Thibet is a continual going up and down; a single day's march leads one through considerable differences of level. This peculiarity adds greatly to the fatigue of the pedestrian, especially when he carries—as we did—a load on his back. But it also greatly enhances the charm of walking because of the great diversity of scenery which one sees each day.

After having crossed the ridge, we found a good straight path through the forest which led to a valley in which, to my great astonishment, I saw a river flowing toward China. At that time I had not yet read the accounts of the few explorers who, years ago, had trodden that same path when this part of Thibet had not yet been taken away from its old rulers and when—as I have already mentioned—foreigners were allowed to visit it.

Like me, they had all been puzzled by the mysterious river which seems to run toward the Mekong, whereas it is known that a gigantic range, crowned with everlasting snow, separates its watershed from that of the Salween. But as my information told me of but a single river, namely the Nu chu, which I was to follow upstream, I concluded that it took a bend round the range I had just crossed. A man whom I met down in the valley confirmed the fact: the river I had crossed two days before, which was then flowing toward the Salween, was the very same that I now saw before me.

The man explained to us that we should cross a bridge nearby and proceed upward to the monastery of Pedo, where we could purchase food. He also told us that the road following the stream led to Atunze (in Chinese territory) across several passes.

The country looked pretty. It was well cultivated and the upper part of the hills was woody and green, although it was winter.

A little farther from the bridge, a rounded spur divided the valley into two parts; the river flowed to the right, and a wide slope on which several villages were perched occupied the left. Behind the villages was a path leading to the mountains. For a little while, I felt tempted to take that road, thinking that it was a short cut to the Salween side. But reflection convinced me that I was still too near Chinese territory to attract attention by following a route of my own. Prudence demanded that I should continue for a time along the path trodden by *arjopas*, where we would pass unnoticed. Exploration, and its joys, would come later.

The sun set after we had crossed the bridge. I meant to pass the monastery at night, and to hide myself early in the morning at some distance from it, leaving to Yongden the task of going alone to purchase some food.

I would gladly have camped near the river where there was a charming natural grove with rivulets of clear water. But the lamasery was still far away, and it was better for the success of my scheme to stop only when we were close to it.

For the first time we made use of one of the rubber bottles we had carried with us, which were ordinary hot-water bottles. When I decided to add two of them to our extremely reduced luggage, I thought that they might help travellers devoid of blankets, as we were, to bear the cold of the winter nights in high altitudes. They could also be used to carry water across the dry regions. Yet, on account of their foreign aspect we dared not fill them before Thibetans, and for that reason we suffered thirst more than once when we could have easily carried with us enough water to make our tea.

We had, however, disguised our bottles in a style akin to that of their owners. Covered with a case of thick *nambu*,[1] plain red for one, and red and yellow for the other, they had become *shabluks*—that is to say, water pouches worn by lamas of yore, whose sham patterns continue to form part of the ecclesiastic garb of present-day lamaist monks. Though clothed in that fashion, there was considerable difference between our bottles, which came directly from a big American firm, and the purely conventional and useless simulacra that hang on the lama's *shamthabs*. However, as we did not mean to exhibit them freely, from a distance they could create a sufficient illusion.

Moreover, any article of our outfit which attracted the attention of the natives was immediately represented to them as having been purchased at Lhasa, and this gave us an opportunity of relating the wonders of the great city where so many foreign goods are offered for sale. People listened to Yongden, or to myself, if the audience happened to be mostly women. We cleverly spoke of other objects much more wonderful, that easily made them forget those found in our bags, and these were prudently hidden again.

Before the beginning of our journey I had settled with the lama that in any story we might invent, according to circumstances, we should never appear as people coming from outside Thibet, but that, on the contrary, those whom we should meet should be made to believe that we had travelled from Lhasa

[1] Thick Thibetan woolen cloth.

58

to the border, and were now on our way home. This gave us a certificate of Thibetan nationality and did away with the curiosity and the suspicion which fastens upon newcomers in the country. This was much safer in every way and allowed us also to speak as having bought at Lhasa the few foreign articles we carried with us.

We filled one of our bottles at the stream and left the pretty grove behind. The *gompa* (monastery) was situated a good distance from the bridge and night came before we had even discovered it. We followed a path cut in a woody slope above the river Nu. As it curved, we saw several fires burning higher up, which reminded us of those which had frightened us the second night after our departure. Most likely travellers camped there whom we should meet if we proceeded, which prospect displeased us greatly. Yet to wait until they had started next morning would have upset our scheme and forced us to pass the *gompa* in the middle of the morning, which we disliked even more. An official was established there, we had been told, and in any case I did not wish in the least to meet the "trapas" of the place. The monks were much more to be feared by us than ordinary villagers, for whereas the latter seldom leave their homes and know but little of the world beyond them, the enterprising clerical fellows travel all over Thibet, in China, India, Mongolia, and even in far-away Siberia. They see a lot of things and a lot of men, *philings* included, and are as a rule much more alert than their lay countrymen. We walked again for a while and reached the border of the woods. The ground had been cleared for cultivation, and our path, which had become very narrow, kept skirting the fences that enclosed the fields. On our left side, its edge ended abruptly above the river bank. The fires had ceased to flare and were luckily far from the road. We proceeded quickly and in the utmost silence. The new moon had set. We vaguely discerned some black form which might have been the walls of the monastery, and deemed it wise to wait until dawn, lest we should mistake our way near the lamasery, where several village paths probably crossed one another, and where dogs would bark if we wandered about.

A cold wind swept the cliff, no shelter was at hand. The best place we discovered was next a stone which screened us a little. I had carried the rubber bottle under my dress to prevent the water from freezing on the way; still, it was far from being even tepid when we drank a draught of it with a handful of dry *tsampa* for our supper. Then I lay down on the ground, keeping in my arm, as well covered as a child, the bottle containing the remainder of the water to drink when we should awake. Small heads of rocks piercing through the earth made a really painful couch, even for me, who from youth upwards had been accustomed to the bare boards affected by the Greek stoics.

When we got up, at the first rays of dawn, we saw the monastery standing a few steps before us and not at all in the direction we had thought it to be when arriving at night.

We passed along the walls and made haste to be out of sight. A well-dressed native chief passed us on horseback, coming from the road that leads toward Bhatang. He threw us an indifferent glance without stopping.

We could now see that there was no suitable place near the *gompa* where I could wait safely while Yongden made his purchases. Our way descended a narrow valley in which flowed a small tributary of the river Nu. Several farms and mills had been built on its banks. We met also an important traders' caravan coming from Lhasa. People were to be seen everywhere. I thought for a while that I could stay higher up in the woods, but already a girl was driving cattle in that direction. We continued to walk, exceedingly annoyed at moving away from the *gompa*, for we urgently needed fresh supplies of food. Healthy pedestrians like us have good appetites, and, at the risk of appearing a character devoid of all poetry, I confess that I ate a large quantity of barley-meal butter, and bread, when fortunate enough to get wheat-flour to make it. And in that respect the lama was very like his adopted mother.

After crossing the small valley, I discovered some large

MY JOURNEY TO LHASA

fields which were not to be cultivated before spring. I remained here a few hours, seated behind bushes, reading a Thibetan philosophical treatise, until Yongden, who had gone back to the *gompa,* returned, loaded like a mule. We then enjoyed an exceptional meal—a broth thickened with wheat-flour. Filling our breast pockets with dried apricots, we started off cheerfully. In the afternoon we again entered a wild region. We met some pilgrims walking leisurely, who belonged to a large party, numbering at least fifty people, whose vanguard we found farther along, already camped, boiling tea in cauldrons the size of tubs.

Yongden was delayed a long time. Some asked him to tell their fortunes, others to foresee happenings of importance for them or their families. Many came forward to be blessed.

Seated on the ground, I watched with amusement the various performances in which lama and believers played their parts with the utmost gravity, tinged, however, by that special good humour and overflowing gaiety which makes life among Thibetans so pleasant.

I delightedly forgot Western lands, that I belonged to them, and that they would probably take me again in the clutches of their sorrowful civilization.

I felt myself a simple *dokpa* of the *Koko nor.* I chatted with the women about my imaginary black tent in the Desert of Grass, my cattle, and the feast days when the menfolk race on horseback and show their cleverness as marksmen. I knew by heart the region I described, for I had lived there long, and my enthusiasm for my so-styled mother country was so genuinely sincere that no one could have guessed my lie. . . . After all, was it entirely a lie? I am one of the Genghis Khan race who, by mistake and perhaps for her sins, was born in the Occident. So I was once told by a lama.

At sunset we again found the dark forest with huge trees. The track was good, and as we had wasted so much time with the pilgrims, we wished to continue walking as long as possible.

Going down toward a ravine in which flowed a small stream, I noticed something lying on the ground, and on nearing it saw that the object was an old fur-lined bonnet, such as is worn by the women of Kham. Yongden lifted it with the iron end of his pilgrim's staff and threw it off the road. The bonnet did not go far, nor did it fall on the ground. It flew rather like a bird, and alighted, if I may use that word, on the broken trunk of an enormous tree.

A strange intuition warned me that the ugly-looking, dirty article was to be of great use to me—that, indeed, it had been *sent* to me—and in obedience to this occult suggestion I went down the track to fetch it.

Yongden did not like to carry it. Thibetans, when on a journey, never pick up even their own hats if they happen to fall from their heads to the ground, and would think still less of taking anyone else's they found on the road. They think that it would bring them bad luck. On the contrary, to find a boot on the road is a good omen and often travellers lift it, worn out and dirty as it may be, and place it for one second on their heads! My companion was free from such superstitions, but the greasy fur disgusted him and he could see nothing wonderful in such a find. A pilgrim, he said, had put it on the top of the load he carried on his back, and the bonnet had fallen off without its owner being aware of it. Either that, or the pilgrim, on account of the prevalent superstition, had preferred to abandon it.

"I do not go so far," I replied, "as to believe that some milliner goddess has sewn it for me seated on a lotus in Paradise. No doubt, a mere human being has lost it, but why has he or she lost it just there?"

"Well," rejoined my young companion, jokingly, "let us think, then, that an invisible friend of yours has pulled it off in order that it may fall on your way to-day. A most precious gift, indeed."

I said nothing more, but I carefully fastened the bonnet on my load and we proceeded.

It had snowed in the forest some days before; white patches remained everywhere. Tired, we stopped at the entrance of a transversal valley from which descended a large torrent flowing toward the river Nu. After a search, Yongden discovered a camping-ground out of sight of the road. But the cold wind swept that leafless spot. We therefore found a second place, lower down and near the track.

Until now our tent had been of little use to us as a *tent*. Since our departure, we had pitched it only once. But it was precious as a blanket. We used to lie down, in Thibetan fashion, with our luggage between us, so that nothing could be taken without awakening us. We both had our revolvers at hand. Our inner belts, containing silver and gold, were often hidden near us between stones or buried under dry leaves, or, if the country seemed safe, we placed them next us. The tent was then spread over the luggage and ourselves as well. When snow had fallen, that white tent spread on the ground, with a few dry leaves and twigs strewn on it, looked absolutely like a patch of snow amongst other patches, and we felt quite safe under it.

So we slept that night under our favourite imitation of "patch of snow" laid near the road. We were really over-confident about the illusion that we created. The trick was no doubt excellent; still, it could not work if we were under the very feet of the passers-by. Before daybreak, some traders passed, and one of them noticed something strange about our "snow patch."

"Is that men or snow?" he asked one of his companions.

"Snow," answered the fellow, who probably had not even looked our way, but saw snow all over the wood. The first who had spoken uttered a sound denoting doubt. We were laughing silently under our tent; but as the man could have thrown a stone at us to ascertain our living or inanimate nature —Thibetans being quick to throw stones, for various purposes —Yongden in a deep, sepulchral voice affirmed, "It is snow."

The loaded mules of the caravan started at the noise and the men laughed heartily. The lama then emerged from the cloth, leaving me under it, and chatted a few minutes with the traders, who were going to Atunze in Chinese Thibet.

"Are you alone?" they asked Yongden.

"Yes," he answered.

And they went their way.

That morning we passed a village and reached a small table-land from which we discovered, far in front of us, a steep hill on which could be seen a threadlike path that could be none other than that over the "To la," which we were to cross.

Those who wished to avoid the tiring climb and a second pass, the "Ku la," farther off, could follow a narrow path along the river. *Arjopas,* we were told, went that way. But I had heard that some parts of this path were exceedingly difficult, and that one had to cling to the rocks, walk on all-fours, and generally perform a series of feats which I did not feel tempted to undertake with a heavy load on my back. Better for us to follow the tiring but safer road. I did not yet know that the days would come when I could not avoid playing the equilibrist on rocks overlooking precipices!

I lacked another and much more useful piece of information. When looking at the hill and the perpendicular, narrow yellow ribbon which crossed it, I thought only of the fatigue of the climbing, and did not suspect that the whole success of my journey would be in jeopardy before our ascent began. I did not know, and so walked gaily down to the bottom of the valley.

We found a pleasant place next a stream, and feeling somewhat lazy, rested there for the remainder of the afternoon and the night. We were even imprudent enough to pitch our tent to make ourselves more comfortable, although we knew that a village was near us, beyond the stream.

Next morning, contrary to our custom, we did not make haste to start. A man came and talked a long time with Yongden, who invited him to drink a bowl of soup. And then we learned that we were loitering just in front of a Lhasa official's house!

We could only curse our folly, but what was done could not be undone. The man who had spoken with my young friend was a soldier, a retainer of the official. Thus, if any suspicion had arisen in his mind, and he reported it to his chief, we could not escape our fate.

I suppose that, when we left the place to proceed through the dreaded village, there was something in our mien of people sentenced to death and walking toward the scaffold.

On and on we went. The track skirted the fields and led rather far from the houses. We reached a *chörten*, around which I walked thrice with an edifying countenance, touching it with my forehead.

Higher and higher we were going; the official's dwelling was now far behind us and nobody had stopped us. Near by was the border of the wooded zone.

"Lha gyalo!" [1] We would shout it loudly when reaching the summit above the village. What joy would then be ours! Once more we were to escape!

"Oi! Oi!"

A villager was running after us across the fields.

"You must come before the *pönpo* [chief]," he said.

These were the very same words with which I had been stopped in Kham, after my hard journey through the snows, and the crossing of the "Iron Bridge."

With perfect composure, Yongden immediately mastered the situation. He put his load down on the ground, in order to avoid the curiosity of the *pönpo* and his servants, who, had they seen it, would most likely have wanted to look at its contents. He did not even give me a glance, as if the thought never occurred to him that an insignificant old woman like me could be worth the attention of a *kudak* (nobleman)!

"Let us go," he said to the man, and the two went off, chatting together.

I humbly squatted on the path, near our baggage. Taking my Thibetan rosary from my neck, I made a pretence of telling the beads.

The words I had heard took me back to my previous adven-

---

[1] "The Gods win!" An exclamation of triumph and good wishes for the victory of the good and the gods, which Thibetans utter loudly, especially at the top of passes and other summits.

ture. Very likely the end, now, would be the same. Once again, all the hardships endured would have been in vain. I saw ourselves escorted back to the nearest Chinese frontier, passing through the villages, a prey to the curiosity of the country folk. Not for one minute did I consider the idea of giving up the game. I had sworn that a woman should pass, and I *would*. . . . But when, and how, if it was not to-day? . . . Some time elapsed. . . . Presently I heard a voice. The sound grew louder. Yongden was returning, chanting a Thibetan liturgy. If he came alone and singing. . . . It was a sudden hope, nay, a certainty, which flashed across my mind! The young lama was before me, a mocking smile on his lips. He opened his hand and showed me a silver coin.

"He has given me a rupee as alms," he said. "Now let us be off quickly."

Yongden had learned that the *pönpo* was stationed there specially to watch over the road and see that no traveller crossing the pass should escape investigation. We could congratulate ourselves on our good luck, but we were far from having finished with incidents of that kind. We had not long to wait before our nerves received a still greater shock.

The very same morning, a little farther on our way, we again heard about a *pönpo* from a soldier who came hurriedly downhill to attend to some relay business.

This one was crossing the range which we had just begun to mount. The news terrified us. No escape was possible. The path lay along a steep slope that did not offer any hiding-place. The coming official would see us both. No doubt he would question us.

These Lhasa men, of whom a large number go to the English stations in the Himalayas and even to India, have many opportunities of seeing white people, and are much cleverer than the common folk of eastern or northern Thibet in detecting them. Anyhow, we could not escape the meeting.

We spent a few hours of terrible mental agony, listening for a noise to warn us of the dreaded apparition, looking desperately to the right and to the left in the hope that, as in the old tales, a rock or a tree would open suddenly and shelter us till the danger was over. But, alas, no miracle happened! Fairies and gods left us apparently unaided.

In the middle of the afternoon we suddenly heard the jingling of bells. Just above our heads, on the winding path, appeared a well-dressed, sturdy man followed by soldiers and servants leading horses. He stopped, astonished at the sight of us. According to Thibetan custom, we threw ourselves hurriedly on the low side of the road, to show our respect. The official proceeded downward and stopped again before us, surrounded by his followers.

Now began the questions about our mother country, about our journey and other things. When all had been said, the *pönpo* still remained looking silently at us, as did all who were behind him.

I felt as if needles were piercing my brain, so awful was the tension of my nerves. Did these men doubt us? That silence must be broken or something bad would come of it. What could I do? . . . Yes, I knew.

With the chanting tone of the Thibetan beggars, only a little moderated by reverence, I implored a charity.

"Kusho rimpoche, nga tso la sölra nang rogs nang [Noble sir, give us alms, please!]"

My voice broke the concentration of the group. Even physically I felt the relaxation. The Thibetans had lost their suspicious manner. Some laughed. The good official took a coin from his purse and handed it to my companion.

"Mother!" exclaimed Yongden, simulating a most happy surprise, "look what the *pönpo* gives us!"

I manifested my joy in a way befitting my assumed personality, with a wish—very sincere, and coming from the bottom of my heart—for the prosperity and long life of my benefactor. The latter smiled at me and I answered the favour of his smile with the most respectful of Thibetan salutes. I put out my tongue as far as I could extend it.

"Jetsunma [reverend lady]," said Yongden, a few minutes later, "you spake truth indeed when you told me, in the forests

of Kha Karpo, that 'you would make them dream and see visions.' No doubt that fat fellow and his retainers, who looked so long at you, have been bewitched."

Standing at the top of the pass, we shouted, loudly and heartily.

"*Lha gyalo! De tamche pham* [The gods win; the demons are defeated]!"

But I did not allude to the two kind *pönpos* in mentioning demons; quite the contrary. May happiness befall them till the last of their earthly days, and thereafter.

CHAPTER III

THE joy which our double victory had left us was not devoid of nervousness. We were now on the alert and expected to confront a *pönpo* at each turning of the path. On our way down, the jingling of a bell that we heard coming in our direction gave us a terrible fright. The bell, however, was attached to the neck of a goat, which soon appeared, carrying some baggage belonging to an aged couple going on a pilgrimage to the Kha Karpo.

The husband was a lean, tall *khampa* with bright eyes in a bold wrinkled face suitable to a retired robber chieftain, and the wife's slightly stooping figure still allowed one to guess what an energetic matron she had been. Together, with the goat bearing its queer head haughtily as if in utter disgust of the masters who had enslaved her frail body but had not tamed her wild little mind, they formed a most picturesque group.

The vivacious animal took the opportunity of our arrival to turn its back and run away. The old people tried to run after it, but they were not a match for that little demon, which trotted a few steps, then stopped and looked at them mockingly, and then started off again. It looked really intelligent and worthy of a better lot than that of a beast of burden. Yongden succeeded in catching it and leading it upward again. The pilgrim pair thanked him profusely. Beholding the goat which now waited patiently for them, the lama addressed the two villagers seriously.

"Be careful," he said, "to be very kind to that beast. It has been related to you in a previous life when it was a human being. On account of some bad deeds it has been reborn in the sorrowful animal kingdom. On account, also, of previous good actions, it has now got the happy chance of going to the holy Kha Karpo. Owing to the merit of that pilgrimage, it will be once more a man in its next life, and you three will meet again, so do your best in order that feelings of friendship may be cultivated between you which will bear good fruits in the future."

The red hat of my companion, perhaps also the dark forest that surrounded us and the first shadow of the evening that spread all around, imparted a peculiar solemnity to that astonishing oracular pronouncement. The old peasants looked deeply impressed and expressed their gratitude to the seer lama who had revealed to them such an important mystery.

Before we started I saw the woman taking a few packages out of the goat's load to lighten it, while the old man patted it.

"The little thing will be happy now," Yongden told me, as we continued to walk down the hill. "They will treat it kindly and allow it to die a natural death.

"Why did I invent that story? Really, I could not tell; it came by itself."

"Could it not be," I suggested, "that you yourself in a previous life were related to the goat?"

My prophet friend stopped, gazing at me, trying to guess if I was joking or speaking seriously. He did not appear to appreciate that relationship much, even in a remote past.

I laughed.

"Well, well," said Yongden, "after all, a good beast deserves much more esteem than many men who are but scoundrels. Let me be the *aku* [1] of the goat, if you like. I do not mind. It was a nice little thing. . . ."

The incidents of the day had put a great strain on our nerves, and in spite of the little fun we had just enjoyed we felt really tired and not in a mood either to walk the whole night or to stay amongst talkative people in a village, even if we could have reached one, which was rather doubtful. Our road lay on the side of the range, which remained most of the time in the shade, so that the streams were scalloped with ice and the ground deeply frozen. That circumstance did not

[1] Aku, paternal uncle.

promise an agreeable camping; nevertheless, we decided to stay in a melancholy valley which crossed our path. Most luckily, wood was lying on the ground in large quantities, but even before a big fire we remained shivering, and the desolate landscape seemed to add to the sensation of icy cold which pervaded us.

To sleep unsheltered in such a spot seemed decidedly miserable. I thought that, although in pitching the tent we lost the benefit of our blanket, we should be more comfortable with a roof over our heads. We therefore filled two rubber bottles with boiling water and slept with them under our dresses, in the well-closed tent, whose thin cloth, however, was a very feeble barrier against the cold.

We did not reach the village situated at the foot of the Ku la until the middle of the afternoon. Yongden visited a few houses to purchase food, and the good people pressed him to stay overnight because, they said, it was too late to cross the pass that day. We knew it, but we had travelled so slowly during the last week that we wished to push a little ahead. Moreover, I had not yet slept amongst Thibetans since leaving Yunnan, and I deemed it prudent to delay until we should be farther in the interior of Thibet before venturing on intimate contact with the people of the country, thus giving them the opportunity of observing us at close quarters.

So Yongden, taking advantage of the fact that I had continued to walk while he was busy making his purchases, pointed me out, already high on the winding path, and declared that we should have thankfully accepted their kind hospitality had we been together, but that he could not now call his old mother back.

We cooked some soup for our supper by the roadside, and crossed the pass at about midnight. It was covered with forests, and a grassy slope free of trees rose from the path itself. Perhaps in daytime one could get a view of the surrounding country from its summit, but it was of course impossible to ascertain it at night.

The climbing had warmed us, and tired us as well, so that

I felt tempted to pitch our tent among the evergreens that grew in clusters on the small flat piece of ground forming the top of the pass. We were neither thirsty nor hungry, and could have waited to drink tea until we had found water lower down on the next day. But Yongden objected that a traveller never spent the night on the summit of a pass, and that we should be frozen to death if we were foolish enough to stop and sleep. It was nonsense; we should obviously have been cold, after the heat produced by our walk had cooled down, but there was no fear of freezing. Be that as it may, it is difficult, even for one who has had a partly foreign education from childhood, to give up entirely the ancestral notions of his native land. True Thibetans never spend the night on the top of the pass, and the height of their mountains sufficiently explains that custom, but I suppose that even in the middle of the summer, and in a warmer country, most of them would still strongly hesitate to depart from their time-honoured rule.

As my companion appeared so reluctant to halt, I did not want to press him. We continued on our way. About an hour later we reached a partly level, wide ground sheltered by huge trees but free from undergrowth. In the night it appeared extraordinarily majestic; a mountain stream roared near by against a wall of whitish rocks and added greatly to the impression caused by the site itself. This was an ideal camping-place and we were not the only ones to appreciate it as such, for, after having wandered about a little, Yongden and I discovered several primitive hearths marking the spots where travellers were in the habit of stopping to make tea. Near one of them we slept without pitching our tent. We had heard about brigands rambling between the two passes, waiting for travellers, and did not want to attract their attention. Still, we lighted a small fire to boil some tea.

I had seldom had a more sumptuous bedroom than that natural and immense hall whose tall pillars supported a roof of thick foliage. It reminded me of the temple-like glade where I had halted one night while rounding the Kha Karpo. But this place was much larger and less gloomy.

The next day, I enjoyed a lazy morning to compensate for our nocturnal tramp. We were eating a flour broth which my naturally excellent appetite, much increased by the pure air and long daily walks, made me find delicious, when a man appeared. He was one of the villagers who had accompanied the baggage of the *pönpo* whom we met on the road, and had witnessed the generosity of the gentleman. To such a man we could not be suspect, and moreover the smell of the broth kept warm on the embers was an attraction sufficient in itself. He came straight to us, sat himself near the fire, and a talk followed our invitation to take his bowl out of his *amphag* [1] and to share our meal. This is never refused by Thibetans, who are capable of eating any amount at any time.

As was to be expected, Yongden had to cast lots and the man went away, after having invited us to his house in the next village, called Gyatong.

We again crossed a minor pass during the morning. Thence a steady descent on a good path led us to a cultivated area. On reaching it, we met a large party of pilgrims, who certainly numbered more than one hundred, mostly lay people, men and women. Some of them stopped my companion for the inevitable business of casting lots. This time, however, the monotony of that work was relieved by the subject proposed to the science of the seer by one of the enquirers. This man had brought with him from his home a small ass which carried his luggage. The object of the *mo* was to know if it was good, or not, to let the animal go round the Kha Karpo with his owner. If it were foreseen that the journey would turn out badly, the beast would be left at Pedo *gompa* and the villager would take it home on his way back at the end of his pilgrimage.

The little long-eared fellow was not to be consulted, but its good luck had led it to a compassionate friend. Yongden afterward told me that he pictured to himself all the steep climbing that would be hard on the tiny feet of the poor donkey,

[1] Amphag, the breast pocket formed by the wide dress of the Thibetans tightly tied with a belt.

the high passes, now covered with deep snow, the frosty nights to be passed in the open, and all the other troubles which would befall the little slave. How much happier it would be to get a month's rest in the pleasant grazing grounds of the Pedo Valley!

So, after appropriate gestures and recitations, the oracle declared that without the least doubt the beast would die if it only came in sight of the Kha Karpo, and that such a death happening during a pilgrimage would greatly diminish the merits and blessed results which each pilgrim expected from his pious journey!

That community of interests was created to insure that not only the master of the animal, but all his companions would look carefully to it that the latter be left behind at Pedo!

Yongden was profusely thanked for his remarkable and most valuable advice, and a few presents entered our provision bags in gratitude. While the young man was delivering his oracle, a well-dressed lama came into sight, accompanied by a few retainers, all riding beautiful horses. As he proceeded I noticed that he was looking at my son. Perhaps he too harboured in his mind some disquieting thoughts and would like to learn the future from the "Red Cap *ñönshe*" whose air, I must admit, announced a high degree of proficiency. But his rank did not allow him to humble his fine travelling robe of bright yellow brocade by alighting on the dusty road. Perhaps he sighed when the ragged seer, who had by then finished lecturing his pilgrims, passed near him without asking his blessing or showing any special mark of respect. Twice he looked backward at him, but seeing me and being probably ashamed to be caught paying attention to a mere *arjopa*, he quickly turned his head, and I saw only his shining yellow back and his large gilded travelling hat of wood which was almost the same shape as the roof of the monastery of which he was the lord.

As it was still early, we did not wish to halt, and preferred to dispense with the invitation we had received. So, instead of looking for the house of our would-be host, we endeavoured to cross the village speedily. We had nearly reached the end of the inhabited zone when, passing by a farm, a door opened in the enclosure of a courtyard, and, lo! the man whom we had already met several times appeared as if out of the wall, like a hobgoblin. I suppose that he must have been waiting for us. Yongden tried vainly to parley with him, but the farmer would not listen. Why did we wish to proceed, since we were certain not to reach the next village before night? The astonished villager put the question to us and we did not know what answer to give him, for authentic *arjopas* sleep in the jungle only when they cannot possibly avoid it. As a rule they halt near some building, and when happy enough to be called inside they never think of refusing the good luck. I was very much annoyed, but feared to seem strange in preferring the jungle to the hospitality of a farm of comfortable appearance. We therefore stepped in, uttering thanks and blessings, and were shown to the top story, where lived the family, the ground floor being, as usual, occupied by stables.

This was the first time I had been the guest of Thibetans in my rôle of a beggar. A Thibetan house had nothing new for me, but my present disguise made things very different from what they had been in the course of my previous journeys. Although on those I did not indulge in Western customs, the servants who followed me, my fine beasts, and my good lamaist attire kept my hosts respectful and distant. I enjoyed all the privileges of quietness and privacy, or as much privacy as there is in the East. And the life of a lama of rank is far from being unpleasant. On the contrary, I could not now expect much attention, but only, at the best, the condescending kindness of these coarse and common folk who would include me in Yongden's train, his dress as a member of the religious order commanding a certain respect.

I was to experience various things which until then I had only observed from afar. I should be sitting on the rough floor of the kitchen, which was dirty with the grease of the soup, the butter of the tea, and the spit of the inmates. Well-meaning women would offer me a scrap of a piece of meat which they had cut on the lap of their dress which had been used, maybe for years, as a handkerchief and a kitchen towel. I should have to eat in the way of the poor, dipping my unwashed fingers in the soup and in the tea, to knead the *tsampa*, and to do any number of things which disgusted me. Yet I knew that such penance would not be without reward, and that under cover of my inconspicuous garb of a poor pilgrim I should gather a quantity of observations which would never have come within reach of a foreigner, or even, perhaps, of a Thibetan of the upper classes. I was to live near the very soul and heart of the masses of that unknown land, near those of its womenfolk whom no outsider had ever approached. To the knowledge I had already acquired about the religious people of the country I would add another and quite intimate one, concerning its humblest sons and daughters. For this it was certainly worth while overlooking my disgust and making the even more difficult sacrifice of delightful hours of solitude in the enchanting jungle.

The man who received us was a rather wealthy villager. Nevertheless, he allowed us to cook our own food, a broth of which he took his share, thinking, perhaps, that it was his due for having supplied a few turnips which he cut without peeling or washing and threw in the pot. In any other country, the sand would have been noticeable in the soup, but I cannot say often enough that Thibet is a land of wonder which changes everything for the best. At least it has always been so for me. The broth was delicious.

Some neighbours called in the evening. They were all informed by our host of the two Lhasa officials' generosity toward us, and Yongden declared boldly that these good gentlemen of Ü and Tsang were religious-minded and that he was accustomed to receive such bounties.

I profited by the opportunity to enquire about places where we could expect to meet other officials. I said that we had exhausted our money and we would want to beg from them food or silver on our way back home. I had invented that story so as to inform myself as minutely as possible about the *pönpos'* residences. The peasants would think my eagerness to know the smallest details of the situation of the *zongs* [1] was due to the necessity of securing food. People who sought with such earnestness to meet officials could not but appear honest and respectable travellers who had nothing to fear from the authorities. Had the Thibetans whom I met during my journey conceived the least doubt about my origin, such enquiry, and the reason given for it, would have immediately dispelled their suspicion.

That evening I heard that the military rolls were filled in the Nu Valley in the very same way as in the north of Kham. A number of villagers were enlisted who could remain at home and continue their ordinary work, but had to join the troops as soon as they were ordered. As wages they enjoyed several advantages—exemption of taxes or of statute labour and sometimes a small salary paid generally in kind.

A thing which had surprised me very much, two years before, in Kham, had been to hear the reports about the uncommonly large number of soldiers stationed at the new Thibeto-Chinese border. One spoke of three hundred men in such a monastery, three hundred in such another, three hundred again in a third, and so on. The repetition of that number "three hundred" first attracted my attention. I was accustomed to find such repetitions in the sacred Scriptures of the Orient. It was a question, in some books, of five hundred followers, five hundred chariots, five hundred sheep, five hundred no matter what. One had to understand that the conventional expression in reality meant merely an indefinitely large number. In later literature the modest five hundred grew to be five thousand, eight thousand, till they reached the eighty thousand of the Mahâyânist Buddhist treatises, to which the good Thibetan translators have still added a few thousands and hundreds of their own. Now, the Thibetan staff seemed to apply the same methods to the reckoning of its regiments. I went to the bottom of the mystery and learned that strict orders were given

---

[1] Zong: originally a fort, but, by extension, nowadays any building that is the seat of an official or of a local chief of tribe.

to the people all along the Sino-Thibetan border to speak of powerful troops stationed in the watch posts. Then, when I myself went to investigate on the spot, and discovered half a dozen or ten warriors where three hundred were said to have their abode, I was told that the remainder were "at home." That meant that the fifty or hundred which made up the mythical three hundred were but villagers who would be provided with a gun and sent to fight if the Lhasa government deemed it wise. In the meantime the actual rulers do not appear to trust their countrymen newly 'liberated" from the Chinese rule. Several times I asked regular soldiers why they were all men from central Thibet, and the answer was always the same: "If the Khampas had good guns they would fire at us." On one occasion some of the regulars from Tsang told me that a few years before, when they fought against the Chinese in western Szetchuan, some of the Thibetan villagers had fled away and, at night, when the Lhasa troops were camped in the conquered place, they returned with Chinese soldiers and fell on them with their swords. In view of this, when it is considered indispensable to arm the reserve soldiers who remain at home, the government supplies them only with old-pattern Thibetan or Chinese guns. Men who held them in their hands smiled when I asked the reason for it. "Those from Lhasa," they said, "do not wish us to be able to match their own soldiers. They know what some of us might do."

The hatred of the new Lhasa masters did not seem to have reached that degree in the Tsarong and Tsawarong valleys; but even though they are patiently accepted, it is easy to understand that they are not much liked.

We left the hospitable farmers at dawn, and proceeded on our way along the valley.

Few landscapes in the world can compete with the graceful yet majestic scenery of the Nu Valley. We crossed large meadows strewn with rocks of different sizes and shapes, where trees of various species grew, here, isolated, there in clusters, yonder forming groves, as if they had been trimmed and planted where they stood by some artistic gardener. An air of gentle mystery, of pristine purity, spread over everything. I seemed to be walking across a picture out of an old book of legends, and would not have been very startled had I suddenly surprised some elfs seated on sun rays, or come upon the Enchanted Palace of the Sleeping Beauty.

The weather continued to be glorious, and, strangely enough, though shallow ponds and rivulets were frozen, the night was not really cold.

The queer glimmers of hidden fires that had puzzled us in the Kha Karpo forest reappeared in the darkest recesses of this natural park. They became so much a part of the nocturnal landscape that we did not trouble any more about them, whatever their cause may have been.

Every day we met groups of pilgrims journeying toward the holy Kha Karpo. Villages were near enough to allow them to spend the nights in shelter. For my part, I preferred to sleep under the trees, shrouded in silence and serenity.

Wild animals seemed scarce in the valley. Once, when I remained awake longer than usual, I saw a wolf passing near us. It trotted by with the busy yet calm gait of a serious gentleman going to attend to some affair of importance. Although it was well aware of our presence, it did not show the least curiosity or fear, but went its way with the utmost indifference, as if intent on affairs of its own.

I have said that, when putting on my Thibetan disguise I used Chinese ink to blacken my hair. It did not prove a very fast dye; a great part of the stuff came off on the turban which I wore after the Lutzekiang fashion. I therefore revived the jet-black colour of my plaits from time to time. Needless to say, during this work my fingers got their share of dye! But this did not matter much, for the personality of the old beggar mother which I had assumed required me to be as dirty as possible, and I frequently used to rub my hands on the smoky bottom of our kettle to match the colour of these of the country womenfolk. So ink could not be conspicuous.

On one occasion when I begged in a village of the Nu Valley, this dye gave birth to a comical, although rather unpleasant, incident.

I had gone from door to door, reciting prayers according to the custom of needy pilgrims. A good housewife called Yongden and me inside for a meal, and poured in our bowls curd and *tsampa*. The custom is to use one's fingers to mix them. So, forgetting all about the hair and ink business to which I had attended a few hours before, I dipped my fingers in my bowl and began to knead the flour.

But what is this? It becomes black; dirty streaks appear and grow wider on the milky meal. . . . Oh, I see! The dye on my fingers comes off. What is to be done?

Yongden, who has just glanced at me, sees the catastrophe. Comic as it is, the situation is nevertheless serious. It could provoke embarrassing questions, lead to the discovery of my identity.

"Eat quickly!" the lama advises in a suppressed but most imperative tone. I try. . . . What a nasty taste!

"Eat, eat quickly!" urges my young companion desperately; "the *nemo* [hostess] is coming back to us." And shutting my eyes, I hastily swallow the contents of the bowl.

We proceeded through this beautiful country toward the monastery of Dayul. Though previous meetings with *pönpos* had all ended nicely for me, I had not the least desire to take willingly more chances of that kind. So, knowing that an official resided at Dayul, I had decided to pass the place at night.

The thing appeared plain enough. Yet for us who did not know the region, who had no milestones as guides and who moved in a dense forest, it was rather difficult to regulate our gait in order to arrive at the monastery at the time chosen. One morning some villagers told us: "You will reach Dayul to-day." This was news, but how vague! Was one to make haste, or to take it leisurely so as to arrive during the day? We could not guess. The Thibetans, like most country people, except the Chinese, have no precise idea of distance. The latter can at any moment on any road tell you how many *lis* it is from one place to another.

Out of fear of emerging from the woods in front of the *gompa* before night had fallen, we spent a part of the day hidden under the trees near the river, eating and musing, with the result that, the monastery being farther than we had supposed, we tramped for a long time at night before discovering it.

Through the Eden-like valley, even more romantic in the darkness, we proceeded in complete silence, straining our eyes in vain in an endeavour to discern shapes of buildings on the opposite shore of the river on which, we knew, stood the monastery. We had nearly become convinced that, having delayed too long on the way, we should not reach it before daybreak.

As the time passed my anxiety increased. I walked nervously ahead when I saw white forms, like walls, in the middle of the widening path. We had arrived near two *mendongs* separated by *chörtens* and surrounded by a large number of mystic flags. We could still see no houses on the opposite bank, but I was too well acquainted with Thibet to have the least doubt that we were in front of the monastery. A few minutes later we reached the bridge spanning the river in front of the *gompa* about which we had been told. We knew that we did not need to cross it, although in addition to an important track going to Dowa and other places, several bypaths existed, on the right bank of the river Nu, which we could have followed. But I had decided to continue on the left bank, in order to avoid the monastery completely.

The night was clear, stars shone in the sky without a cloud, yet their dim light did not allow us to see far ahead. The path we had followed for many days seemed to end near a second bridge, about which I had heard nothing. Anyhow, no other passage appeared possible and we were in a great hurry to be far from the *gompa*.

The bridge once crossed, we found ourselves walking on stones amongst which water streamed everywhere. We pushed on for some distance; then I became convinced that we had missed the way. We went back, crossed the bridge again, and, while nearing its end, we heard a feeble noise. In no time we hid ourselves behind a wall close to the river. Then I looked around me. Heavens! We were in a small courtyard! A few steps away people were probably sleeping who might awaken and discover us.

Taking the utmost care to avoid being heard, we went out and walked toward the *mendong* to look for another way. But except for the two bridges, it really seemed that there was none.

We hardly knew what to think. We might have been misinformed or have misunderstood the directions that had been given to us, but we could not remain there to ponder over the matter. We must make haste to leave the vicinity of the monastery and go wherever we could, at the risk of trying to find the right way again on the morrow, if we had missed it, or even of being compelled to change our itinerary.

Then Yongden went to scout beyond the bridge which was in front of the *gompa*. At length I vaguely discerned the whitish mass of the monastery outlined in a recess of the hillside. It reminded me of the *chagzam*[1] and of my last failure . . . and at this particular moment such a memory had nothing pleasing in it! Under the feet of the lama the planks of the bridge made an awful noise. Then silence fell for a long time, until finally I heard the noise made by the young man in returning. It is impossible, I thought, that nobody has been awakened. Soldiers or servants will come. I awaited a shout calling the night traveller, commanding him to come forward, show himself and tell why he was roaming at that hour. I feared even worse; shots in the night; a bullet which, perchance, might hit Yongden . . .

The report of the scout was not encouraging. He had seen but one path leading from the shore to the *gompa;* the tracks probably started from behind the buildings.

[1] Chagzam, the "Iron Bridge," which I crossed in rather dramatic circumstances in a previous journey.

Whatever it might be, we did not want to risk ourselves near the monastery.

The noise made by my companion had rendered a quick flight still more urgent. We ran toward the first bridge we had crossed, passed again through the water and amongst the stones and reached a small shrine built under a tree. There our path divided in two. We turned to the left without knowing why, climbed a steep winding path, and arrived at a village. Beyond it, higher up, we lost ourselves amongst irrigation canals and fields built terrace upon terrace. Where were we to go? . . .

Once more Yongden put his load down beside me and started scouting. I sat on crumbling stones, fearing, each time that I moved, to slide down the slope. A cold wind arose; I shivered, crouched amongst the baggage. Suddenly a dog barked above me and continued for a long time, tiring my over-strained nerves. Was the lama in that direction? Would he find the road? He did not come back. Several hours went by, as I could see by the radium dial of my small watch which I consulted again and again. What had happened to him?

Far away big stones began to roll down. . . . What was that? A small landslide only, or an accident? . . . In the dark, a slip caused by a shadow is enough to send the wanderer rolling down to break his neck on the rocks or be drowned in the river. I stood in readiness to go and look for the young man. He stayed too long; something bad must have happened. I went a few steps; all was darkness around me. How could I discover him? And if he came back while I was away, how frightened he would be at the sight of the loads abandoned and myself gone. And would either he or I be able in the darkness to find the place where we had left the luggage? If no one remained there, who could signal as faintly as possible to the one who came back? Prudence commanded me to stay, and my inactivity added to the anxiety which tormented me.

The scout appeared at last. I had guessed right. He had fallen and been carried down with sliding stones. Happily, he had stopped on a small platform, while a boulder jumped near him and continued its course down. He was a little excited, as well he might be, after such a narrow escape, but his main thought was about the road. He had found none. The situation was critical. We could not think of remaining perched on that bare slope where we could be seen from all sides at the first gleam of dawn.

We must go down, I said, if need be; as far as the *mendong* in front of the *gompa*. In that way, if people see us in the early morning we will not appear strange, and can pretend that we have slept at the monastery or near it. There was nothing else to do. We once more crossed the village, but the night faded as we wandered. As soon as we had reached the last house it was daybreak.

It was necessary, now, to go farther down. If asked whence we were coming, we could answer quite plausibly that we were coming from the monastery. There remained only to ascertain if the path on which we were was the right one.

Yongden left me seated against the fence around a field, and, going up again to the farms, he knocked at a door. A half-awakened man opened a window of the upper story, and from him, the lama learned that we had but to climb again to about the place where I had spent a part of the night, and keep on to another village.

I quickly took up my load, and I for the third time, and Yongden for the fifth, together crossed that tiresome village. We proceeded as silently and as quickly as we could, deeming it prudent to avoid the inhabitants. As for the man of whom my son had asked his way, he could speak of but one lonely lama pilgrim, for he had not seen me.

We arrived at the top of the hill, where we found several big houses. One of them looked particularly large and well built. Most likely it was the abode of one of those petty princes who, before the Lhasa government had annexed eastern Thibet, were independent rulers, each one on his own small territory. Or it might have been that the Lhasa official lived there, and not in the monastery, as we had understood.

From there we could easily see Dayul *gompa* beneath us. People were already afoot. A woman appeared and I went piously round a *chörten*, which is the proper thing for a pilgrim to do at the beginning of the day. There was a crossroad here, but my young friend did not see it. He thought that my wanderings meant that I had found no path on the other side and disappeared at full speed up a road opening on his right. I followed hastily to tell him that he was turning his back to the river Nu, but before I could join him a man barred his way and politely, yet with an inquisitive look which turned my blood cold, asked him several questions about his country, his journey, and the like; but to my astonishment he did not look at me. Nervous, overtired by his exertion during the previous night, Yongden answered blunderingly. I was dying of fear!

We learned that we had made a mistake, and had taken the Chiamdo road, instead of that of Zogong. We retraced our steps, but now we had been seen and that villager with his suspicious look and his inquisitive questions knew which way we had gone.

What a result for all the trouble we had taken during a whole night!

At sunrise we saw once more Dayul *gompa*, all white in its nest of green woods. I feared the man would inform the *pönpo*. I calculated the time he would take in going down to the monastery, seeing the official, saddling a horse, and for a rider to catch up with us. It could not have taken very long. Yet nobody appeared behind us. . . . But yes, there is a peasant! . . . He carries a bag; he is on foot. . . . The *pönpo* would not send a man after us with a load on his shoulders. . . . He overtakes us; he is gone. . . . The path is empty behind us. We continue our walk.

A jingling of bells makes us start. A horseman approaches. I straighten my back. I do not want to faint, but I feel the blood leaving my brain, everything around me swims and darkens. I have just the time to move to the side of the path, to avoid being knocked down by the horse. The man has passed us; the tinkling grows fainter and finally ceases.

We are still far from being completely reassured, but emotion and a long tramp have exhausted our strength. Below the road, cut high on the hill, a series of large natural terraces descends in steps down to the river.

They, also, in the rosy light of the early morning, remind me of fairyland gardens. Autumn leaves blaze in their golden and purple tints around the dark greens of the fir trees. Strewn on the grass, sprinkled in places with a fine snow, they make a carpet such as no emperor has ever seen in his throne room.

I tell Yongden to follow me down. We quickly boil our tea and eat some *tsampa* with a ferocious appetite. Emotions may tire me, but can never prevent me from eating or sleeping. Sleep is especially needed. And now the sun is shining and will keep us warm.

We continued on our way in the afternoon and reached a hot spring. There are quite a number of them all over Thibet, but we had not yet come across any since we left Yunnan. I felt delighted at the prospect of a warm bath. A rustic basin had been built with stones for that purpose, near a rocky wall which sheltered it. I had only to wait until night to enter the water without any fear of allowing the colour of my skin to be seen by occasional passers-by!

Judge of my annoyance when a family of pilgrims—father, mother, and three children—came and pitched their camp next us! I had not the least doubt that they would all sit in the basin, for Thibetans are very fond of hot natural baths, and as they had not the same reasons as I for waiting until night, I would get the water in which they had already bathed! Although the spring bubbling at the bottom of it sent a continual stream through the small artificial pool which overflowed through a specially built canal, I did not like that idea at all. But, of course, all happened as I had foreseen. Yongden, whom I told to hurry to enjoy the clean water, reported to me when he returned that his bath had been shortened by the entrance of the father and three sons into the water!

I could but wait, and I waited long. The happy sensation produced by the hot water in that cold country kept the four Thibetans under its spell for more than one hour. Night had fallen and a cold wind promised little comfort for the moment, since on coming out of the bath I should have to dry myself in the open with my one-foot-square towel! Still more delay was caused by my desire to allow time for the water of the bath to be changed, but I started at last for the spring, after having been earnestly entreated by Yongden to avoid washing my face, which had now become nearly the orthodox colour of a Thibetan countrywoman.

A few days later, on a sunny morning, we were walking leisurely on the bank of the river when two lamas dressed in lay clothes reached us, coming up from behind. They asked about our country and many other details for a rather long time, and one of them stared at me with peculiar insistence. They said that they were in the service of the Governor of Menkong and carried a message from him to the officer residing at Zogong.

We both noticed the way one of them had looked at me, and, as anybody in our circumstances would have done, we began to fancy the worst. Maybe some rumours had spread after our leaving Menkong and had only recently reached the Governor, who had dispatched these two to inform his colleague and order him to ascertain who we were.

Previous disquieting meetings had come to a quick end. But this one left a lasting terror in its wake. Zogong, where we should know our fate, was still far away, and each day brought the same question. Were we not walking toward our doom?

We reverted to our nocturnal tramps. We had become again the scared game dreaming of the hunter. One morning at dawn a party of pilgrims met us and stopped to exchange a few words. According to my custom, I continued to walk slowly ahead while Yongden was talking with the men. When he rejoined me he was more frightened than I had ever seen him.

"They are people from Riwoche," he said. "Who knows if they have not seen you when you went there with Thobgyal? . . . You are quite famous in that region."

Riwoche is the site of a once celebrated monastery, now half ruined. I had stayed there twice during a previous journey in Thibet after having entered the forbidden zone through the Iron Bridge.

Our fears grew. . . . Hour by hour they became greater. At the sight of each group of men or women who happened to pass us we trembled, thinking of the catastrophe that awaited us. Truly, this way madness lay.

In that mood we reached a bridge on the river Nu, near a big village called Porang.

"Let us take a chance," I said to my companion. "On this side of the stream we run the risk of meeting old acquaintances from the province of Kham, because that is the way by which they go to Kha Karpo. We shall also have to cross Zogong, where these lamas have perhaps spoken about us, even if they have not been sent to catch us. Here is a bridge—there are few in Thibet—showing that there is a trail of some importance on the other bank. The Giamo Nu River flows in that direction. Let us try to reach it and we will then see what can be done."

We therefore crossed the bridge and bravely climbed the trail beyond it, without knowing where it would lead us.

That evening we slept at an isolated farm, and on the morrow, continuing through wild forests, we crossed the Ra Pass. We had been told at the farm that the region beyond was completely uninhabited except for a few *dokpas*, who moved with their cattle along the valleys enclosed between two high ranges.

Our good luck brought us on the second day near to an encampment of cowmen. They gave us some butter and *tsampa*, but did not allow us to sleep in their hut. There were about forty armed men assembled around it, and I guessed that they were preparing a robbing expedition, so they naturally did not wish to discuss their plans before unknown travellers. We begged from other camps near by and were given a good deal of cheese, butter, and *tsampa*. After a night spent in the open, we started, heavily loaded, but certain that starvation was not imminent!

The country we were crossing had none of the charms of the Nu Valley. It was colder and often barren. The trails were difficult to find.

In the morning, after having set out from the *dokpas'* camp, we crossed a clear river, climbed a very steep path, and then missed our way. We had already wandered about two hours when some sharp-eyed cowboys discovered us on the slope of the mountain. They themselves had wandered far from their camp with their cattle, and now were almost beneath us, but at a considerable distance. Their shouts arrived faint and indistinct, and at first we did not understand that they were addressed to us. By straining our ears we succeeded in catching some words. We were to turn back, and then to proceed upwards.[1]

From the Pang *la*, an endless descent through forests led to large rocky caves inhabited in the summer by cowmen. At that time of the year a torrent near by supplied them with water, but it was now quite dry, so that in the absence of water we continued our way, although the shelter of these roomy caves tempted us. Farther down we reached at dusk a hamlet composed of three farms. The looks of the men who came out to examine us and enquired about our beasts and luggage were not very reassuring, but, though they were a rough lot, they treated us well in the end.

In the evening, as we were seated with them near the fire, some one spoke about Lhasa, and, incidentally, uttered the

[1] Besides being prompted by their natural kind-heartedness, Thibetans are always ready to direct a wayfarer because such an act is considered by them as highly meritorious and bearing good fruits in this life and the next one. On the contrary, to mislead any traveller is believed to have serious results; the "consciousness" (*namshes*) of one who has done so will roam painfully in the *Bardo*, after its separation from the body, at death, being unable to find the road leading to a new rebirth.

89

dreaded word *"philings."* They had heard about their existence from some of their relatives and friends, who had been
to Lhasa or in China, but they had never seen any and none
had ever visited their country. Yongden boasted of having
met two of them in northern Thibet, but for my part I humbly
confessed that I had never caught sight of any!

Two days later, from the summit of a sandy hill, we discovered, several thousand feet below us, a narrow glittering ribbon.
It was the Giamo nu chu, the upper course of the Salween.

We had heard that somewhere in that region there was a
place called Tsawa, where the river could be crossed by a cable
stretched from one bank to the other. But as passengers were
very few on that out-of-the-way path, the ferrymen lived far
from the river and came there only when they were informed
that a number of people meant to cross. We poor lone pilgrims might have remained for weeks in front of the rope but
for the happy circumstance that a lama had performed some
religious ceremonies at the house of the very farmer whose
guests we had just been, and was returning to his monastery
on the other side of the Giamo nu chu, with a dozen of his
followers.

We waited only one day for his arrival in a pretty, sheltered
place between picturesque red rocks. The weather was glori-
ously bright and the temperature mild.

To cross a river hanging to a cable was not new to us. We
had done it in other places. But at these other places, two
different cables, one for each direction, were used to carry the
passengers, who, starting from a point much higher than the
landing-place, glided swiftly, as if on a switch-back.

Here there was but a single cable fastened to poles fixed at
the same level on either bank, and it sagged terrifyingly.

Only the strongest of the countrymen dared to venture to
cross by it unaided, for the climbing up from the bottom of
the sag by the sheer strength of one's wrists was rather a feat.
Most of them were therefore hauled up by ferrymen, as were
the animals and baggage.

When my turn came, a Thibetan girl and I were bound with rough straps, and tied together to a wooden hook that would glide on the leather cable. Dressed up in that way, a push sent us swinging in the void, like two pitiable puppets.

In less than one minute we were down in the middle of the dip, and then, from the other bank, the ferrymen began their work. Each jerk they gave at the long towing rope caused us to dance in the air a most unpleasant kind of jig.

This went on for a little while; then we felt a shock, heard a splash below us, and slipped back at full speed into the sagging dip of the cable.

The towing rope had broken!

The accident in itself did not endanger our lives. Men would come to fasten the rope that they were drawing out of the water. But giddiness might overcome us, suspended as we were two or three hundred feet above the swift current.

The way in which we were trussed up afforded security for a conscious passenger in an erect position whose hands had a strong grip on the strap under the hook. But this was not to be depended upon in the case of anyone who collapsed or dropped backward. My nerves are solid. I had no doubt I could stand there even for hours.

But what of my companion? She was rather pale and looked with frightened eyes at the point where the strap to which we were suspended was fastened to the hook.

"What is the matter with you?" I said. "I have called my *Tsawai lama*[1] to protect us. You need not fear."

With a slight motion of the head she indicated the hook. "The strap is coming loose," she said, trembling.

If the strap came loose . . . then we would fall in the deep river. . . . Tied as we were, swimming was out of the question. Even could I disentangle myself and drag the girl for awhile, there was no landing in that gorge where the river flowed between gigantic walls of rocks. I looked attentively at the knots, but could notice nothing wrong.

[1] Spiritual father.

"Shut your eyes," I said to the girl. "You are giddy. Nothing is loose. We are quite safe."

"It is loosening," she repeated, with such a convinced tone that I began to doubt. This Thibetan lass who had often crossed rivers in that way naturally knew more than I did about knots, straps and hooks.

It was, therefore, only a question of time. Would the men have repaired the towing rope and taken us on land before all the knots gave? It might have been the subject of a bet. I thought it over, and smiled inwardly. The slow way in which the ferrymen were working was rather irritating. At last one of them proceeded toward us, hands and feet up, the way flies walk on the ceiling. We swung again, and more than ever.

"She says that the knots of the straps are coming loose," I told him as soon as he reached us.

"*Lama kieno!*" [1] he exclaimed. He gave a hasty look in the direction of the hook. "I cannot see it well," he said. "I hope it will hold fast till you arrive at the bank."

He hoped! . . .

Bless the fellow! I also "hoped."

He went away, working with his hands and feet, just as he had come. When he had joined his companions they began to haul us again. Would the knots bear these repeated jerks? We continued to "hope" they would.

At last we had safely landed on a projecting rock of the cliff. Half a dozen women took hold of us, expressing their sympathy in loud exclamations. The ferryman who had untied us had ascertained that the knots had never loosened, and were cursing the girl whose notion had given them such a fright. The poor thing did not need that addition to her nervousness. She became hysterical, weeping and shrieking. It was a scene of picturesque confusion.

Yongden seized the chance of this general commotion to beg for "his aged mother, who had suffered such agony while

---

[1] "Know it, O Lama!" a call asking one's spiritual father to cast his look on one who stands in distress and needs protection, but the habit of repeating it frequently has made it a mere interjection.

hanging to that rope, and needed a good meal with which to refresh herself." All those present gave really liberally and we set out loaded with a fresh supply.

I had already noticed that my headgear, arranged after the Lutzekiang fashion, attracted a good deal of notice. We began to be rather far from the country where it was worn. It now looked conspicuous, and people questioned me about my native land. The day after the crossing of the Giamo nu chu at Tsawa, the *nemo* of a farm where we had slept, and other people there, made several embarrassing observations about the way in which my hair was dressed and my turban fixed. At any rate, I needed a Thibetan hat, but none could be bought in the villages which were on my road, men and women countryfolk going bareheaded. The time had truly come for the plain bonnet of Kham, of a shape known and worn all over Thibet. I had done well to have washed it and kept it carefully in my luggage. As soon as I began to wear it all questions and curiosity were at an end. Later on I had another reason to bless it. When I crossed high passes amongst glaciers and snow, and when the blizzard raged around me, then the poor fur-lined bonnet kept my head and ears warm and protected me against frost and wind.

Who could still doubt that it had been *sent* to me, as I felt on the day we found it in the forest? I often asked Yongden this question and we both smiled in answer. But I would not dare to affirm that at the bottom of my heart, after having experienced the various kinds of protection which it offered me, I did not feel still more inclined to believe that it had truly been *sent* to me by some mysterious friend.

At any rate, I like to fancy it.

We were now in a more populated region. The whole of the low ground was cultivated, and the higher part of the hills completely bare. Our road crossed a large number of minor ranges which cut across the Giamo nu chu valley. Each day we had to climb up and down several thousand feet, and sometimes that drill was even performed twice in the course of the same day.

A new subject of anxiety agitated our minds. We had heard that the Lhasa government had sent officials in remote parts of the country to establish a new system of taxation. These *pönpos,* moving across the country with hosts of retainers, each more inquisitive and arrogant than his master, constituted a real danger to us. We devoted nearly all our time to discussions as to the best way of escaping unwelcome meetings. It did not seem easy, though, to reach the Po country which we had decided to cross on our way to Lhasa. We had the choice of two roads. We could go to Sangnachöszong [1] or wind a long way northward through the Sepo Khang Pass. But Sangnachöszong was the residence of a *pönpo,* and on the other road the envoys of the Thibetan exchequer were reported to be wandering in the neighbourhood of Ubes. The gentleman seated in his house appeared more easy to avoid than his colleagues, who might be met on the road unexpectedly. This ought to have decided me to turn in that direction, all the more because the way was direct and saved us a long march in rounding a range. But I knew that Sangnachöszong had been visited by some foreigners, while I had never heard that any had ever crossed the Sepo Khang la and the neighbourhood,[2] and this decided me to prefer the latter.

In a country so little known as Thibet it seems better to avoid following tracks that have already been trod, every time one has the chance to do so.

Anyhow, I was still undecided when, after having slept at Yu, I ascended the pass which led to the junction of the roads of Sangnachöszong and of Lankazong. Evening came while we were crossing a cold slope whose streams were but thick blocks of ice. Happily we found, a little out of the way, an abandoned *dokpas'* camp and we spent the night in one of the

[1] More exactly Sang ngags chös zong, the fort of the doctrine of the secret spells, or, as others call it: Tsang kha chu zong, the fort of the pure spring.

[2] Information gathered later on confirmed the fact that none had yet crossed that mountain range.

huts near a blazing fire. The morrow we crossed the pass. A terrible storm rose in the evening and raged throughout the night. In the darkness we failed to discover the road to the village which we knew was near, as we had heard dogs barking.

The violence of the wind did not allow us to open our loads to get out our tent-blanket and throw it over us. We remained squatted, shivering till daybreak, when the wind gradually abated. Then we saw that we were less than half an hour's walk from the village, near the gorge in which ran the road to Sangnachöszong.

We had now to make a decision. I turned again toward the Giamo nu chu. The country and its people interested me. I did not want to miss the unique opportunity to see some more of it and them, or to cut my journey short. As for the Ubes *pönpos*, I would take my chance.

Since landing on the right bank of the Giamo nu chu our existence had become that of true Thibetan wayfarers. We no longer hid ourselves in the forest. On the contrary, lingering in the villages had become a pleasure to us. Each stage brought us amongst the countryfolk, and we stayed all night with them, witnessing their customs close at hand, and listening to their talk about the events happening in Thibet. No traveller other than one who was really believed by them to belong to the same peasant stock could have gathered the same treasure of observations that I collected.

Such a life could not be lived without bringing adventures in its train, and they were often adventures of a most unexpected kind. Nearly every day supplied its contribution, pleasant or otherwise, but always full of humour. I have amassed in that region a store of fun sufficient to keep one merry for years. It would be quite impossible to relate *in extenso* all these incidents, but the account of a few will give the reader some picture of country life in Thibet.

One morning while kneeling on the pebbles, filling my wooden bowl at the river, I hear a voice behind me.

"Where do you come from, Lama?"

I turn my head and see that a peasant has approached my adopted son. A few words are exchanged, and these are always the same at every encounter: "What country do you come from? Where are you going to? Have you anything to sell?"

But this time, after having satisfied his curiosity with the answers given to him, the man does not go away. He remains silent for a few seconds, spits, and then begins:

"Lama, do you know how to tell fortunes?"

Good! Here is another of them! Telling fortunes, we are doing it all the time, and at any rate we cannot complain, for if our rôle of prophet is somewhat monotonous, it certainly yields a useful profit and admirably conceals our identity.

Yongden allows himself to be entreated. Yes, he does know the art of *mo*, but he has no time; he is in a hurry. . . .

The peasant persists, exclaiming: "Lama, three days ago one of my cows disappeared. We have been looking for it in vain. Has it fallen down a precipice? Has it been stolen?"

He sighs and, lowering his voice, continues, "The people on the other side of the river are awful brigands."

For my part, I cannot help thinking that "the people on the other side" may have the same flattering opinion of their compatriots opposite, and that both parties have undoubtedly very good reasons for their views.

"They are quite capable," the man continued, "of having killed and cut my cow in pieces, and taken it away to eat. . . . Lama, consult the oracle! Tell me what has become of my cow and whether I shall find it again. . . . I have nothing to offer you just now, but if you will go to my house I will give you and your mother something to eat, and you can both sleep there to-night."

I am the mother. The people of this country are astonishingly clear-sighted! It is useless to lie to them. They invent many more wonderful stories about us than any we could possibly concoct ourselves.

96

Mendicant pilgrims, such as we appear to be, never refuse an invitation of the kind just issued to us. I have no desire to appear a suspect, especially since I have learned of the presence of the two officials who are retaking the census of the villages in the district.

I sign to Yongden to accept the fellow's offer. He puts his load down upon a flat rock, saying with a condescending air, "Well, I suppose I must grant your request, since it is the duty of a lama to be compassionate."

Many edifying phrases follow, and then the ceremony begins. Muttering the sacred formulæ, but shortening them as much as possible, my young companion counts and recounts the beads of his rosary. I can follow his thought. He is asking himself: "Where is this unlucky cow to be found? I know nothing about it. That is not the question, however. What is the best thing to say to the poor fool who is asking me?"

The old Thibetan is squatting there, silent and attentive, awaiting the verdict of fate. At last the oracle is pronounced.

"Your cow," the lama says, "has not been eaten. It is still alive, but runs the risk of an accident. If you start looking for it at once, going down the river, you will find it, but everything depends upon your cleverness."

The vagueness of the last two sentences affords a wide margin for different interpretations. A prophet should never be too precise. The day is not far off when we are to have an amusing proof of this.

Somewhat reassured, the peasant describes his dwelling minutely. We shall find it, he says, on the river bank. We start off upstream, while he hastens in the opposite direction. About half an hour later we see the house indicated.

A painter would have found a charming subject for a landscape in this Thibetan farm, resting against a high background of greyish rocks, in the midst of a wood of golden leaves. In front of it flowed the low, wintry waters of the Salween, translucid and peaceful, scalloped with ice. In all probability, no white traveller had yet seen it in this part of its course, winding between barefaced gigantic cliffs whose sharp crests point high toward the open sky.

I would gladly have rested there upon the sun-baked stones, to savour the beauty of the surroundings, the joy of the passing hour and the intoxication of adventure which had led me hither. But it was not the time to indulge in revery. The personality of a decrepit beggar, which I had assumed, does not go well with poetic fancy.

Attracted by my companion's shouts, some women show themselves on the flat roof of clay. They listen rather distrustfully to the account of our meeting with the master of the house, and how he was led to offer us hospitality. However, after lengthy explanations they allow themselves to be convinced. We are led first of all into the yard, and after a fresh examination of our faces and some more questions we are permitted to climb the ladder leading to the roof-terrace on which the family apartment is situated, the ground floor being occupied by stables.

A ragged cushion is brought for Yongden, the lama. As for me, the old and unimportant mother, I simply seat myself on the ground. We have to tell the women around us the names of all the holy places we have visited or are about to visit (for the most part, of course, wholly imaginary) and assure them that we have no merchandise to sell, not possessing so much as a blanket (which is on this occasion nothing but the truth).

The weather is fine but cold, and, being seated motionless in the open air, I begin to shiver. As for our hostesses, they do not appear to feel the touch of the cold north wind which has arisen. In order to work the more easily, they draw their right arms out of the sheepskin coat, their only garment, which is held to the waist by a girdle, displaying dirty breasts which no ablutions have ever touched!

After having been there for about two hours, something happens. The master of the house reappears, driving the recovered cow in front of him. There is general excitement.

"Oh, Lama," exclaims the peasant as soon as he has joined

us on the terrace, "you are a true, a great *ñönshes chen!* [1] All
your words, without exception, have come true. The cow
was found in a very dangerous position. She was stuck fast
in a narrow path cut by a landslide. She could neither go on,
nor turn back, nor climb up to the top of the cliff. . . . It was
all I could do to get her out. Just as you said. . . . Yes, you
are undoubtedly a learned *ñönshes* lama!"

We enjoy this unexpected triumph. A good meal will probably follow to feast the recovery of the lost cow and pay honour to the seer who has brought about this happy result. In
the meantime a woman brings some tea, that buttered and
salted Thibetan tea, a soup, maybe, rather than a beverage,
but so truly refreshing to the tired and benumbed traveller!
A bag of *tsampa* is put down beside us, and we can dip into
it at will. I eat as much as I can.

Our host remains thoughtful. He asks Yongden: "Lama,
can you read?"

"Certainly," answers the latter, proudly, "I can read, and
write, too."

"Oh! Oh! You are indeed learned. Perhaps you are a
gaishes. [2] I thought you might be."

He rises, goes into the combined oratory and storeroom—the
usual arrangement in Thibetan farmhouses—and brings out an
enormous volume which he places with deep respect upon a
low table in front of my companion.

"Lama," he says, "look at this book. It is a book that
brings the most wonderful blessings and all sorts of prosperity
to those for whom it is read. You shall read it for my benefit."

Yongden turns his head toward me with a disturbed glance.
What have we fallen upon now? The task to be imposed
upon him offers no attractions. He is tired and in great need
of rest and sleep. Nevertheless, he must answer the old fellow,
whose eyes are fixed beseechingly upon him.

"It is a big volume," he says. "The reading of it would

[1] Nönshes chen: a great seer.
[2] A doctor of philosophy and literature.

require several days, and I must leave to-morrow. But I can open it.[1] The blessing will be quite as efficacious."

As this is a current practice in Thibet, nobody makes any objection. The book is opened ceremoniously, incense burned, a fresh supply of hot tea poured into our bowls, and Yongden begins to read in a very loud voice, after having ordered me imperatively: "Mother, recite *Dölma!*" [2]

I obediently intone a psalmody bearing no relation to the words read by my adopted son, the aim of which is merely to keep me occupied so that the women cannot worry me with their questions. It is by injunctions of this kind that the young man habitually spares me the fatiguing experience of long useless conversations, in the course of which either my pronunciation, or the literary turn of my speech might excite the wonder of the villagers.

At the sound of the noise we are making, some neighbours appear and wag their heads comprehendingly and approvingly. I must have repeated *Dölma* at least twenty times, and the *Kyapdo* [3] about five hundred times. The sense of the words I am repeating arrests my thoughts.

"In order that you may awaken to the supreme deliverance, free from fear and grief, turn your steps toward Knowledge!"

I ponder, and my pious murmurs cease. The lama notices this, turns his head toward me, and thunders out the words:

"Just as, in the sky, the clouds form and melt away, without our knowing whence they come or whither they go, and without there being anywhere a dwelling-place for the clouds, so do phenomena appear through a combination of causes and vanish through the operation of other causes, without our being able to assign any of them a place where it may dwell.

[1] Literally, "open its mouth," which means to remove the cloth in which the book is wrapped and read the first pages of it, or the first line of each page.

[2] A hymn of praise to the goddess Dölma known in Sanskrit literature as Tara.

[3] Kyapdo: "prostration," because that recitation is often accompanied by repeated prostrations.

... Fleeting in their essence, impermanent, are all these components of elements."

It is by the reading of such treatises as these, although, be it understood, they do not comprehend a single word of them—that the country folk of Thibet expect their cattle to multiply, their sick to be cured, and their commercial enterprises to succeed. Strange people and strange country!

I start, aroused from my revery by the martial tone with which the reader has pronounced the declarations of the Sacred Writings, and I resume my chanting with, *"Aum mani padme hum!"* My ears are tingling. I feel exhausted. If only I might sleep!

Night approaches. We have been reciting this sort of office for several hours. The head of the family reappears, bringing a plate of barley and a bowl of clear water, which he puts down near the book.

"Lama," he begins, "it is not light enough to read any more. I beg you to bless my house and my goods so that they may prosper, and to give us all holy water that we may be preserved from sickness."

He is really tenacious, this worthy farmer! The recovery of the cow must have inspired him with a blind confidence in the magic power of Yongden. Now, faith in a lama is always shown in Thibet by the donation of gifts, and the latter vary in value according to the extent of this faith. The old farmer is well off; that is to be seen by the number of cattle he has just had brought in from his pastures. Undoubtedly we shall be liberally provided with food for our journey, and a few coins will be added to the present.

I see by the expression on my companion's face that he enters into the spirit of the joke and is slyly rejoicing over the windfall which awaits us.

Behold him, grave as an archbishop, patrolling the different rooms of the dwelling, reciting words of benison from the liturgy. Sometimes he pauses for a moment, and I know that during the brief silence he is breathing an earnest wish for the material and spiritual welfare of our hosts, for if he smiles at the childish credulity of his unlettered compatriots, Yongden is profoundly religious and a member of a mystic sect in his country. When the tour of the house is finished, the peasant points the way to the stables. They extend far and are never cleaned out, and this prolonged circuit in the sticky mud at last proves irritating to the officiating priest. The adventure has ceased to be amusing. He throws the grain broadcast upon the heads of sheep and goats that are startled, horses that prance, and cows that remain stolidly indifferent as if disdainful of all religious rites. Then, believing he has finished, he approaches the ladder and mounts a step or two. But the proprietor, who has accompanied him as incense bearer, hurries up behind him, seizes him by one ankle, and points out that the pigs have not had their share of blessing. He has to go down again. The unfortunate lama finishes as soon as he possibly can with the foul-smelling animals, which utter weird sounds as he angrily throws forth a hail of barley at them. With muddy shoes and cold wet feet he at last attains the roof. Now it is the turn of the human beings! The water in the bowl is blessed according to the orthodox rite. Then the family, headed by the father, advances in line to receive a few drops in their hollowed palms. The water is swallowed, and the moisture left in the hand is used to wet the head. The neighbours join in this procession.

When the devotions are at an end the evening meal is served. It is a soup of dried nettles without any meat. We are far from obtaining the feast we had anticipated, and it augurs badly for the present that will be offered on our departure. One may well fear that it will be no more substantial than the soup. Nevertheless, one never knows. Thibetan peasants have strange ideas. My concern about the alms we will or will not receive amuses me. I have developed the true beggar's mentality since I began to play the part of a poverty-stricken wanderer! But our begging is not, after all, wholly a sport. It has a serious side, for the offerings which fill our wallets relieve us of the necessity of buying food and showing that we possess money, and therefore help to preserve our incognito.

Finally, we are allowed to go to sleep. In the room which we are now permitted to enter there is a scrap of tattered sacking upon the earthen floor. It is about as large as a towel, and this is the bed destined for me! Yongden, by virtue of his clerical dignity, is treated somewhat better. He will have the use of a ragged carpet which will preserve him, as far as his knees, from contact with the bare earth. As to the legs, they do not matter. The lower classes in Thibet always sleep doubled up, like dogs, almost in the form of a ball, and they never possess carpets or cushions as long as their own bodies. To sleep with the body fully extended is regarded as a luxury pertaining to "the Quality" alone.

I lay down after having merely unfastened the girdle of my thick robe. In Thibet the poor do not undress when they go to bed, especially when they are guests in a strange house in the course of a journey. Shortly afterwards my son joined me, and with as little toilet preparations as myself he stretched himself upon his bit of carpet. We were both asleep when a noise and a bright light awakened us.

But are we really awake? The picturesque spectacle which we perceive between our half-closed eyelids almost makes us doubt it. The room we are in is that in which the two daughters of the house and the maidservant sleep. They have all three just come in, and, to light themselves (lamps and candles are unknown in this part of the country), they have thrown shavings of resinous wood into the brazier in the middle of the floor. I see them unfasten their girdles, shake their blackened arms out of their sleeves, drag hither and thither the greasy and matted sheepskins which are to serve them for bed and blankets. They move about, chattering, their silver necklaces tinkling upon their bare breasts. The flames which first gleam and dance and then darken to mere glowing embers, surround them with a weird light. They look like three young witches preparing for their Sabbath.

Before the day has dawned I nudge Yongden quietly to awaken him. We must complete our toilet before the light permits the others to notice too many details about us. For

me, this consists first in darkening my face with the black I
procure by rubbing the bottom of our only saucepan with my
hand. This precaution prevents my too fair skin from astonishing the natives. Then, beneath our robes we must arrange
the belts containing our gold and silver, our maps, thermome-
ter, miniature compasses, watches, and other objects which
must on no account be perceived.

We have scarcely finished when the mistress appears. She
calls her daughters and the servant; the fire is rekindled, the
saucepan containing the remains of last night's soup placed on
the brazier, and a few moments later we are invited to hold
out our bowls for its distribution. The bowls were not washed
last night; it is not the custom amongst Thibetan villagers.
Each one possesses a special bowl which he never lends. He
licks it carefully after every meal and that is the cleansing
process. Poor me! I lack practice in the art of licking my
bowl; it is still smeared over with a layer of soup and of tea
which has frozen during the night. But protesting nerves
must be subdued and the rising gorge swallowed, for the success of my journey depends upon it. Let us shut our eyes
and drink off our soup though it is even more nauseating
than last night's, because of the water added to make it go
further.

Our packages are soon tied up. No present is forthcoming,
and I regard with a look of amusement the discomfited countenance of my lama who has poured forth so many blessings,
chants, and official ministrations of all kinds. It is useless to
delay any longer. The whole family comes for one more blessing by the imposition of hands, and I can guess that Yongden
would willingly administer a sound cuffing to the old miser
upon whose shock of hair he lays his hands.

We go down the ladder again, pass in front of the horses
which eye us curiously, the goats whose odd and diabolical gaze
seems to jeer at the crestfallen lama, and the ever placid cows.
Once outside, we walk for a while in silence. Then, out of
sight and earshot, Yongden turns suddenly and, having made

some cabalistic signs in the direction of our host, he bursts forth:

"Oh, you rogue, you base deceiver, in whose service I toiled a whole day long! . . . Telling me to go down the ladder again to bless his pigs, forsooth! I take back all my blessings, unworthy old miser! May the wool never grow on your sheep's back, your cattle prove barren, and your fruit trees be blighted!"

His comical indignation, which was only half feigned, amused me very much. For, after all, my companion was a real lama, and he had been cheated of dues that were justly his. But he himself could not long withstand the funny side of the adventure, and we both burst out laughing in the face of the wintry Salween, which seemed to be singing as it wended its way over its pebbly bed: "That's the way things are done in the fine country of Thibet, my adventurous little strangers; you will see many more such!"

That very day, after having again crossed a pass, we reached the vicinity of the dreaded Ubes. We delayed our walk through the village until dusk, and then, leaving behind a group of houses in one of which we supposed that the Big Man was sleeping, we allowed ourselves a short rest in a narrow crevice of the hill, the dry bed of a summer stream.

At dawn the first rays of light revealed a decorated building which was doubtlessly the present abode of the official. As it was still early, we were lucky enough to meet no one in the vicinity.

We made great haste, and when the sun rose we had already put about two miles between us and the dangerous spot. We joyfully congratulated each other on our escape.

In the middle of the afternoon, while we were still in this gay mood, we were told that the *pönpo* had moved three days ago from Ubes to another village situated farther on.

We tramped on again at night till we had passed the place. Perfectly convinced, this time, that our troubles were over, we slept happily in a chaos of rocks and thorns. The following morning, after ten minutes' walk, we reached a large house sheltered in a recess of the mountain. About thirty good horses were tethered outside. Country people were already crowding in, bringing grain, grass, butter, meat, and so forth.

This was the place where the official had actually put up! A stalwart head servant supervised the entrance of the things brought by the villagers. He stopped Yongden, and after a talk which appeared to me endless, he ordered a man to give us a meal of tea and *tsampa*. We could not refuse this kind offer. Beggars like us could but rejoice at this piece of good luck. We made a pretense of it, seated on the steps of the kitchen, smiling, laughing, and joking with the attendants of the gentleman, but all the while we felt rather inclined to take to our heels!

The thing which proved most tiresome, and even at times became excessively difficult in the life I was now leading, was the part that I was always obliged to play in order to preserve my incognito. In a country where everything is done in public, down to the most intimate personal acts, I was forced to affect peculiar local customs which embarrassed me terribly. Happily, our way lay at times through large tracts of un-inhabited land, and the greater freedom which I enjoyed there somewhat relieved my painful nervous tension. There, especially, I was able to avoid the indescribable soups which the kindly but poverty-stricken fellows, our hosts, bestowed upon us, and which we had to swallow down with a smile, for fear of suspicious comments. Once only did I depart from my accustomed attitude of the beggar to whom everything tastes good, but that day! . . .

We have arrived toward nightfall in a little village. It was very cold and the stark surroundings afforded no shelter. We had already been refused hospitality at several houses, when a woman opened her door to us—the rickety door of an exceedingly miserable dwelling. We entered; a fire burned on the hearth, and in this frosty weather this in itself afforded comfort. The husband of the woman came back shortly after-wards, bringing out some handfuls of *tsampa* from the bottom of a beggar's wallet, and we realised that no supper could be expected from people who had nothing to eat themselves. After a few words of praise for the generosity of an imaginary chief who has given him a rupee, Yongden declares that he will buy some meat, if there is any to be had in the village.

"I know of a good place," said our host at once, scenting a windfall. From the corner where I was crouching, I insisted that it should be of good quality. Most Thibetans eat without any repugnance the putrefied flesh of animals which have died of disease.

"Do not bring back the flesh of an animal which has died, nor a piece which is decayed," I said.

"No, no," said the man. "I know what I am about. You shall have something good."

About ten minutes passed. The village is not large, and the peasant soon returned.

"There," he said, triumphantly, drawing a large parcel of some kind from beneath his sheepskin robe.

What can this be? . . . The room is lighted only by the embers of the fire, and I cannot clearly distinguish anything. . . . The man seems to be opening something, probably a cloth which he has wrapped round his purchase.

Ugh! . . . A most fearsome odour suddenly fills the room, the smell of a charnel-house. It is sickening.

"Oh," says Yongden, in a voice that trembles slightly, concealing the nausea that he is obliged to repress. "Oh, it is a stomach!"

I understand now. The Thibetans, when they kill a beast, have a horrible habit of enclosing in the stomach, the kidneys, heart, liver, and entrails of the animal. They then sew up this kind of bag, and its contents go on decaying inside for days, weeks, and even longer.

"Yes, it is a stomach," repeats its purchaser, whose voice also trembles somewhat, but with joy, seeing the mass of foodstuff falling out of the now opened bag. "It is full," he exclaims, "quite full! Oh, what a lot!"

He has placed the horror on the floor, is plunging his hands into it, taking out the gelatinous entrails. Three children who were asleep on a heap of tatters have awakened, and are now squatting in front of their father, watching him eagerly with covetous eyes.

"Yes . . . yes, a stomach!" repeats Yongden, in consternation.

"Here, mother, here is a saucepan," says the woman, kindly, addressing me: "You can prepare your supper."

What! Am I to handle this filth? I whisper hastily to my son, "Tell them that I am ill."

"It always seems your turn to be ill when something unpleasant befalls us," Yongden growls, under his breath. But the boy is resourceful; he has already regained his self-possession.

"The old mother is ill," he announces. "Why do you not make the *tupa* [thick soup] yourselves? I want everybody to have a share."

The two peasants do not wait to be invited a second time, and the youngsters, realizing that a feast is in course of preparation, stay quietly by the fire, having no desire to go to sleep again. The mother takes up a chopper and a rustic chopping-block made out of a log, on which she cuts the carrion into small pieces. From time to time one of these drops upon the floor, and then the children fall upon it like young puppies and devour it raw.

Now this foul soup is boiling, and a little barley meal is added. Finally the supper is ready.

"Take some, mother; it will do you good," say the husband and wife. I confine myself to groaning, in the corner where I have stretched myself.

"Let her sleep," says Yongden.

He cannot himself be excused. *Arjopas* who spend a rupee on meat and do not touch it do not exist. To-morrow the whole village would be talking about it. He has to swallow down a full bowl of the evil-smelling liquid, but beyond that he cannot go, and he declares that he, too, is not feeling very well. I do not wonder at it. The others feast long and gluttonously upon the broth, smacking their lips in silence, overcome with joy at this unexpected *bonne bouche,* and I am overtaken by sleep whilst the family is still masticating noisily.

We travelled across more hills and more valleys; we passed by more *gompas.* We sat with more peasants, and met two *pönpos* on the road, one of whom bestowed on us most useful presents of food. Thus we progressed in the direction of the Sepo Khang *la.*

At the foot of the pass one of those mysterious and inexplicable incidents was to befall us, such as sometimes bewilder the traveller in Thibet. A long tramp had brought us to a gorge in which a clear stream flowed toward the invisible Salween, which we were again approaching for the last time.

It was scarcely noon, and we felt reluctant to waste a whole afternoon in a village house when we could still have gone on for several hours. We had been informed that it was impossible to cross the range in one day, even if we started before dawn, so that we were bound in any case to spend the night on the hills. We therefore thought it wiser to continue on our way, and if the cold prevented us from camping, we could walk on through the night, as we had often done. But before starting on this long tramp I wished to eat a good meal. Water was now at our feet, and we could not guess when we should again run across a stream. Yongden gladly agreed to make a halt, and as soon as we had reached the bank we put our loads on the shingle, and my companion began to light a fire with the few twigs that I had gathered under some trees which grew at the end of the fields.

A little boy whom I had noticed on the other side of the river then crossed the bridge and ran toward Yongden. He bowed down three times before him as Thibetans do in their greetings to great lamas. We were most astonished. What could have made that child give such a deep token of reverence to a mere beggar pilgrim. Without giving us time to put any question, the boy addressed Yongden.

"My grandfather, who is very ill," he said, "has told us all, this morning, that a lama coming down that hill, was to make tea in the dry part of the river bed and that he wanted to see him. Since the sun has risen my brother and I have watched in turn at the bridge to invite the lama to our house. Now that you have come, please follow me."

"It is not my son whom your grandfather expects," I told the boy. "We are people from a far-off country. He does not know us."

"He said the lama *who would make tea on the stones,*" insisted the child; and as we did not comply with his request he crossed the river again and disappeared between the fences of the fields.

We had just begun to drink our tea when the boy reappeared, accompanied by a young *trapa.*

"Lama," the latter said to Yongden, "be kind enough to come to see my father. He is very ill and says that he is about to die. He only waits for a lama who will arrive to-day and who is the one and only person who can direct him to a happy place of rebirth in the next world. He told us all this morning that you would come down that hill and make tea, here on the stones, near the river. All has happened as he said. Now please be kind to us and come."

Neither Yongden nor I knew what to think about this queer affair. We persisted in believing that the sufferer meant some lama whom he knew and had some reason to expect on this road. Nevertheless, seeing the *trapa* weeping, I advised my companion to pay a visit to the sick villager. So he promised to go as soon as we had finished our meal.

The boy and the young *trapa*—his uncle, I understood— went to report our answer to the farmer. But presently I saw another boy seated near the bridge observing us. These people were certainly afraid that Yongden would fail to keep his promise, and therefore kept him in sight. No escape was possible, and why indeed should Yongden have disappointed an old invalid? The latter would evidently see that my son was not the one he expected, and all would end with no more than ten minutes' delay.

All the family had assembled at the door of the farm. They greeted Yongden with the greatest respect. My companion was then led into the room, and while he went toward the cushions on which the farmer lay I remained near the threshold with the women of the house.

The old man did not really appear as one who is near death. His voice was firm and his intelligent eyes showed that his mental faculties were in no way dimmed. He wished to rise and bow down to my son, but the latter prevented him from moving out of his blankets, saying that sick people need only *mean* the respectful salute.

"Lama," the farmer said, "I have been longing for your coming, but I knew that you were to come and I waited for you, to die. You are my true *tsawai lama;* [1] no one but you alone can lead me to the 'Land of Bliss.' Have compassion on me, bless me, do not refuse me your help."

What the old man wished was for Yongden to utter for his benefit the mystic words called *Powa* which are pronounced at the deathbed of a lay lamaist or of any monk who is not an initiate, when the latter is quite beyond all hope of recovery.

As I have said, the old Thibetan did not seem to be near to death, and for religious reasons whose explanations would be out of place here, my companion hesitated to yield to his wishes. He tried in vain to hearten the sick man, assuring him that he would not die, and offering to recite the spells which "mend" life and give it new strength. This the farmer, however, obstinately refused, maintaining that he knew his hour to be at hand and had only awaited the spiritual aid of his lama to take his departure.

He then began to weep and order those present to entreat the lama on his behalf. The family did so, sobbing and weeping, with repeated prostrations, until, overpowered, Yongden finally gave in. Then, deep moved he recited the ritual words

---

[1] Either the head lama of the sect to which one belongs, or the head lama of the monastery of which one is either a benefactor, a monk, or a serf. But in this case it means a spiritual father and guide with whom one has been connected in that way for several lives.

which loosen the ties of the "*namshés,*" [1] and lead them safely through the labyrinthine paths of the other worlds.

When we left him the old farmer's face expressed a perfect serenity, a complete detachment from all earthly concerns, having, it seemed, entered the true Blissful Paradise which, being nowhere and everywhere, lies in the mind of each one of us.

I shall not venture to offer any explanation of this peculiar incident. I have related the fact thinking that it might interest those who pursue psychic researches, but I would feel exceedingly sorry if my account provoked commentaries disrespectful to the memory of the departed Thibetan. Death and the dying are never to be made a subject of raillery.

Those who had told us that the road across the Sepo Khang hills was a long one, were certainly right. We walked on from the dawn, meeting nobody and mistaking our way on several occasions at the intersection of trails leading to *dokpas'* summer camps. At dusk we were still far from the pass. A blizzard then rose, as we climbed a steep and waterless slope. There was no camping-place in the vicinity, and we had almost decided to retrace our steps and shelter ourselves much lower down at a place where we had seen some empty huts, when we heard the tinkling of horses' bells and three men appeared on the way up like ourselves. They were traders, and told us that a little farther along on the road there was a farm wherein we could get shelter.

It was pitch dark when we arrived. I understood from the large stables, that the place was a kind of inn for the use of travellers crossing the pass at a season when camping in the open is rather dangerous. We were admitted to the kitchen with the merchants who fed us with soup, tea, *tsampa* and dried fruits. These men belonged to a village in the same neighbourhood as the sick farmer. Passing there in the morning, they had heard all about Yongden, and brought

[1] *Namshés:* consciousness, which is multiple. Not in any case to be translated by *soul.*

us the sad news that at dawn, when we ourselves had left the village, the old man had smiled and died. The traders had been deeply impressed by the account of their friend's last hours. The thoughts of all being turned toward religion, they begged Yongden to preach them a sermon, which he did.

The kitchen, the only living room of the farm, was very small, and with the blazing fire that burned quite near us, we were half roasted. Then, when the time came to sleep, we understood that the owner and his wife wished to remain alone. The traders went down the ladder to the stable, where they slept near their beasts. As for us, we were told to accommodate ourselves on the flat roof. What a change from that ovenlike kitchen to the cold air of a frosty night, with a blizzard raging, at fifteen or sixteen thousand feet above sea level! It was not the first time that I had experienced this kind of hospitality. More than once villagers had invited us, treated us to a good supper, and then sent us on the roof or into the courtyard. Nobody apparently thought much of it in Thibet!

But that night I lacked the courage to lie down in the open air, and I begged permission (which was granted) to sleep next the kitchen in a shelter shut in on three sides.

The next day we crossed the pass and descended to the Sepo monastery, beautifully situated in a lonely spot with an extended view in front of it. The traders were on horseback, and had reached the *gompa* long before us. They had stayed there for a while and had told the lamas about Yongden, so that when he arrived, meaning to purchase some food, he was cordially welcomed and invited to remain a few days to discuss matters concerning the Buddhist doctrine with some of the monastery's learned inmates. As for myself, I could also get lodging in a guest house. But as I had not accompanied my adopted son to the monastery, and had continued my way, I was already out of sight amongst the hills, so Yongden declined the kind invitation. I regretted it afterwards; but as my rôle of a lay woman would very likely have kept me away from the place where the *literati* of the monastery would hold their meetings with Yongden, I consoled myself with no great difficulty.

A little later in the evening, we met a woman going to the *gompa* who told us that we could find a shelter in a partly ruined house that was easily seen from the road. The country was once more a complete desert, and we could not hope to reach the lower valley on the same day. It proved more and more true that the crossing of the Sepo Khang *la* was a long one. We walked about an hour longer without discovering the house, but at last reached it when it was nearly dark.

It had been a really large and well-built farm with a good number of stables, sheds, storerooms, servants' quarters, and a pretty apartment upstairs for the owners. Everything was now in a dilapidated condition, but with a little work it would have been quite possible to make the necessary repairs, for no essential parts of the building were ruined.

We had nearly finished our meal when the woman who had told us about that house arrived with a young boy, her son. She was the owner of the farm and had left it, though there were good fields around it, after a terrible drama.

A few years before, a gang of robbers from the Po country had attacked this isolated farm and there had been a terrific struggle. Four of the masters, the woman's husband, her two brothers, another relative, and a few servants had been killed, while others were wounded. The robbers also had left several dead on the ground. Since then the unhappy housewife and her family lived in the village near the monastery. The fear that a similar outrage would happen again, naturally kept her away from her farm, which gradually fell into ruins.

But another and still stronger fear prevented her from returning to her former house. The farm was believed to be haunted by evil spirits. The violent death of so many men had attracted them, and, with the ghosts of the murderers and their victims, they roamed about the buildings. For this reason the woman had come back from the *gompa* to ask the lama to spend the night in her house, to exorcise it.

She could have requested the services of the lamas of Sepo,

and most likely some of them had already performed the required rites on her behalf; but, as I have already mentioned, "Red Cap" lamas are deemed more powerful exorcists than their colleagues of the yellow sect. Moreover, Yongden, for obvious reasons, had a real success as a lama "Holder of the Secret Spells." Had he established himself somewhere, clients would have flocked to his residence. But he hated that kind of trade; he had seen it from too near.

Nevertheless, kindness compelled him to comply with the wishes of the woman. He told her that if she wished to cultivate her property again, she could do so without fear of any denizen of another world, but that serious precautions were to be taken against robbers.

The following day we arrived in the Dainshin province, and here again, as along the Salween, I was the guest of many. I never regretted my roundabout tour in that country. It is out of the way of the great trade routes, and absolutely unknown to foreigners. Yet it is a well-cultivated area. Large and prosperous monasteries are seen in several places, the villages seem to be well built, and the people are agreeable. I saw some interesting soda fields from which Thibetans get the stuff they mix with their tea when boiling it.

Once we passed a rich traveller on the road, carrying presents to a *gompa*. He gave us two rupees each, without our asking for money. We were naturally most astonished at this unexpected windfall.

We did not always take our disguise as beggars very seriously. Once in the heart of Thibet, we preferred to save time by purchasing our supplies. Nevertheless, unsolicited alms came our way several times. Never in my life have I made so economical a journey. We used to laugh as we tramped along the road, recalling all the stories we had read of travellers who started out with many camels laden with heavy and expensive stores and luggage only to meet with failure more or less near their goal.

I could have done the whole journey without any money in

my pocket, but as we were extravagant beggars, indulging in molasses cakes, dried fruits, the best tea, and plenty of butter, we succeeded in spending one hundred rupees in our four months' journey from Yunnan to Lhasa. One need not be rolling in riches to travel in the blessed lands of Asia!

CHAPTER IV

I HAD been told at Tashi Tse: "To go to Po *yul* you can choose between two roads. One follows the valley, the other cuts through the hills. The first one crosses many villages and passes near several monasteries. Robbers are not much to be feared on that side; at the worst the traveller may meet some petty thieves—three or four men roaming together at night, who do not generally kill those whom they attack. It is also easy, on that road, to get food either by begging or by purchasing it. The second is a mountain track, and, although fairly good, it runs through a wilderness. Until the first villages of the Po *yul* [1] are reached, you will tramp in a desert probably without meeting a single soul. And this is the best that can happen to you, for those you meet might be highwaymen from the Po country, coming and going on some looting expedition. They would certainly not trouble about the contents of your beggars' bags, but might possibly kill you, vexed to have been seen and anxious to avoid any further talk. You will also have to pass two very high passes, and a large tract of land between. Snow has not yet fallen heavily this year. You may succeed in crossing the range, but you must be ready to face the worst, for snow might close the road of the first pass, after your passage, so that, if you found the second closed also, you would be caught in a trap. If you risk the adventure, you must take a large supply of food with you. You may possibly meet a few *dokpas* camped between the two ranges, but they will neither give nor sell any food. They have scarcely enough for themselves to last until next spring."

I did not give much time to pondering over this news. The valley road was marked on all the maps, but that does not necessarily mean, where Thibet is concerned, that any for-

[1] *Yul* means country.

eigner has followed it. It often happens that the line marked
on the map by the map-maker is traced, not from his actual
knowledge, but according to information received from natives,
and Thibetans are rather vague, if not quite fanciful, in
describing the roads and the country which they cross. Anyhow the *rong lam* [1] in question was, I could well believe,
rather well known by the Chinese. The other one, on the
contrary, was unexplored; maps ignored it completely, as well
as the passes which it crossed. These passes were, no doubt,
those at the foot of which sprang the river Po, referred to by
the English general who, strange as it might appear, had a
good deal of responsibility in the choice of my present itinerary.

His name was Sir George Pereira. We often spoke of him,
Yongden and I, and we meant to relate to him our prowess on
our return. We were far from thinking that he would die on
a road of the Chinese Far East, about the time we entered
that Po *yul* which we had looked at together on the map.

General Pereira had arrived at Jakyendo when I had just
returned there after a tour in that part of Kham that extends
from the grassy desert to the southern trade road—the one
going from Chiamdo to Lhasa. That trip, during which I had
gathered most interesting information, ended suddenly, as I
have related. I was stopped and prevented from proceeding
southwards toward the Salween. No doubt the general had
learned this from the servants or other people, but, as I did
not take him into my confidence as to my unpleasant adventure, he never alluded to it in our talks.

He spent a fortnight in an apartment situated opposite to
mine in the same courtyard, and we often met to take tea or
to visit some place of interest. He was a well-bred, elderly
gentleman, a charming scholar, a geographer, and a tireless
globe-trotter. He was suspected at Jakyendo of being charged
with a secret mission by his government. Many things were
rumoured of which I cannot say whether they were true or
not. It was a matter of indifference to me.

General Pereira was on his way to Lhasa by the northern

[1] Valley road.

trade route, and he openly spoke of it.[1] Although a Danish traveller had been stopped but a few weeks before on that very same road, the general was certain that orders had been sent to the Thibetans to receive him with due regard, and thus it turned out.

He carried with him a quantity of maps, and himself surveyed the country through which he went, working strenuously a part of the night to put his notes in order, and taking but little interest in the picturesque aspect of the customs, feasts, and the like of the country.

Very kindly he put his maps and some of his notes at my disposal. I copied from them a number of useful points for the future journey I had already planned. Some of these rough map sketches have accompanied me to Lhasa, hidden in my boots, and, thanks to them, I have been able to verify on my way how incomplete the geographical knowledge of that part of the world still is.

One afternoon, after having had tea together, we were speaking about Thibet. A map remained open on a table, and with the tip of his finger Sir George Pereira followed the thin line marking the supposed course of the Po.

"Nobody has ever been there," he said. "There may be several accessible passes above the spring of the river. . . . It would be an interesting way to Lhasa."

Did he speak on purpose to give me a hint, or had his words no special meaning? I never knew.

More than once I had considered the idea of crossing the Po country. It was an old idea of mine, for I had discussed it with Yongden three years before, in the Kum Bum Monastery, but the vague facts I had gathered about Po *yul* from traders of central Thibet or the people of Kham had been rather discouraging. Many maintained that the Popas were cannibals. Others, more moderate in their opinions, left this

[1] Since then I have learned that the general's itinerary was entirely different from that which he declared he would follow when leaving Jakyendo. He proceeded by the southern road which crosses an inhabited country. The Thibetan government supplied him with conveyances all the way.

question unsettled. But all united in affirming that anyone foreign to the Po tribes, who entered their country, was never seen again.

So I hesitated a little before risking this adventure, when the words of the general decided me—"Nobody has ever been there. . . ." All right. I would see these ranges and these passes! Truly it would be "an interesting road to Lhasa"! Hearty thanks to you, sir, who on purpose or by chance did me a real service.

I was now at the foot of the hills about which I had dreamed for years. Hesitation was impossible.

Tashi Tse, where I chose the road which was to lead to so many adventures, is an important village situated in a wide valley near a *zong* [1] built on an isolated hillock.

Tashi Tse means the prosperous summit, or the summit of prosperity. Both translations can be justified on the score of grammar. Since the bottom of the valley does not in the least correspond to one's geographical notion of a summit, one is compelled to look to the other translation, which, alas! appears as inexact as the first one. The poor countryfolk of the region are, I have heard, far from having reached the height of prosperity.

Taxes, statute labour, and a number of other ways of plundering them, which the villagers lament, fill the strong box of the *pönpo* perched on his hillock, and it is very likely that it is to his paltry citadel we must look to find the "prosperous summit."

I reached the place rather early in the afternoon and had time to go round a-begging, the purpose of which was to deceive the official or his men if they happened to hear about my presence. The poor peasants, to whom my apparent poverty and my beggarly attire gave confidence, described their distress in that country where the soil does not produce every year enough grain to pay the tax in kind.

To leave the country, to look for better land or less exacting lords, is not permitted. A few ventured the flight and estab-

[1] Zong: a fort, but nowadays any dwelling seat of an official.

lished themselves in neighbouring provinces. Having been discovered, they were taken away from the new home they had created and led back to Tashi Tse, where they were beaten and heavily fined.

Now many who had thought to imitate them, too frightened by the fate of their friends, remain resigned, all energy destroyed, growing poorer each year, expecting no deliverance in this life. Others looked toward China. "We were not illtreated in this way when the Chinese were the masters," they said. "Will they come back? Maybe . . . but when? We may die before . . ."

And so, in the evenings, around small fires in their miserable huts, these women, whose tears have reddened their eyes, gaze before them in the dark, picturing the range after range of hills between them and the land where the Lhasa troops have driven away their old suzerains.

The distance which separates their country from that certainly not perfect, but more hospitable, land, is not great, but how is it possible to travel quickly without being detected, if one must take the grandmother who walks so slowly, the little ones so soon tired, and the infants who must be carried? And then, what of the ass and of the only cow, whose loss would mean utter ruin for those who would already be compelled to leave so many things behind . . . ?

How sorrowful was this "prosperous summit"!

I spent the night in a house where thoughts such as I have mentioned haunted the minds of my hosts. The husband and his wife were rather ill-assorted as to their age, and my foolish companion repented bitterly for days having mistaken the rather young man for the son of the housewife, whereas he was her husband. The grandmother knew that, once she were dead, the couple would try to escape with the children from their jail. The poor old thing, in other circumstances, would certainly have liked to live longer, but now she wished to die, so that her children might be free to start toward happiness, or at least a lesser misery. She wished to die, but she, too, dreamed of happiness, and as she was not to know the earthly one which perhaps awaited her family, she begged the lama at night, when the others had retired to sleep, to perform the rite which would bring her a happy rebirth in *Nub dewa chen*, the Western Paradise. Her daughter was a kind-hearted woman. She did not, of course, desire the end of the tottering, white-haired grandmother, nor did the good young husband. Yet, with the increasing poverty and the taxes . . . and . . . and . . . ! I could have wept.

How heart-rending was the sorrow of these humble folk! It is on such occasions that one would like to be a God and to have at one's command an inexhaustible treasure of welfare and happiness to pour out to all alike: intelligent and simple-minded ones, so-called good and so-called bad ones, so that all should smile and rejoice! Why could I not flood with true felicity that melancholic Tashi Tse, "the prosperous summit."

I started a little before daybreak, missed the road in the darkness, and did not cross the river as I ought to have done. When I became aware of it the bridge was far behind. To retrace my steps might have attracted the notice of some servants of the *zong*. I did not like to risk it, and so one way only remained—to cross in the water. The stream flowed rapidly; it was large and deep but clear. One could see the bottom, and did not risk losing unexpectedly one's footing, as happened to me in the upper course of the Mekong during a previous journey. On the whole, the crossing had nothing that could frighten Yongden or myself, who had many times, on horseback or on foot, forded foaming torrents. But the banks were widely scalloped with thick ice which told of the temperature of the morning bath with which the deity of Tashi Tse meant to increase our comfort.

I went upstream looking for a ford, and reached a fork of the river. The small branch was shallow, nearly frozen over, but, for that very reason, the passage was still more painful. In several places the frozen sheet broke under me and I fell amongst splinters of ice which cruelly cut my bare feet. Then followed the real bath, with dress lifted up and the water just a little lower than my hips.

How welcome would have been a warm Turkish towel when we reached the stony shore! Such luxury, of course, was quite far out of reach. True I had in my bag a one-foot-square towel, but I used it only when in hiding. Thibetans do not dry themselves after crossing a river, or, if they do, they use a flap of their wide robes. I tried to imitate them, but as soon as it became wet my thick dress of coarse wool stiffened and froze.

We went along the river till noon; we then felt hungry and deemed it wise to have a meal before leaving the valley, for we could not guess if water would be found soon on the hills. Previous experiences had taught us the torment of remaining thirty-six hours without drinking. We preferred to avoid risks of that kind.

A torrent crossed our road. Once upon a time, in a dreadful rush, it had rent and carried down a mountain and covered the plain, far away, with countless rocks and boulders. Now, at its winter low-water level, it divided in several rivulets which went winding among the obstacles accumulated in the days of its strength.

I hastily collected whatever dry twigs or cow dung I could find among the stones, and Yongden lit a fire. Foreseeing greater hardships than ever on the desert road of the high passes, we decided that day that a specially good meal was required: first the soup, then the tea. As a rule we had only one course, either soup or tea. The ordering of the menu was mine. Thibetans begin with tea and end with soup.

The soup? Under what name could it appear on a bill of fare? Would *"potage Vatel"* do? I disclose the receipt. From a bag of the most orthodox local fashion—that is to say, greasy and black with dirt—I take out a small piece of dry bacon, the gift of a kind-hearted householder. My young companion cuts it into a dozen tiny bits, which he throws in the pot full of boiling water. Then a pinch of salt, and a sigh: "Ah! if we had a radish or a turnip!" But we lack these

123

delicacies and the minute slices of bacon dance alone a lively jig in the boiling broth, a turbid liquid the smell of which reminds one of dishwater. Nevertheless, that scent is not unpleasant to the needy vagrants which we have become. Pure air and long tramps are the best appetizers, and we have eaten nothing since the meagre soup, with turnips but without bacon, that our host had given us the day before.

Now a few handfuls of flour beaten up in cold water are thrown in the pot. A few minutes later we begin to eat. "How particularly good is the soup to-day! Really delicious!" But as, in spite of my long stay amongst Thibetans, I still keep a vague remembrance of French cooking, I add, "My father's dogs would never have eaten such a thing." I laugh and extend my bowl to have it filled again.

Now it is the turn of the tea. I tear a small piece of the hard compressed brick made as much of branches of wood as of tea leaves. It is crushed into the water; salt and butter are added. It is like a second soup, all the more because we add *tsampa* in our bowls. Now the lunch is ended and we feel perfectly refreshed, capable of climbing as high as the sky. We look boldly to the first range silhouetted against the horizon and behind which we shall meet so many others.

We have loaded our bags upon our backs and hold in our hands our long pilgrim staffs. Let us go! I am entering a virgin country and only a few natives have ever contemplated the scenery yonder, which I shall see this very evening.

We found a hamlet higher up, in an immense upper valley that ascended slowly toward distant ranges, where it became a desert covered only with grass and shrubs. At first we could see trails followed by cattle-keepers in the summer, but soon they disappeared under the grass or in the stony patches, and we were left to our own cleverness to find our way.

Once we discovered, far away at the foot of the hills, an intermittent smoke. It might be *dokpas* encamped there for the winter; or, as the smoke looked so white, perhaps it was the vapour of some hot spring, as there are a good number of these in Thibet. To go to that place would have taken several hours, and I could not afford this. Although the weather was fine, snow seemed to be expected before long by the people of the country, and I was anxious to be quickly over the first high pass at least. I therefore pushed on, going straight toward the ridge I could see before me.

The slight slope over which we were proceeding was not flat ground, for hillocks, miniature ranges, and ravine springs cut it here and there. We plunged into one of the latter, and found its bottom filled with the frozen water of a torrent whose slippery surface made our progress difficult. When we emerged we saw that the large valley turned aside. We had been told to follow a river, but now we saw two—one very far down in a gorge, and another which wound close to us amongst short grass and moss. The information we had gathered mentioned also a *dokpas'* camp, deserted in the winter, where we could spend the night in shelter. I was very desirous to reach it, for at that height the night would be extremely cold. I decided to follow the more important of the two streams, which very likely had its source farther away and probably in the main ridge. Thus we continued to walk. The sun set and a sharp cold wind arose. . . . We had not found any *dokpas'* huts. We began to think of stopping and making a fire in some sheltered place, to spend the night there, for the higher up we went the more severe would be the cold. As for water, there was none save the river, far, far below us. But we could easily do without evening tea after having had such a meal as our last lunch. We were discussing the place where we might stay, when I noticed a long distance before us, on the other bank of the river, a yellowish spot which could not be autumnal foliage, because we were above the zone of the trees, and which, I felt, was neither a rock nor any natural object, but a thing made by man—maybe a thatched roof. Curiosity, rather than real hope, prompted us, and we walked quickly forward instead of camping. Gradually the spot became bigger, but we still could not see clearly what it was. A little later it appeared as thatch raised on beams. It was a roof, then, the *dokpas'* camp! When at last we confronted it across the stream, we realized that it was not a roof, but merely straw that had been put high up on some crossed beams to prevent the wild beasts, antelopes, and others, feeding on it during the winter, when the camp was abandoned. We felt a little disappointed.

"No matter," I said to Yongden. "It is worth while taking the trouble to go down to the river and climb up the opposite bank. We will get a few bundles of that straw down, build a kind of shelter with them and spread some as mattresses on the frozen ground. That will keep us warm. We will also fill our pot with water when crossing the stream, and make some good tea."

It was a long way to the bottom of the gorge, and then up again by an exceedingly steep slope to the encampment. But we reaped the full reward of our toil, for, to our happy astonishment, we discovered on a small headland a real camp with a number of roofed pens for the cattle, and in one of them a separate place for the use of the men. It had a hearth, and dried cow dung lay in abundance all over the camp. We had reached a paradise!

Most probably we were the only human beings on that hill, but not forgetting the warning we had been given about robbers, before we slept we set a kind of a trap between ourselves and the entrance. A man entering the hut could not have taken three steps without catching his feet in one or another of the ropes, stretched invisibly near the ground, and on his falling the noise would have awakened us. What mattered most was to avoid being taken by surprise. Once awakened . . . Well, we each had a revolver and that still better weapon, in the East—and perhaps everywhere—the "winged words" of the divine Ulysses and the artifices of the goddess Juno. I relied more on these latter for my safety than on anything else, and the day was near when they would justify the confidence I placed in them by giving me the victory over a gang of Popas brigands.

In spite of the cold wind which made me shiver, I remained a long time outside, wandering through that summer resort of the wilds, beautifully lighted by an enormous full moon.

How happy I was to be there, *en route* for the mystery of these unexplored heights, alone in the great silence, "tasting the sweets of solitude and tranquillity," as a passage of the Buddhist Scripture has it!

We ought to have left the *dokpas'* camp in the middle of the night to cross the pass at noon. But we were tired, and the warmth that we felt, lying next to a big fire, kept us sleeping longer than we had planned. I shrank also from the idea of starting without eating and drinking hot tea, for on the higher level we would find no fuel. What would happen? What would the road be like? We could not guess. Was the pass even practicable? People had only told us that it might be. Yongden, of course, felt reluctant to go so far to fetch water, inasmuch as the few places where the stream flowed freely in daytime might be covered with ice after dark. Anyhow, he went, and we drank our tea. But the day broke before we had left the place.

Later in the morning we reached a *latza*, which, from a distance, we had taken as marking the top of the pass. Behind it extended a completely barren valley enclosed between a high ridge of crumbling reddish stones on one side, and perpendicular cliffs of various pretty greyish and mauve shades on the other. In the middle of this valley we again saw the river, the water of which we had drunk at our breakfast. It fell nearly straight down in a narrow gorge from the upper valley to the lower one. I looked for traces of *dokpas'* summer encampments—those low stone walls forming enclosures in which cattle are penned, but there were none. I could understand from the barrenness of the landscape that cattle were probably never brought so high.

A nearly straight reddish line—the sharp summit of a ridge it seemed—blocked the horizon at the end of that desolate valley. The distance without being considerable, appeared great enough to people ascending with loads on their backs, in the rarefied air of these high altitudes. Still, the hope of seeing the end of the climb gave us courage, and we endeavoured to accelerate our pace. One thing, however, made me uneasy—I did not discover any *latza* on that ridge, and Thibetans never fail to erect at least one, at the top of a pass. The explanation came when we had reached the point from which we had supposed that we would descend the opposite side of the mountain.

How could I express what we felt at that moment? It was a mixture of admiration and grief. We were at the same time wonderstricken and terrified. Quite suddenly an awe-inspiring landscape, which had previously been shut from our sight by the walls of the valley, burst upon us.

Think of an immensity of snow, an undulating tableland limited far away at our left by a straight wall of blue-green glaciers and peaks wrapped in everlasting, immaculate whiteness. At our right extended a wide valley which ascended in a gentle slope until we reached the neighbouring summits on the sky line. In front, a similar but wider stretch of gradually sloping ground vanished in the distance, without our being able to discern whether it led to the pass or to another tableland.

Words cannot give an idea of such winter scenery as we saw on these heights. It was one of those overpowering spectacles that make believers bend their knees, as before the veil that hides the Supreme Face.

But Yongden and I, after our first admiration had subsided, only looked at each other in silence. No talk was needed; we clearly understood the situation.

Which was the way, we did not know! It could just as well be to our right, as ahead of us. The snow did not allow one to see any trace of a trail. It was already late in the afternoon, and to miss the road meant to remain wandering all night on these frozen summits. We had a sufficient experience of mountaineering in Thibet to know what it would mean—the exploration would be ended at its first step, and the explorers would never live to tell their tale.

I looked at my watch; it was three in the afternoon. We had still several hours of daylight before us, and, happily, the moon would shine brightly at night. We had not yet cause to be really alarmed—the important thing was to avoid missing the road and to make haste.

I looked once more at the valley on our right, then decided: "Let us proceed straight forward." And so we went.

I grew excited and, although the snow became deeper and deeper, I walked rather quickly. We had not been able to follow the advice of the Tashi Tse villagers and carry much food with us. Our host could only sell us a small quantity of *tsampa*. His neighbours had hardly enough for themselves. They informed us that we could buy some from the servants of the *pönpo*. To avoid giving them cause to talk we had said that we would go to the *zong* early the next morning, which, of course, we didn't! My bag was, therefore, rather light, whereas Yongden, carrying the tent, its iron pegs, and sundries, was much more heavily loaded.

I forged quickly ahead. Dominated by the idea of reaching the top of the pass, or of discovering if we were going in a wrong direction, I tramped with the utmost energy through the snow that reached my knees.

Was the lama far behind? I turned to look at him. Never shall I forget the sight! Far, far below, amidst the white silent immensity, a small black spot, like a tiny Lilliputian insect, seemed to be crawling slowly up. The disproportion between the giant glacier range, that wild and endless slope, and the two puny travellers who had ventured alone in that extraordinarily phantasmagoric land of the heights, impressed me as it had never done before. An inexpressible feeling of compassion moved me to the bottom of my heart. It could not be possible that my young friend, the companion of so many of my adventurous travels, should meet his end in a few hours on that hill. I would find the pass; it was my duty. I knew that I would!

There was no time for useless emotion. Evening was already beginning to dim the shining whiteness of the landscape. We ought by then to have been far beyond and below the pass. I strode on, now through the snow field, jumping sometimes with the help of my long staff, proceeding I could not say how, but progressing quickly. At last I discerned a white mound and emerging from it, branches on which hung flags covered with snow and fringed with ice. It was the *latza*, the top of the pass! I signalled to Yongden, who appeared still more distant and tiny. He did not see me at once, but after a while he too waved his staff. He had understood that I had arrived.

There the scenery was grand beyond all description. Behind extended the waste I had crossed. In front of me was a precipitous fall of the mountain. Stretching far below, black undulating crests vanished into the darkness. The moon rose as I looked around in a trance of admiration. Its rays touched the glaciers and the high snow-robed peaks, the whole white plain, and some silvery unknown valleys toward which I was to proceed. The impassive landscape of the day seemed to awaken under the blue light which metamorphosed it, sparks glittered to and fro, and faint sounds were wafted by the wind. . . . Maybe elves of the frozen waterfalls, fairies of the snow, and djin-keepers of mysterious caves were to assemble and play and feast on the illuminated white tableland; or perhaps some grave council was to take place between the giants whose heads wore helmets of cold radiance. What mysteries could not have been discovered by the inquisitive pilgrim who, hidden, dared remain there motionless till dawn. Not that he could ever have related the wonder of the bewitching night, for his tongue would soon have been stiffened by the frost!

Thibetans do not shout *"lha gyalo"* after dark. I complied with the custom and threw only in six directions the old Sanskrit mantra, *"Subham astu sarvajagatam* [May all beings be happy]."

Yongden, who, after having understood that he neared the *latza*, had taken courage and quickened his pace, caught up with me. We began to descend. Traces of a track were visible now and then, for on that side of the mountain the snow was not deep and the ground, a yellowish gravel, was often visible.

What might have been the exact level of the pass we had crossed I would not venture to tell, as I could not make any observation. Still, from the comparison of the plants and various other particulars, one who has tramped for years through many mountain ranges, in the same country, may make a rough guess. I had carefully looked at the lichens, and observed a few other things; and I felt nearly certain that the pass was about 19,000 feet high, even higher perhaps than the Dokar *la* I had crossed about two months before, higher than the Nago *la* and others that reached from 18,299 to 18,500.

Although we knew that we should have to walk a part of the night before we should reach a spot where fuel would be available, we rejoiced at having found the pass open and at having crossed it safely. In this agreeable mood we reached a valley whose bottom was almost entirely covered by a frozen stream. There, on the ice, no trace of a track was of course visible, and we began again to roam to and fro in search of some sign to show us our direction. To follow the course of the frozen river was the safest way, if we did not find any better one. It would take us to a lower level, no doubt, but it could also happen that the stream would disappear into a narrow gorge or fall over a cliff. Still, I had decided to continue on the ice—at least as long as the valley was open. But then I found the track again, near the foot of the hill, and we had only to follow it down, proceeding slowly.

The walk was rather agreeable beneath a beautiful moon. Here and there we began to see a few bushes scattered in pasture grounds. Otherwise the country was quite barren. We could not think of stopping without lighting a fire, for motion alone kept us warm. No shelter whatsoever was in sight, and the cold wind from the snow rushed through the valley, which had now become rather wide.

We tramped until two o'clock in the morning. For nineteen hours we had been walking, without having stopped or refreshed ourselves in any way. Strangely enough, I did not feel tired, but only sleepy!

Yongden had gone in the direction of the hills in search of

fuel, and I found some near the river, in a flat place, which must have been a camping-place in the summer, where travellers from the Po country go to the Dainshin province, either to trade or on robbery expeditions.

I called the young man back, gathered as much fuel as I could, and, certain that nobody was wandering in that wilderness, we decided to pitch our tent in a low place among a few bushes. The flint and steel which, according to Thibetan custom, Yongden carried attached to his belt in a pouch, had become wet during our passage across the snow fields, and now it did not work at all. This was a serious matter. Of course we were no longer on the top of the range and we had only a few hours to wait before the sun would rise; but even if we escaped being frozen, we were not at all certain that we should not catch pneumonia or some other serious disease.

"Jetsunma," [1] said Yongden, "you are, I know, initiated in the *thumo reskiang* practice. Warm yourself and do not bother about me. I shall jump and move to keep my blood moving."

True, I had studied under two Thibetan *gompchens* the strange art of increasing the internal heat. For long I had been puzzled by the stories I had heard and read on the subject and as I am of a somewhat scientific turn of mind I wanted to make the experiment myself. With great difficulties, showing an extreme perseverance in my desire to be initiated into the secret, and after a number of ordeals, I succeeded in reaching my aim. I saw some hermits seated night after night, motionless on the snow, entirely naked, sunk in meditation, while the terrible winter blizzard whirled and hissed around them! I saw under the bright full moon the test given to their disciples who, on the shore of a lake or a river in the heart of the winter, dried on their bodies, as on a stove, a number of sheets dipped in the icy water! And I learned the means of performing these feats. I had inured myself, during five months of the cold season, to wearing the single

---

[1] "Jetsunma" or "Jetsun Kusho": "Reverend lady" or "your reverend ladyship," is the highest honourific title of address for a woman belonging to the religious order.

thin cotton garment of the students at a 13,000-foot level. But the experience once over, I felt that a further training would have been a waste of time for me, who, as a rule, could choose my dwelling in less severe climates or provide myself with heating apparatus. I had, therefore, returned to fires and warm clothes, and thus could not be taken for an adept in the *thumo reskiang,* as my companion believed! Nevertheless, I liked at times to remember the lesson I had learned and to sit on some snowy summit in my thin dress of *reskiang.* But the present was not the time to look selfishly after my own comfort. I wanted to try to kindle a fire that had nothing miraculous about it, but which could warm my adopted son as well as myself.

"Go!" said I to Yongden, "collect as much dry cow dung and dry twigs as you can; the exertion will prevent you from getting cold. I will see after the fire business."

He went, convinced that the fuel was useless; but I had got an idea. After all, the flint and steel were wet and cold. What if I warmed them on me, as I had dried dripping sheets when a student of *thumo reskiang? Thumo reskiang* is but a way devised by the Thibetan hermits of enabling themselves to live without endangering their health on the high hills. It has nothing to do with religion, and so it can be used for ordinary purposes without lack of reverence.

I put the flint and steel and a pinch of the moss under my clothes, sat down, and began the ritualistic practice. I mentioned that I felt sleepy on the road; the exertion while collecting fuel and pitching the tent, the effort to kindle the fire, had shaken my torpor, but now, being seated, I began to doze. Yet my mind continued to be concentrated on the object of the *thumo* rite. Soon I saw flames arising around me; they grew higher and higher; they enveloped me, curling their tongues above my head. I felt deliciously comfortable.

A loud report awakened me. The ice on the river was rending. The flames suddenly died down as if entering the ground. I opened my eyes. The wind was blowing hard and my body burned. I made haste. The flint and steel and moss would work this time; I was convinced of it. I was still half dreaming, although I had got up and walked toward the tent. I felt fire bursting out of my head, of my fingers.

I placed on the ground a little dry grass, a small piece of very dry cow dung, and I knocked the stone. A spark sprang out of it. I knocked again; another sprang out . . . another . . . another . . . a miniature fireworks. . . . The fire was lighted; it was a little baby flame which wanted to grow, to eat, to live. I fed it and it leaped higher and higher. When Yongden arrived with a quantity of dry cow dung in the lap of his dress and some branches between his arms, he was joyfully astonished.

"How have you done it?" he asked.

"Well, it is the fire of *thumo*," I answered, smiling.

The lama looked at me.

"True," he said. "Your face is quite red and your eyes are so bright . . ."

"Yes," I replied, "that is all right. Let me alone now, and make a good buttered tea quickly. I need a very hot drink."

I feared a little for the morrow, but I awakened in perfect health when the sun touched the thin cloth of our tent.

That very day we reached the end of the valley we had followed from the foot of the Deo *la* and entered another wider valley, enclosed between high ranges. No trace of human being was to be seen; the country was truly what Thibetans call *satong*.[1] The sun shone, although clouds wandered to and fro in a sky of a lighter blue than it had previously been. That immense space in which we were the only living beings, as if we had been the first inhabitants and masters of the earth, was extremely pleasant to the eye! We had no fear of missing our way, for we had as guide a clear river descending from the range that blocked the end of the large valley.

The ground was neither sandy nor very hard, and its imperceptible slope helped our progress. This empty land had a very peculiar and refreshing charm. After a few hours' march I observed some black spots scattered over the grass. I was

[1] Empty land.

far from being certain of their nature, but after what I had heard at Tashi Tse about *dokpas* spending the winter shut in between the high ranges, I guessed that these black spots were yaks. In the northern desert of grass one meets herds of wild yaks, numbering several hundred animals, but such is not the case in the region which we were crossing and I looked for the dwelling-place of the beasts' owners.

For at least another hour we proceeded without discovering any habitation. At last I saw a camp built of stones heaped together without any kind of mortar, as is usual in the Thibetan highlands. A few huts were huddled together, with enclosures around them to pen the cattle. And a wall, a little higher than the breast, enclosed the hamlet which was sheltered from the winds which swept through the valley. A *chörten* and a short *mendong* testified to the religious feelings of the few inhabitants of the place. But in Thibet, as elsewhere, external demonstrations of piety are not always accompanied by an effective practice of compassion, benevolence, and like virtues. When Yongden begged a shelter for the night and some food, he was told to pass on his way and to go to the next camp.

The next camp was discovered late in the evening, and the answer was still less courteous. However, before reaching it I had seen a place where we should have been well protected against the wind. It was the place where the *dokpas* of the valley put the bones of their dead.

When I speak of bones one must not fancy a charnel house. There is not such a thing in Thibet.

Thibetans prefer cremation to all other ways of disposing of dead bodies, and their great lamas are incinerated in a big cauldron filled with butter. But that kind of fuel is far too expensive for the common people, so in the barren regions, where wood is not available, the dead are placed on the hills and abandoned there to the vultures and other wild animals. In central Thibet the prevalent custom is to cut the corpse into pieces before leaving it on the cemetery ground. When the flesh has been eaten by the animals and the bones are dry, the family collects them, or a part of them, and hands them to a lama, who pounds them, mixing their dust with clay, and moulds a number of miniature *chörten* called *tsa-tsa.* It is in this shape that the pulverized bones of the ancestors are kept in places built for this purpose near the villages, or deposited in caves and other clean spots.

Sufficient room still remained in the *tsa-tsa* hut which I had discovered to allow us to lie down, but there was nothing fit to burn near it, and as the *dokpas'* door remained closed we had to choose between the night under a roof without fire and without meal, or the open air with both. We chose the open air, and spent the night in a small rocky place surrounded by bushes.

The next day we continued to follow the river until we arrived at a bridge. Bridges are few in that country and I was most astonished to see one on that but little trodden summer track. Yet you must not fancy a structure such as Westerners are accustomed to meet on the roads of their countries. Four or five trunks of fir trees, long and thin, resting on two piles, a few flat stones placed on them here and there to step on—such was the bridge! It was used, I should imagine, when the melting snow considerably increased the volume of the water. At any other season men and beasts forded the stream.

That bridge, poor as it was, would not have been built without reason. The track certainly passed over it, yet I saw it continuing clearly marked on the side where we stood. I was puzzled. Should we cross, or not? We decided to cross, fell amongst thorny bushes growing in marshy ground, and, being tired out, had nearly decided to camp, leaving to the morrow the care of looking for a road, when we saw a few boys tending cattle. I went toward them and learned that some *dokpas* had a camp on the opposite bank of the river, which we had just left. The children told me also that I had arrived at the foot of the three passes that led into the country of Po. One of them was blocked by the snow; they were certain of it. Regarding the two others they could give no information. It might be that one of them, or both, were still open.

Then a woman who had seen us from a distance joined the boys and repeated what they said about the passes. She advised us to continue our way as far as we could on the track of the Aigni *la,* and to rest a part of the night wherever we found water and wood, so as to be able to begin to climb again before daybreak, for it was a long way to the top of the pass, and even if it was open we would find high snow toward the summit. The prospect was agreeable indeed for people who had just struggled hard to go over one high range! Really the woman's news was not cheerful.

Yet we were prepared for such news, having been told that a second pass, difficult to negotiate, even if it was not entirely blocked, lay on our way. We realized the necessity of progressing quickly toward the villages of Po, for we had but a small quantity of food left, and our appetites, after daily mountaineering, were enormous. Why did we not rejoice to near that last range and to think that the next day we should very likely climb down into that Po *yul* of which we had spoken and dreamed for years? I could find no reason, except for our recent rather trying experience at the Deo *la.* We had not much time, however, to waste in analysis of our feelings; the most important thing was to reach the summit of the hill early on the morrow, in order to have as long as possible to look for the road, if doubt rose about it, or if we were hindered and delayed in any other way. So we had decided to continue our way and to camp higher up, when a man carrying a load of wood emerged from the thickets.

Yongden was once more compelled to relate the false stories of our pilgrimages, native land, and other kindred matters. Then, in his turn he questioned the *dokpa* about the passes. The answers he got confirmed what we had successively heard from the boys and from the woman. The man also advised the passage of the Aigni *la.* He said that it was longer than that across the Gotza *la,* but much less steep and easier on the opposite side of the mountain which we had to climb down.

We also would find on that side, he continued, some cow-men's summer huts, empty at the present season, which would afford us shelter.

I felt most anxious to put some questions about the springs of the river flowing all along the Po country; but, as beggar pilgrims, unless they have already travelled the road before, are not supposed to have any geographical knowledge of what exists in the region which lies ahead of them, and as, more-over, they do not care in the least for such things, it would have been imprudent to ask anything directly. I turned the difficulty, pretending to be concerned with very material cares.

"What about water?" I enquired. "Will we get some beyond the pass?"

"Have no fear!" answered the man. "You will follow a river to a place where there are pasture grounds. I only know so much. I have never been further."

"Is there water also on the Gotza *la* side?" I asked again.

"Yes, but the stream is much smaller."

"And what about the third pass?"

I was insisting too much, I felt, but as snow and other cir-cumstances prevented me from wandering at will on the moun-tains, I wished to get whatever information possible, and would have chosen the Gotza *la* had I had some reason to believe that journey to be more interesting.

"What?" replied the man, frowning. "You cannot cross the Yöntsong *la*. It is blocked by the snow. . . . *Dokpas* say there is a large river on that side. . . . What does that matter to you?"

Yongden quickly interfered.

"Ah," he said, laughingly, "you do not know the old mother. She always fears to miss her tea. Her eyes are continually in search of water and a place to stay to make tea. If I listened to her we would spend more than half of the day drinking!"

The *dokpa* echoed the lama's laughter.

"Ah! ah!" he said. "Truly tea is a good thing, especially for women who do not drink as much spirit as we do."

But Yongden had a sudden inspiration.

"Elder brother," he said to the man, "it is a good thing to acquire merits by performing good deeds. It is useful for this life and the next.

"You see, I am a lama and here is an old woman, a *nagspa yum*,[1] my mother. We are both *neskorpa*,[2] and to help us would be, without any doubt, a most meritorious action. Get horses for us and lead us to the top of the Aigni *la*, for we are very tired indeed."

It was a rather bold attempt. To persuade a *dokpa* to do such a service free is, as a rule, impossible. Hidden in our belts we had valuable arguments which could have decided the man easily and spared a lot of diplomacy, but we did not deem it safe to produce them in that country. Seated on the ground, I observed with interest the mental wrestle of the two cunning fellows. But the *dokpa* was not capable of competing with my adopted son, who, in some ways could have taught Ulysses himself. Yet his victory was not complete; he obtained only one horse, which we were to ride in turn, he and I, and the *dokpa* would carry our load on his back. Such a piece of good luck, however, seemed wonderful.

As it would be out of the question to take the horse that evening and camp on the road, and as, on the other hand, Yongden did not like to part with the *dokpa* lest the latter escape from his influence and break his promise, he asked to be allowed to spend the night in the house. The *dokpa* thought a second or two, and granted the request.

Now we had to recross the river, the cowmen's camp being situated on the bank we had left at the bridge. I feared to take off my high felt boots and show my white legs. These would, no doubt, be noticed, so, pretending that, on account of rheumatism, I could not tramp in iced water for fear of severe pain, I turned my steps toward the bridge, although it was rather far. But the good man, who had already had

[1] *Nagspa yum:* The wife of a sorcerer who has herself received a special ordination.

[2] A *neskorpa:* Literally, one who circulates from one place of pilgrimage to another one—a pilgrim.

a little religious talk with the lama, declared that he would take us, one after the other, on his back, and put us down on the other side of the stream.

I was greatly pleased to be relieved from a rather long walk, but at the same time I felt embarrassed about my revolver, the bag in which I carried our small provision of gold, and the belt filled with silver which I wore under my dress.

When I am on that man's back, I thought, he will think that I am rather heavy for my size and feel that I have hard objects on my breast under my robe. . . . If he thinks of hidden money that may be our death. Had our future guide been alone, I could have more or less easily changed a little the place of the various dangerous objects so that they could not be so easily detected, but the woman and the boys who followed us, chatting, deterred me.

Anyhow, simulating the gesture familiar to all Thibetans, of one who (I beg your pardon, my readers!) feels uncomfortable on account of lice and looks for the unpleasant animals in his dress, I succeeded in pushing my automatic pistol under my left armpit, the small bag of gold under the right one, and in lifting the belt a little higher up. Nobody, of course, had given any attention to my actions, the motive of them being clear and habitual to all.

Our arrival at the *dokpas'* encampment did not excite much curiosity. Yongden and I were quite commonplace, poor travellers. A man led us to a small hut which had sheltered goats—the ground, covered with a thick layer of *rima*,[1] clearly told its tale. Maybe the beasts would share it with us next night—such familiarity between animals and human beings is not rare amongst Thibetan cowmen. I nearly regretted having met these boys and the woman who first delayed us on our way. Had they not seen us, we should have camped alone amongst the bushes, in a much cleaner place than this goatpen, and we could have explored the hills at leisure. Now we should be compelled to keep strictly to our rôle of destitute

---

[1] *Rima:* Goat or sheep dung.

neskorpa, for the people of those parts have a sinister name as robbers.

In Thibet, unless one is convinced that he has been seen by none, it is always safer to stay with the people of the country, even if it is certain that they are regular thieves or highwaymen. The reason for it is that Thibetans, unless they are drunk, fighting for their own lives, or have some other exceptional reason, shrink from killing. That feeling is the result of the Buddhist teaching of the respect for life which has permeated the mind of the Thibetans, although only very dim notions about the Buddha's doctrine have spread in their country. But if the man whom they have robbed is set free and can indicate the scene of the robbery, the robbers run the risk of being denounced by him to some chief. Of justice there is not much in Thibet and officials do not, as a rule, listen to the travellers who have met with misfortune on their way, unless they be rich traders from whom valuable presents may be expected. Anyhow, villagers or *dokpas* prefer robberies to take place at a distance from their homes, so that they can answer all enquiries which may be made with: "We do not know about the thing. We are not the thieves. They must have been travellers from another country who were on their way."

The highwaymen of Thibet do not form a special class of people exclusively employed in brigandage. In some parts of the country all men, without exception, are robbers, even to the extent of leaving husbandry entirely to the womenfolk, a more profitable work claiming the males of the tribe! This is perhaps an uncommon case; but in the outer provinces many peasants or cowmen with all the appearance and ways of honest folk, occasionally unite in a gang to form a plundering expedition in a neighbouring district or to attack a caravan, and, in any case, are prompt to despoil the travellers who cross their path. The terrible or amusing stories I have heard about attacks on the hill roads, or in the desert steppes, the number of the robbers' victims I have seen, compel me to believe that insecurity prevails to a large extent in the fairyland of Thibet;

but I owe it to its inhabitants to testify that personally, though I have had a few disquieting meetings, I have never suffered any loss. I may say the same about China, although I have travelled in the midst of the civil war as well as through the wildest regions of the remote Szetchuanese and Yunnanese far west. Some will think that I have been uncommonly lucky. I shall not disagree; but luck has a cause, like anything else and I believe that there exists a mental attitude capable of shaping circumstances more or less according to one's wishes.

Thibetans are simple men. Brigandage is for them merely an adventurous sport, in which they do not discover anything fundamentally wicked so long as it does not cause death. No one is ashamed to practise it. The shame is for the one who has been robbed, who has not been able to defend himself by sheer strength or by cleverness.

"Elder brothers, give me a man to accompany me for a few days to the shore of the lake," I said once, when spending the summer amongst the famous Gologs robber tribes, "and, during my absence, look after my camp, my luggage, and my horses. You old brigands know the tricks of the trade! Shame on you if some one is able to take away what is around your tents!"

They laughed heartily, not offended in the least, but rather proud of my appreciation of their valour as bandits. After all, they may have unconsciously felt the power of my sympathy, and my love for their land and for themselves—wild children of the wild heights!

To return to our *dokpas'* camp. We knew that we would be safer in their midst than isolated at some distance, and we hoped also to be able to go round a-begging and get some food as alms, for to show money in such a place would have been unwise. However much one may trust in one's good luck, one must not forget to be sensible.

I asked for some burning pieces of cow dung to kindle a fire, and enquired about the dogs. Might I safely go to the river to fetch water? But a woman brought us curd and tea, and I delayed lighting the fire until I had refreshed myself. During that time the chief of the family had come and talked with Yongden. Feeling satisfied with what he had learned about us, he deemed us worthy to be shown into his own dwelling. We were told that we did not need to worry about fire and water, for we should get our meals in the house of the master.

The large kitchen we entered was like villagers' kitchens all over Thibet. The hearth occupied a large place on the bottom of it. All around, the walls and shelves, some in wood, others in stone, supported various household utensils, big store boxes, bags of wool to be spun, sheepskins, and sundries, all covered with a thick layer of dust and blackened by the smoke. Windows there were none, the smoke hole being at the same time the light hole. But between the roof and the top of the wall there was a gap which allowed a certain amount of light to enter the room. Moreover, with the exception of the upper classes living in towns, Thibetans are accustomed to dark dwellings.

The sun had already set when we entered the kitchen. A big fire was burning, and on a large iron tripod something boiled in a huge cauldron, which was evidently of great interest to the inmates of the house, for they all eyed it with the greatest attention.

We were received rather politely. The head of the family spread a ragged carpet for the lama in the most honourable place, next the hearth, and the women who spun at the lower end of it told me to sit on the floor next them.

Then began the tiresome talk, always the same, about our country, our pilgrimages, and the like. Moreover, the master of the house and the other members of the family wished, as usual, to take the opportunity of a lama's presence to get from him an amount of ecclesiastic service at least equal to the value of the hospitality they gave him.

Again Yongden had to pay in prophetic oracles, blessings, and the like for the tea, the *tsampa,* and the shelter we both enjoyed.

He did not like, he told me later on, the look of his host, thinking that he had all the features and the ways of a robber. Partly because, as I have said, we really needed some provisions, and partly to impress upon the minds of the *dokpas* that we were real paupers, he asked leave for a time to go on a begging round through the encampment. Such being the current practice of *arjopas,* nobody showed any astonishment.

"My mother is tired," he told the people of the house. "She will sleep now, because we must start at night for the pass, and she needs rest." And addressing me, "Come here, mother!" he said. "Lie down! I shall not be away very long."

He went and I took his place on the carpet, my head resting on my own bag which was placed against my son's in such a way that it was not possible to move one of them without shaking the other one. Travellers in Thibet become experts in such devices, for, unless they spend the night at the house of relatives or well-known friends, they must always fear petty thefts.

I made a pretence of sleeping, but remained, of course, fully awake, observing the doings of our hosts, listening to their talk, ready for any event. I did not move when I heard the head of the family saying to the others in a low, subdued tone, "What can they be carrying in their bags?" Maybe he was prompted by mere curiosity, but it was doubtful. Would things turn out badly? . . . I waited.

He spoke again with those next him, but his voice was so low that I could not understand what he said, and through my lowered eyelashes I saw the tall fellow coming slowly, noiselessly toward me. I noticed also that he had no arms upon him. As for myself, my revolver was at hand under my dress, but it would have been of no use in a camp full of cowmen. Strategy would be a better weapon and I wondered what trick I could invent if the situation required it, when the man extended his large hand and cautiously felt the bag which I had used as a pillow.

I moved a little and he drew back his hand immediately, saying, with a vexed intonation:

"She is waking up!"

But I had found my stratagem.

"*Lags, lags, Gelong lags* [Yes, yes, reverend monk]!" I said, imitating the voice of one who speaks half in dreams. I then opened my eyes widely, looked around as if bewildered, and asked in a natural way: "Is my son, the lama, not here? Oh, strange! I have just heard him telling me: 'Awake mother! Awake quickly! . . . I am coming!'"

"He has not yet come back," answered the *nepo*,[1] who looked rather frightened. "Do you wish me to send for him?"

"No, no," I replied. "I do not want him. I would not dare to trouble him. He is a learned and saintly *gelong*.[2] He will come soon, I know. . . . I am all right here with you all, near that good fire. . . ."

"Have a cup of tea," said a woman.

"Yes, I will. Most kind of you," I answered, politely, producing my bowl.

Yongden entered the room. His arrival, coming on top of this incident, caused a sort of sensation.

"I heard you well, *Gelong lags*," I said, "when you told me to awaken, and I did so. I really thought you were in the room. Is it not so, *nepo?*"

"It is so, it is so," grumbled the *nepo*, whose mind was very likely a little agitated.

Yongden understood that something had happened that he could not guess, but which he must follow up with me.

"Good! good!" he said in the deep voice of the lamas when they chant in the choir. . . . "Be awakened! . . . Be awakened! . . ." His eyes turned in all directions, and seeing nothing in particular to justify that order, he looked rather comical. He had collected some butter and a little *tsampa*, and even a small piece of silver that he could not refuse without arousing suspicion.

The story behind it was a sad one. The only son of a cowman had died some months ago, and a lama belonging to a monastery situated far beyond the passes had performed the

[1] Master of the house; the mistress is called *nemo*.
[2] A lama who keeps the rule of celibacy.

rites for the dead. Nevertheless, the sorrowful parents were not satisfied, and still entertained some doubt about the situation of their little one. The boy was about eleven years old when he departed to the next world, and they begged Yongden to stay a few days to perform a supplementary ceremony. As he declined, explaining that for various reasons he must proceed quickly, they had instantly begged him to utter at least the mystic sentence that lights the lost wanderer through the various roads of the beyond and, as if taking him by the hand, leads him to the Western Paradise, the Land of Bliss.

Who could refuse these simple-minded ones the innocent illusion that meant so much to them? And so, accompanying his religious performance with a sermon on morality addressed to a number of *dokpas,* men and women, Yongden had seated the little cowboy on a lotus in the Heaven of *Chenreszigs.*

The *nepo,* now even more convinced of the greatness of the lama, drove me away from the carpet where I had remained seated, listening to the story of the dead boy.

"Go, go, mother! Sit behind now. Let the lama be comfortable!"

I moved back to the bare floor, in obedience to custom, casting on Yongden a glance which ordered him to say nothing and to be seated on the carpet.

The mystery of the cauldron was now revealed. The cover was removed and a long iron hook was dipped into the boiling broth. It brought out the heart, the lungs, and the liver of a yak, together with its stomach and bowels, which had been filled with meat and *tsampa* to make a kind of sausage. The whole flabby mass was placed on a large wooden tray, carefully covered with a piece of sacking . . . and put aside.

Then *tsampa* was poured into the broth, and ten minutes afterwards, the lama first, then the *nepo,* and I amongst the last, filled our bowls. In view of the effort which I should have to make to climb the pass, I endeavoured to feed myself as much as possible, and drank off three full bowls.

After the meal the *nepo,* evidently pleased to chat with a

traveller who could tell of so many distant places of pilgrimage, began an endless and most uninteresting talk. I hardly listened to it, thinking of the country of Po, from which I was separated only by a single range, and recollecting various observations made during the day, when a few words made me start as if I had been struck.

"I have heard," said the *nepo*, "that some *philings* have been to the Kha Karpo."

Philings? . . . to Kha Karpo! . . . Was it possible that rumours had spread about us? Or could it be that the official had searched for us on the direct roads to Lhasa, and that we owed our liberty solely to the devious route we had chosen? Who could tell? But if such was the case, they would be on the lookout around Lhasa, and would perhaps catch us near our goal.

Yongden tried to gather where the news came from. As usual in Thibet, the man did not know. He had heard it from some travellers, who might themselves have heard it from others. News hawked in such a way might well be several years old and have no connection whatsoever with us. An English consul and his Thibetan wife had toured the Kha Karpo three or four years ago. Perhaps they were these *philings*. Or had the American naturalist, whom we had left in the Lutzekiang, attempted to pursue his researches in the now forbidden zone? We could not guess, and the unpleasant feeling of hunted game, from which we had been freed for a few weeks, troubled us once more.

Yongden was no longer in the mood to continue entertaining the *nepo* with stories of remote places of pilgrimage. He declared that he wanted to sleep.

But the *nepo*, without appearing to have heard him, produced a request. The *dokpas*, he said, felt much anxiety about the snow which had fallen in but small quantity that year. The ground remained dry and would not store sufficient moisture to ensure a full growth of the grass on the pasture land. And what of the cattle which needed abundant food, after the half-starving period of winter? Would the snow fall soon?

147

. . . The lama could tell. He could also, by his art in the secret spells, cause it to come down from the sky and cover the earth. . . . Would he not do what was required to bring about that happy result? . . .

Yongden was tired out, but it was unsafe either to displease the *dokpas* or to let them believe that he was not a quite capable lama.

"Several days are needed," he answered, "to perform these rites, and as I must proceed to Po *yul*, I cannot call down the snow that will block the very passes which I must cross. What you ask is rather a complicated piece of business."

All those present agreed that it was.

"Let us see," continued my young friend. "Yes . . . in that way . . ."

He produced a small piece of paper out of a sack and asked that barley be brought to him, if they had some. He then placed a few grains on the paper and holding it outstretched on his open palms, lapsed into a deep meditation. A chanting followed whose slow rhythm and whispering sound gradually grew louder and louder until it rolled like thunder beneath the low, ramshakle roof of the large kitchen.

The *dokpas* looked really terrified.

Yongden stopped abruptly, which caused everybody, including myself, to start up.

Then he divided the grains that had been used for the performance of the rite into two parts, putting one half aside in a corner of his handkerchief, and leaving the remaining part in the paper which was folded in a peculiar and complicated way.

"Here, take it," he ordered the *nepo*, "and listen! You will open that paper to-morrow at sunset, and throw the grain it contains toward the sky in the four directions. I myself will at the same time recite the *ngags* [spells] needed to make an abundant fall of snow. Now, if you open the paper *before* sunset, before I have uttered the *ngags;* the deities, not being propitiated in the proper way, will feel irritated and revenge themselves upon you all. So be careful!"

The man promised to follow exactly the orders he had received, and at last the thought arose in his mind that he had perhaps exacted from the lama more than the value of the meagre hospitality he had shown us. So he told his wife to fetch a piece of meat that we might carry as provision on the road. The woman brought a quite excellent piece, but her husband snatched it out of her hand before she had time to present it to the lama, hung it up again, and carefully chose a skinny bit which he gave with the utmost gravity to my companion. We were hard put to it not to laugh aloud, so much had we enjoyed the fun.

"I cannot," declared Yongden, who is perfectly conversant with the religious monastic rules, "thank you for a gift of meat, which is an impure thing, the result of the great sin of killing. It would be as if I rejoiced at the slaughter of that animal, because I have a piece of its flesh to eat. But give me some *tsampa* and I will bless your home."

The words of the lama were most edifying and strictly orthodox, but they had still another quality, in that they were to provide us with some barely flour, which, however small in quantity, would prove very useful.

A big bowl heaped high with *tsampa* was placed before him. Yongden threw a few pinches of it in various directions, called health and prosperity on the host, his family, and his belongings. And before the *nepo* had time to take back the flour, which he had only lent for ritualistic purposes, my son poured the contents of the bowl into our bag, which I had promptly extended toward him, kneeling in a most devout attitude.

We now hoped that the old miser, who looked rather astonished at the sight of his empty bowl, would allow the lama to rest. We were anxious to sleep a few hours before starting on a new tiring march whose end we could not foresee. The pass might be blocked, or other obstacles might arise on our way. Who could ever tell? As for the *dokpas*, we felt safe. I had very well understood the cunning of Yongden, who wished to prevent any of the cowmen from following us. The next morning the story of the grain would spread, and everyone would feel far too interested in its success to attempt anything that could hinder the magic work which was to bring the desired snow. Then, when the grain had been thrown toward the sky, the *dokpas* would wait for the result for at least another full day. We should be far away by that time, amongst other people. At least, so we believed, but events were to take a very different turn.

Two women arranged the couch of the *nepo* for the night. I cannot say the "bed," for Thibetans, as well as a large number of Asiatics, including Japanese, have no bed. Rich Thibetans sleep on thick cushions covered with fine tapestry; poor ones on the bare floor or ground. Between these two extremes there exist countless degrees of thickness and beauty in the cushions, until one comes to a single piece of ragged sackcloth or of greasy sheepskin. But in any case, the blankets, or whatever takes their place, are put aside during the day and brought out when they are needed for the night.

When all was ready, the old *dokpa* took off his robe, keeping on his trousers, according to the general custom of Thibet, where women as well as men sleep with the upper part of the body naked. Then he slipped between the sheepskins which were spread at the best and warmest place near the hearth. A bucket was placed in the middle of the room to spare the people of the house the trouble of going out at night. I had never seen such a thing elsewhere. Village people, as a rule, have regular closets, partly for cleanliness' sake, but especially to accumulate manure for the field, that supplied by the cows, sheep, and goats being reserved as fuel. *Dokpas* in the solitude, who have large spaces before them and no agriculture whatever, do not feel the need of special accommodation and as a rule retire outside their tents at night as well as in daytime.

Most of the men and women had not waited for the master to lie down. Young married couples rolled themselves in a large blanket with their children between them; elder people or bachelors rested alone; and the youngsters heaped themselves together like so many puppies, laughing and fighting for their share of the covering rags, till sleep silenced them.

CHAPTER V

HOW many hours have I slept? I cannot guess. I feel as if I had shut my eyes only a few minutes before.

"It is time to start," repeats the man whose voice has awakened me. He throws a few branches amongst the smouldering embers; the flame illumines the sleepers, some of whom grumble and roll up more tightly in their blankets. We are quickly ready. Dressing consists merely of tying our belts and our garters, for our loads have not been opened. We are off in no time.

"*Kale pheb*,[1] lama!" says the *nepo* from between his sheepskin covering as we pass the door.

The moon, screened by a high peak, sheds but a dim light upon the valley. The wind blows hard. I feel exceedingly cold and my fingers freeze. Even wrapped as they are in the long sleeves of my thick dress, I have difficulty in gripping my staff. The shallow river which was flowing the day before at the place we crossed it is here covered with thick ice. On the opposite bank the narrow trail winds between thickets. It branches several times, and other tracks cross it. We should very likely have wasted a good deal of time in that labyrinth, had we not been guided. I decline, as does Yongden, the invitation to ride. It is too dreadfully cold. I prefer to keep on walking until the sun rises.

The landscape, as much as I can see of it, is very different from that which extends between Tashi Tse and the summit of the Deo *la*. The latter was truly majestic, whereas the narrow valley which we now follow breathes occult hostility and treachery.

After a few hours' walk, a pale-green dawn breaks and rather adds to the uncomfortable impression produced by

[1] "Proceed slowly," a polite farewell to departing guests.

151

the landscape. There is but little snow on the track we are following, but enormous quantites are heaped in the gorges which score its sides.

The sun rises shyly amidst the clouds. We cross small pastures covered with wet grass, wintry and yellowish. I ride for a while, but soon get off and linger behind, leaving the horse to Yongden. The *dokpa* who walks at his girth annoys me with his uninterrupted twaddle. I like silence when wandering across the hills. So many voices may be heard there by trained ears and an attentive mind.

A little later, snow begins to appear on the path and grows deeper as we continue. A gigantic white mound marks the beginning, says our guide, of a summer track leading to another pass. Seeing it, I understand that I must give up all idea of roaming about on the range, as I should have liked to do. Explorations in those regions ought to take place during the very short period between the time when the mud caused by the melting of the snow and the summer rains is somewhat dried, and that of the first important snowfall, an interval of scarcely six weeks.

That year, owing to that scarcity of snow which alarms the *dokpas*, the Aigni *la* is easily practicable. We reach its *latza* before noon.

Our guide has laid down the lama's load, which he had carried until then. He is about to leave us and take his horse back to the camp.

Although our disguise and our care for our safety did not allow us to be over-generous, I had always meant to give a little present to the good man. Yongden's sermon on the merits inherent in the services rendered gratis to lama pilgrims was aimed only at convincing the *dokpas* of our poverty. The night before, when all had been asleep, I whispered in my young companion's ear what he was to do. And now he obeys my instructions.

Slowly he produces two coins from his purse and, wrapped in a piece of paper, a pinch of dried cypress leaves.

"This money," he declares, solemnly, "is all that I have got.

I have received it from the *pönpo* of Tashi Tse, for the welfare of whom I read the Sacred Scripture at the *zong*. You have helped us both, my mother and me. I therefore give it to you as well as that *sang*[1] which comes from the far distant holy *nes* [place of pilgrimage] called Kha Karpo."

Though the price we give for the hiring of a horse with its driver is small, money is so rare amongst *dokpas* that the man cannot but be satisfied. We are confident, also, that he will hide the silver and keep silent about it, lest some one should rob him of it. Thus do we mingle prudence and righteousness.

Yongden adds some words meant to impress the man and his friends, to whom he will doubtless repeat them, and to let them know that we are not devoid of protection in the country we are entering. This detail may easily influence the *dokpas* and prevent them from following us.

"Take the money, elder brother," insists the lama. "We have arrived on the territory of the Po *gyalpo* [king]; his *anchös* [chaplain] is an old friend of mine. We both belong to the Sera monastery at Lhasa, so, if I am in need, he will ask the king to help me."

"Of course he will, *kusho* [sir]," agrees the man, in a respectful tone which shows how much the poor travellers have progressed in his esteem. "But I prefer to take the *sang* alone. It is most precious. As for the money, if I accepted it I would lose the merit of having served a lama. . . . No, I shall not take it. I like better to keep the merit. It is useful for the next life as well as for this one. . . . Please give me your blessing, *kusho*. I must make haste now. *Kale pheb,* Lama! *Kale pheb,* mother!"

With that he was gone, happy with the dust of a few dry leaves and the belief that he had sown a few seeds of future

[1] *Sang:* dried leaves burned as perfume in purifying and exorcist rites, as is incense in the Roman Church. Cypress and fir trees are more generally used, but, on some hills, azalea leaves and young fern shoots are burned. In the Himalayas a kind of "feverfew" is also gathered for the same purpose.

felicity in this world or in another one. The poor thing! My hearty good wishes followed him.

We stood near the *latza*. We had not shouted the habitual *"Lha gyalo!"* as Thibetan custom requests. We had nothing of that joyful excitement which makes one enthusiastically salute the conquest of the summit at the end of an exhausting climb. Accustomed to long tramps, that short ride had been a real luxury to us. For the first time since we had left China, we had reached a pass without fatigue, and perhaps it was that which prevented us from being cheerful.

Anyhow, it was neither the time nor the place to tarry and ponder over psychological problems.

"Lha gyalo!"

The shout was rather listless.

"It will snow," said Yongden, who looked unusually grave.

"I suspect it since the sun has risen in such a melancholy way," I replied. "But will it snow to-day? Could our *nepo* have thrown, before the appointed hour, the grain you gave him yesterday?"

The joke found no echo in the lama.

"Let us be quick," he said.

I did not like to see him in such a gloomy mood, so I continued: "Do you remember that *Nagspa* lama of the *KoKo Nor* who could, so the cowmen said, make the snow and rain and hail fall or stop at his will? He has taught me some of his *ngags*. Let us bet on the result. You have called the snow. I will try to prevent it."

The young man did not even smile.

"The poor fellows need snow for their pastures," he said. "Let them have it." And he began to stride down the steep white slope.

His strange attitude impressed me! Why was he so greatly concerned about snow? We had seen much of it in previous journeys. It was not a thing to frighten us, especially as we were so near the villages. Perhaps he felt unwell.

I hastened to join the lama, who was already far below. In spite of my efforts the distance between him and me increased rapidly—which annoyed me. I tried to run straighter, avoiding the loss of time caused by long windings. Then, I suppose some invisible and compassionate little mountain fairy, seeing my trouble and wishing to do me a gracious service, pulled me by the foot. In the tenth part of a second I fell and slid just as in a toboggan race, yet with the noteworthy difference that I was myself the toboggan and its driver, all in one! I had happily succeeded in grasping my staff low enough to use it to steer. In such wise, dispensing with any "tacking," I passed Yongden with the speed of an express train and pulled up far ahead of him.

He hurried as quickly as he could and joined me as I shook off the snow that covered my dress and my load. Satisfied with my answer that I had not hurt myself, he declared that my performance looked quite pretty and had spared me a good deal of exertion.

It had another result, which I appreciated still more, for Yongden had recovered his good-humoured laugh.

What vague premonition had for a moment thrown a gloom over the cheerful mind of my young companion? I did not venture to offer any explanation. But truly we were approaching rather trying circumstances.

Judging from the scenery, I could guess that the country toward which we proceeded was entirely different from the upper Salween basin in its physical aspects.

The air was charged with moisture, the ground wet, even slightly marshy, in some places. Snow had already fallen in quantities and the *dokpas* of the region had no reason to feel anxious for the growth of the grass, as did those living on the opposite side of the mountain range.

Soon we entered the zone of trees and followed the shore of the river springing at the foot of the Aigni *la.* It led us to large pasture lands which occupied the area at the intersection of three valleys. We had walked down through one of them, another opened just opposite, beyond the pastures, and a stream, larger than that coming from the Aigni pass, issued from it. The third received the united waters of

the two rivers which would, far away, flow into the *Yeru
Tsangpo* (Brahmaputra) and bring the melted snows of the
mighty range I had crossed into the Indian Ocean.

I had now been able to discover one of the springs of the
river Po, whose upper course is unknown to geographers. The
second interested me greatly. It originated, it seemed, in the
vicinity of the pass which the *dokpas* had named Yön tsong *la*
and which was blocked for the present. That much-to-be-
regretted circumstance left me no hope of climbing it to inspect
the range on that side. But I wished at least to follow the
river up as high as I could, and to gather whatever observations I might be able to make in my humble way. I was far
from suspecting that this bit of rough scouting, such as I had
so often done in Thibet, was to lead me into a short but rather
exciting adventure which turned out all right, but could have
ended otherwise.

Briefly, I explained my intention to Yongden.

Still more laconic, he answered curtly: "It will snow, and
we have no food."

These were words worthy of some reflection.

The snow? . . . I did not fear it. As for the food, I opened
the bags, inspected their contents with the lama, and we agreed
that there remained a sufficient quantity for three meals. Three
meals meant three days, for we had not come to these Thibetan
wilds to indulge in gastronomy. Moreover, I did not intend to
linger in the upper valleys; a mere glance would satisfy my
curiosity and enable me to supply a few general facts to those
interested in that virgin river.

"Forward! . . ."

After sunset the snow began to fall, lightly at first—just a
few butterflies whirling among the black trees. Then it gradually became more and more dense, one of those slow snowfalls, whose flakes descend from some inexhaustible heavenly
store, shrouding the mighty peaks and burying the valleys.

"Let us pitch the tent," I said. "We will light a fire inside
it and have tea."

We really needed some refreshment. Since the evening soup of the day before, eaten at the *dokpas'* camp, we had taken no food.

Dry wood was scarce. To cut and collect some while the snow fell kept us busy for a long time. Nevertheless we gathered enough small branches to boil the tea. Our frugal meal having been hastily eaten, we threw the remaining embers outside, for the heat melted the snow on the thin cloth and water dripped freely on us. It also became evident that our pilgrim staffs, which were used as tent poles, could not bear the weight of the snow for long. Since we could not run the risk of breaking them, we established, with the cloth only, a kind of sloping shelter fixed with a few stones on an adjacent rock. We then lay down beneath it, and as it was not very cold we soon fell asleep.

A sensation of painful oppression awakened me. I lifted my head, and immediately knocked it against our roof. Overloaded with snow, it had sagged and we were being buried. There was, for the time being, nothing tragic about the matter. Anyhow we had better be quick and get out while it was still easy.

I pushed Yongden, who was asleep. He needed no explanation to understand the situation, which was plain enough! I only said:

"Let us turn slowly and then get up together, pushing the cloth with our backs. . . . Ready? . . . Gee up!"

We were out of our grave, and none the better for it. Snow fell and we had no hope of fixing another shelter, for we would have been buried again before long. No rest being possible, it was better to walk and keep warm.

We tramped the remainder of the night and all the next morning without making much progress. The soft snow made walking difficult. Then, when we had reached a higher level, we began to slip on the miniature glaciers formed by previous snowfalls, that had repeatedly melted and frozen again and which were now treacherously hidden under a thick new layer.

A *sa phug* [1] which we discovered a little after noon was hailed with joy.

We established ourselves on its dry ground. Our tent, hung like a curtain to some roots above our heads, added to the protection afforded by the cave. No fuel was available, but we ate a little *tsampa* and quenched our thirst with snow which we melted in our mouths. Then, overtired, after two nights spent nearly without rest, we slept soundly till the morrow at dawn.

When we awakened, the snow was still falling. We could see that it had not ceased the whole night, for it was heaped much higher in front of our prehistoric refuge and formed a wall that had kept us warm during the night.

I decided to leave our bags in the *sa phug* and to attempt a reconnaissance higher up. We should walk the more easily, carrying only our mountain staffs. As we were compelled to retrace our steps to reach the Po villages, we would pick up our baggage again on our way down. As for thieves, they were not much to be feared in that deserted land, on the road to a blocked pass.

We started. Snow continued to fall in the same slow, inexorable way, as it had done for more than forty hours. We found it forming impassable barriers at some points where it had accumulated on old layers already thick. It was impossible to follow any regular direction. With great exertion I reached a ridge from where, through the moving curtain of the white soft flakes, I faintly discerned summits which looked like sloping, undulated tablelands. But who knows if the snow had not leveled the ground and changed their aspect? It is a common thing, well known to all alpinists, that mountains which assume rounded lines in their wintry garb show, in the summer, sharp spurs and rocky peaks like needles.

I went down with still greater difficulty than I had experienced in climbing up, and endeavoured to reach another spot from which I hoped to ascertain if a stream joining the main river issued from what appeared to be a small gorge. I was pushing forward when I heard a cry behind me. Yongden,

[1] The *sa phug* is an earthen cave, the *thag phug* a cavern in the rock.

while looking for a short cut, had slipped and fallen into a ravine. This was not very deep, yet, shut between nearly vertical banks, its access was anything but easy. When, after a few minutes, I reached my poor companion, he looked pitiable enough, lying in his ragged lama dress on the white snow stained with drops of blood.

"Nothing, nothing serious at all," he said, answering my questions. "I must have knocked my head against a rock when rolling down. The skin is a little cut, but there is nothing more. Do not be afraid. The shock only made me giddy."

Then he moved to get up, uttered a moan, whilst he became pale, shut his eyes, and whispered: "Oh! my foot!"

He tried a second time to stand, but without success.

"I cannot," he said, the pain bringing tears to his eyes. "I cannot stand."

I felt terrified. Had he broken his leg?

What should we do in that case, alone in that wilderness, without food and the snow growing higher hour after hour?

I immediately took off his boot and examined his foot. Happily, the bones were unbroken. He had merely sprained his ankle and somewhat bruised his knee. The accident in itself did not endanger his life or his general health. At least, it would not have done so in any inhabited place, but out here. . . .

He understood as well as I did the gravity of our situation and again endeavoured to rise. With my help he succeeded and remained on one foot, leaning on his staff.

"I shall try to carry you," I said. "We must go back to the *sa phug*, and there we will think over the matter."

In spite of my good will and strenuous efforts I was soon compelled to realize that I lacked the strength necessary to carry my adopted son across deep snow, with stones and pits hidden under it, which made me stumble frequently. Yongden, who had reluctantly obeyed my express command to let himself be carried, then endeavoured to proceed, leaning on me and on his staff, creeping rather than walking, and stopping every ten minutes. Drops of perspiration caused by the painful effort fell from the lama cap which covered his forehead. It took us hours to reach the *sa phug.*

I massaged Yongden's ankle, and bandaged it with his belt. I could do no more.

As on the day before, we had no fuel and shivered as we lay on the frozen ground. The snow which we had eaten to quench our thirst on the road, as well as the icy water brought from the stream to drink with our meal, had increased the painful sensation of internal cold that kept us awake.

Yet, had it not been for my concern for my young companion, I should have found a peculiar charm in my situation. Indeed, that charm was so powerful that it triumphed over my preoccupations and my physical discomfort. Until late that night I remained seated, motionless, enjoying the delights of my solitude in the absolute silence, the perfect stillness of that strange white land, sunk in rest, in utter peace.

And the snow still continued to heap itself around us.

In the morning, when I opened my eyes, the first thing I saw was Yongden standing on one leg, leaning on his staff, with his back against the earthen wall of the *sa phug.* His attitude reminded me of that of certain Chinese spirits in the Taosse Temples, and he would have been quite comical in any other circumstances, but tears were in his eyes.

"I cannot walk," he said in despair. "I have already tried several times, but I cannot stand on my foot."

His ankle was swollen. The foot remained twisted out of its normal position. It was impossible to start.

We spent the first morning hours in discussion. I thought of leaving my companion with the baggage and the handful of *tsampa* that remained and of trying to reach some village to ask for help. But Yongden doubted whether anyone would follow me and take trouble for mere beggars, as we appeared to be. As for showing money or offering a reward of some importance, such a thing would prove more dangerous than anything else. Perhaps my son was too pessimistic in his opinion of the Popas, but more serious objections could be raised against my plan.

We did not know how far the villages were, and which were the roads that led to them. Two days ago, when coming down from the Aigni *la*, we had seen three tracks. All traces of these would now be hidden beneath deep snow. The river remained the only guide, and it was not a reliable one. It could not fail to flow down to the inhabited region, but we were not certain that we could follow its course all the way. Mountain streams frequently enter narrow gorges, while travellers' paths cling to the hills far above them, although they both meet again miles away.

What if I missed the right path and had to retrace my steps? I might wander several days, meet with an accident as my companion had done, or starve and fail to reach my goal.

I could not deny that Yongden's apprehensions, gloomy as they might appear, were well grounded. As for me, I felt very frightened at the idea of abandoning the lame young man in that cave, where wolves, bears, snow leopards, or other hungry beasts might attack him at night, while he could not even stand on his feet to protect himself.

So time passed while we made plans and rejected them, one after another. I eventually decided to follow the valley down as far as I could, in search of *dokpas*. I would return by evening. I walked the whole day, seeing two deserted encampments, but not one living being. I was overcome with sorrow at the thought of the lama who had remained shivering in the *sa phug*. How much better he would have been in one of those abandoned huts, in which fuel left by the *dokpas* could have warmed him! At any rate, I ought to bring some back with me. But how could I carry it? I had no bag nor any piece of cloth with me, and only a thick woollen material could prevent the cow dung from becoming wet on the way. As I had no choice, I took off my upper dress made of coarse Thibetan serge, packed the fuel in it, tied the load with my belt, and, having fastened it on my back, I started.

It was an exhausting tramp. The snow had not ceased to fall, and my thin Chinese underdress was but an insufficient protection against it. Before half an hour elapsed I felt as if I were in an icy bath.

Night came while I was still far from the cave. I could not miss my way, the stream being there as a guide, but in the darkness I failed to find the exact place of the *sa phug*. Had I proceeded too high up the valley, or was I still below the spot where the cave was situated? I realized that I did not know.

I was on the point of shouting to the lama when I discerned a small light a little higher up. No doubt Yongden was there and he had lighted, to guide me, the roll of taper which we had in our bag. Such, indeed, was the case.

"I was half dead with fear," he told me, when I joined him. "I fancied the very worst, when evening came and you did not return."

The fire, and a bowl of hot tea in which we threw a few pinches of barley flour, cheered us, even though our wretched plight had grown rather worse. Our food supply was now reduced to three or four spoonfuls of *tsampa*, and a little tea dust. We were still in ignorance as to the distance that separated us from the villages, and the path that led directly to them, and poor Yongden was still unable to walk.

"Do not worry about me, Jetsunma," said the lama as I was drying myself near the fire. "I know you do not fear death, and I do not fear it, either. I have massaged my foot again and again to-day and now I will put a compress of hot water on it. Perhaps I shall be able to walk to-morrow. If not, you must go away and try to save yourself. Do not be sorry on my account. All that happens comes from some cause. This accident is a result of my previous deeds. No gods or men or anybody but myself are responsible for it, and it would be useless to lament about it. . . . Now let us sleep. . . ." And we both slept soundly while the snow still fell and fell, without ceasing.

The next day Yongden could stand. I tied his bag and mine in one load, which I carried, and, as I had done when leading him back to the *sa phug* after the accident, I helped the lama to walk. We were progressing at a snail's pace. When we again reached the wooded hills I cut a branch at the end of which I fixed a short piece of wood and wrapped it round with our empty provision bags to form a kind of cushion. This provided the young man with a primitive crutch and he could thus proceed without my help.

During my scouting tour the day before I had seen the valley narrowing in a way which made me fear that we could not proceed close to the stream. I had more confidence in a track which we had seen climbing through the forest when coming down from the Aigni *la*. It branched a little before entering the pasture land and very likely it followed the same direction as the stream higher up, having been cut through the jungle because the bottom of the valley was not passable. We could, no doubt, have found some short cut to it without going as far as the spot from where we had just noticed it, but it would have been imprudent to attempt steep slopes through the bushes with Yongden who had great difficulty in walking, even in the trodden tracks.

So we went a long way, knee-deep in the snow, until we reached the path which was well marked by a neatly cut line between the trees.

The weather cleared at that time, and had it not been for the difficulty of proceeding in the snow that sixty-five hours of continual fall had accumulated, and the sorrow I felt at seeing the painful efforts made by Yongden, the walk would have been rather pleasant. We were now in the midst of fine alpine scenery which must have been charming in spring and later summer, after the wet season. Unfortunately, I began to share something of the physical misery of my friend. That morning I had noticed a small gap in my boot through which my right big toe began to appear. Hours of tramping had transformed the little hole into a wide mouth that opened and closed at every step, as if my leg ended in a strange animal, feeding on snow as it went. As for my left foot, it did not fare much better, for the sole of the boot had become almost entirely unsewn on one side. I began to suffer cruelly. Fresh snow is especially dangerous; it burns and causes sores. Thibetan hillmen, though their skin is rather tough, take great care to avoid direct contact with it.

It was getting late, and we had abandoned all hope of reaching a village that day. No trace of cultivation, no cattle were seen, and it also seemed that we would find no shelter. For we had searched in vain for the *dokpas'* summer huts which, according to the man who had accompanied us to the top of the Aigni *la,* existed on the path going down to the inhabited valleys. Covered with snow, they were perhaps not easy to discover. Or could it be that, unlucky till the end, we had missed our road? That question formed the topic of the few words which we exchanged. We had given up asking each other about our respective efforts and pains. We knew that we were both struggling with all our might and unable to relieve each other's suffering. Prattling about it was useless. Later on, we also dropped, as idle and tiring, the question of the *dokpas'* huts or whether we had missed our way.

Night came and snow began to fall again. The sky was pitch dark, but a dim, dull light, that made me think of Hades, seemed to ascend strangely from the white ground and issue from the snow-clad trees.

White from head to foot, mind and body benumbed, we continued at a limping gait our silent tramp. In that fantastic landscape, we looked like two queer ghosts *en route* to answer the call of a Thibetan wizard, or the ragged attendants of some needy Father Christmas of the wilds.

Father Christmas. . . . An association of ideas took possession of my thoughts. Were we not in December? Yes. But the concordance of dates between the Gregorian and the Sino-Thibetan calendar, which I had used for years—was not clear in my memory. I would consult, when free to do so, the Chinese-foreign calendar I had in my bag.

Gradually Yongden fell behind and I continued to drag myself aimlessly along. Villages, huts, any kind of shelter, seemed out of reach. To camp in the deep snow was impossible. . . . Then . . . what . . . ?

A sudden shock shook me from my torpor. I had knocked myself against something hard. I looked. It was the top of a rustic fence. . . . A fence! . . . The *dokpas'* summer camp, of which our guide had spoken! We were on the right way, and here was a shelter to sleep in!

I could hardly believe it. I laid my hand on the wood and followed along it as if I feared that fence and huts would vanish, slipping away from my hold. I arrived at the gate of the enclosure and from there vaguely discerned a large square cabin and several smaller ones.

I shouted the good news to the lama:

"*Diru! Diru! Kampa chik dug!* [Here! Here! There is a house!]"

Without waiting for him I entered the camp. Next the men's room was a horse shed. I put my load down under it and began immediately to clear away the snow heaped high before the door. Yongden arrived while I was thus busied.

We happily found a good quantity of firewood and dry cow dung under the shed, and we first lighted a fire there, the room itself being too dark to locate the hearth. As soon as the burning branches gave us some light, we carried them into the hut, which we found rather large, with a fireplace and, on both sides of it, boards covering the ground to sit and lie on. The happiest discovery was another supply of fuel. After the nights spent in the *sa phug,* the warmth that spread into the closed room thrilled voluptuously in me the epicure which is always lurking in the corner of the most ascetic hearts.

Before sleeping, we drank a bowl of hot water sprinkled with *tsampa,* leaving the tea for to-morrow's meal, and Yongden put a hot compress around his foot. I consulted my calendar; it was the 22d of December.

Yongden's foot was less stiff and less painful on the following morning. But the young man still needed his crutch. And I was now in trouble, in my turn, for I could not proceed without sewing new soles on my boots. The day before, my toes had been burnt and half frozen. Blisters and bleeding sores made my gait as lame as that of my son. It would have been really dangerous to start, practically barefooted, on a new tramp in the snow.

Nothing in his monastic study had prepared the lama for a cobbler's work, and he found it very difficult. As for me, I knew nothing whatever of this craft, and the only help I could give him was to unstitch the worn-out piece of leather.

It was one o'clock when the boots were ready. We hesitated to start. The existence of a *dokpas'* abandoned summer camp at this spot had shown us that we were still far from the permanently inhabited region. Most likely, travelling at such a slack pace, we should not reach it before darkness came. That meant one more tramp at night and we began to feel the effects of prolonged fasting on our overtaxed endurance. On the other hand, to rest the remainder of the day was to increase the length of our starvation. The choice between these equally unenjoyable alternatives was hard. The bright fire tempted us; we decided in favour of the warm shelter during the night and a very early start before daybreak.

The weather did not clear; it snowed without interruption. A little before sunset, Yongden, who wished to ascertain if the condition of his sprained ankled had improved, went to another *dokpas'* enclosure situated in the same clearing, and told me that he had seen from there the path we would follow on the morrow.

The fire was revived long before daybreak. We turned our tea bag inside out and shook it over the kettle so that the last atom of tea dust would fall into the boiling water. Then, after a brief, purely liquid breakfast, we proceeded straight to the place Yongden had marked the day before. It was still dark and snow fell heavily. The path seemed to be narrower than it had been above; but Thibetan tracks grow as the forest makes them, and the forest is a capricious road-builder.

We walked painfully until nearly noon, and then, to our

dismay, we realized that we were going in a wrong direction. We ran into thickets and steep slopes, with no more traces of a path. Had we wandered after having started in the right direction? I doubted it. Most likely we had been wrong from the beginning, entering one of those trails on which cattle roam in the hills, of which a number are always to be found near pasture grounds. Be that as it may, we could but retrace our steps to the *dokpas'* encampment. Any attempt to look for the track from our present position would but lead us still farther astray.

We had not gone far. Neither the lama, who still used his crutch, nor I with my sorely bleeding feet, could progress quickly. But far or near, it was the time needed to reach our starting-point that was of importance. The consequence of such a mistake for people who had already fasted three days was really serious.

We did not always find our tracks easily. The snow had partly effaced them, and Yongden had frequently to rest, which caused more delay.

The ranges which we were crossing were covered with forests of holly-oak trees, and reminded me once more of Christmas. It was Christmas Eve, and I pictured the joyful agitation of so many in Western lands, and the sorrow of too many others who do not even receive "the crumbs which fall from the rich man's table." How far I was from all these things, in that solitary woods! I broke a small branch of holly-oak, meaning to give it, later on, to a friend of mine, if I escaped from these mountains and that snow which seemed determined to keep me. But so unexpectedly do things happen, that when I brought the holly of the virgin Po forest to the Western land, the man for whom it was meant had departed for a still more mysterious land than that of the Popas.

A bowl of hot water was again the only refreshment we could get when we arrived at the *dokpas'* hut. I wanted to go scouting immediately, for we ought at any rate to avoid another mistake the next day. We both began to feel very giddy. We heard strange sounds of bells; and although we did not suffer many pangs of hunger, it was certain that unless we got some food before long, we should lack the strength necessary to reach the villages.

Yongden insisted on going himself to look for the road, while I rested near the fire. I yielded to his kind entreaties, and the poor fellow started again over the snow, his staff in one hand and his crutch under the other arm.

Time passed. The lack of provisions dispensed with the trouble of cooking. I had but to fill the kettle with snow, to melt it and boil the water. Then I could lie down and think!

I fancied a few of my acquaintances in my place. I saw some of them swearing at God, the devil, their companions, and themselves. I saw others weeping and praying on their knees. Most of them, I know, would have blamed my quietness and that of my young companion. . . . A *pâli* verse sung sweetly in my memory:

"Happy indeed we live, among the anxious unanxious. . . ."

It was nearly dark when Yongden returned. This time he said that there could be no mistake. He had but faintly seen a trail the day before and had taken it for the main path. Darkness and snow, when we had started, had prevented us from discovering the mistake, which was really an absurd one, for the true track, although its entrance was hidden by fir trees scattered all around the clearing, was not very difficult to find. Nevertheless, he had followed it for quite a long time. There was no need to worry about the matter. It was really the right one.

The news was most comforting, but I did not like the look of the young man. He was pale, with glowing and feverish eyes. He drank two bowls of hot water and immediately fell asleep.

I remained for a while watching him. He was restless and from time to time he moaned. Gradually, however, he became calmer and I closed my eyes to sleep.

A noise of steps on the boards and a confused muttering

awakened me. The dim light of the smouldering embers disclosed the lama tottering toward the door, his staff in his hand. Where was he going? In no time I was on my feet.

"What is the matter with you?" I asked. "Are you ill?"

"Snow is heaping up . . . heaping up," he answered with a strange voice, as if dreaming. "We sleep here, and it falls. . . . Let us start. . . . It will be too late. . . ."

He was only half conscious and undoubtedly under the influence of a nightmare. I tried to calm him, to persuade him to lie down again. He did not appear to understand, and was lost in his own idea. He wanted to start. I could see that he was raving. His hand was burning with fever. It was the result of the long tramps in the snow, the fasting, and the pain caused by the sprained ankle.

With sudden violence he reached the door and opened it.

"Look," he said, "it snows!"

Heavy snow was falling. A new white mound could be seen blocking the passage which we had cleared several times since we had first arrived at the camp. A draught of cold air blew into the hut.

"Do not stay here," I commanded the lama. "You are ill. The cold will make you worse!"

"We must start, start at once," he repeated obstinately, and, trying to drag me away, he cried: "You will die, Jetsunma! Come quick! . . . Come!"

I gave him a push, kicked the door shut, and endeavoured again to make him lie down near the fire, in spite of his struggles. Fever and the wild idea of saving my life had increased the natural strength of the sturdy young fellow. He staggered on his bad foot and did not appear to feel the pain.

What would happen if he succeeded in breaking out? I remembered, terrified, that the clearing ended in a precipice only a few feet away.

I succeeded in throwing a few branches on the fire, and the sudden bright light broke the trend of Yongden's feverish vagaries.

"What? . . . What? . . ." he said, looking around. And he no longer resisted my efforts to make him lie down.

I made a big fire and placed some fresh snow on the young man's head. He then fell asleep again, but I dared not relax my watch and remained seated the rest of the night.

Did I doze and dream? . . . I heard the feeble jingling of a bell, lower down the hill. Who could be travelling in that snow, and at that hour? . . . I listened, fearing that some one might enter, but after a time the jingling died away.

Such was my Christmas Eve in that land of Po.

When day broke I did not dare to awaken my companion. Sleep is a powerful medicine and I placed more faith in it than in the few tabloids I carried with me.

It was already late when he opened his eyes. I saw at once that he was better. He had but a faint remembrance of what had happened in the night, and thought it was altogether a dream. We prepared the hot water that once more constituted our breakfast.

Had we had only a little butter or one or two pinches of *tsampa* to throw in it, we might have felt a trifle refreshed, but that plain water, even boiling hot, was nothing of a cordial.

As I expressed my feelings aloud, ending jocularly with the wish that some compassionate mountain god might bring us even the smallest piece of butter or fat, Yongden looked at me in a peculiar way.

"What is the matter?" I asked.

"Well," he replied, hesitatingly, "if you were not too particular about the fat, I might be the mountain god."

"What do you mean . . . ?"

He laughed.

"You are somewhat Thibetan in your ways, but perhaps not enough to do what a true Thibetan, in your case, would do. . . ."

"Go on. Have you something left in your bag . . . ?"

"Yes," he answered. "A bit of bacon with which I rub the soles of our boots to keep them waterproof, and some bits of

170

skin [1] which were left from the new soles I cut the day before yesterday."

"Throw them all in the pot and add a little salt if there is any left," I ordered, the soul of a true Thibetan arising in me.

He did so, and half an hour later we were tasting a turbid beverage whose flavour was a matter open to discussion. But to a certain extent it satisfied the craving of our empty stomachs.

Christmas merriment continued.

The weather cleared and the sun appeared shyly soon after we had left the *dokpas'* camp. As we descended we found the snow less deep. The path continued through thick forests, and we met another *dokpas'* encampment, which was not a good omen for the nearness of our goal. A little below it, we crossed a third feeder of the river Po, a small torrent rushing down from the side of the Gotza *la.* We also saw the path which led to the pass itself.

Neither villages nor fields nor anything that could suggest the neighbourhood of human habitations could yet be discovered. Evening would come soon. . . . Was our fast to continue?

Below the path, in a narrow clearing, I noticed a small hut which I pointed out to Yongden. Would it be wise to stop there? We had just time to collect some wood before darkness had set in beneath the big trees. To mention food was useless. That topic seemed as if it were to become forever foreign to us and we were to live like the gods of the ethereal regions, feeding on scents and pure air. We grew bewildered. We should not reach a village that day.

On approaching the hut, we were most astonished to see a man standing at its door. This was our first meeting with a Popa in his own land, and the strange stories about robbers and cannibals that are current all over Thibet about that

---

[1] One must understand that it is a soft skin that has undergone no preparation whatever.

dreaded tribe, rose immediately in our memories. Yet we did not show any sign of our thoughts. I simply asked, politely:

"Kusho [sir], may we be allowed to enter to make a fire?"

"Come in," answered the Popa briefly.

We went down the road, crossed the clearing, and our astonishment became still greater when we saw about a dozen men seated inside the cabin around a fire. What could they be doing in the midst of the forest?

We were politely welcomed. The men manifested extreme surprise and looked at one another with an air of mystery when they heard that we had crossed the Aigni *la*. Yongden deemed it useless to tell them about our supplementary promenade in the other valley, so that they thought we had come straight down from that pass.

"Certainly," they said, "you both have got powerful *Po lha*[1] and *Mo lha*.[1] Without their help you would have perished in the snow, for the pass is now completely blocked."

The special heavenly protection which we enjoyed impressed the Popas in our favour. A place of honour was given to the lama next the fire, and we were invited to produce our bowls for some tea, while the men apologized for the lack of *tsampa* to eat with it. They had just finished their meal when we arrived. Even without *tsampa*, the generously buttered tea refreshed us delightfully.

After some more enquiries about our country and our pilgrimages, one who appeared to be a personage of superior rank amongst the other Popas asked the lama if he knew the art of *mos*; and all of them appeared greatly pleased when he answered that he did.

What followed was first-rate material for a novelist, and at the same time threw some light on a picturesque and interesting side of Thibetan home politics.

As nothing, or but very little, is known, in the West, about the true condition of Thibet, a few explanations are needed here to make the matter understood.

It is an error to fancy Thibet as a homogeneous whole under

[1] Gods of the paternal and maternal ancestors.

a central government. Outside of the Ü and Tsang provinces, the various tribes have always lived in independence under a number of petty rulers who were styled *gyalpos* (kings). During the Chinese suzerainty the imperial officials did not interfere much with these local customs, but since they have been driven away by his troops, the Lhasa ruler has undertaken to bring under his direct authority the whole of the Thibetan territory which has escaped Chinese control.

Those tribes who have greeted the departure of the Chinese officials as meaning entire freedom for them do not feel in the least inclined to accept as governors men from Lhasa who lack the prestige of the Chinese *literati*, representatives of the great Chinese Emperor, who is, according to lamaist belief, an incarnation of the God of Knowledge and Wisdom: Janpeyon![1] The Dalai lama is worshipped by them as a spiritually exalted personality only, and though some of them may even go as far as to bow reverently to him from a distance, they strongly resent the appointment of governors or other dignitaries to rule over them, and especially their power to tax them and carry away to Lhasa the product of their levies.

So, the inhabitants of Chös Zong had simply stoned their governor appointed from the capital, and besieged him in his *zong,* where he had run in haste for shelter.

The enraged official had, however, been able to flee at night from Chös Zong and to dispatch secretly a messenger to ask help from the Kalön lama, a kind of Viceroy reigning over eastern Thibet, whose seat is at Chiamdo. The men of Chös Zong had in their turn learned of the departure of the messenger, and fearing that on the order of the Kalön lama soldiers might be dispatched to their country on a punitive expedition, they had sent some of their friends to overtake the messenger, seize the letter he carried, and "suppress" its bearer.

Our hosts were notabilities of the proud city which had stoned the alien governor. There was no question of canni-

[1] Better known in the West under his Sanskrit name of Mañjushri, a Bodhisatva of the Mahayanist Buddhism, very likely a deified hero.

balism or of robbery; the lama was merely required to tell whether the messenger would be caught.

The joke this time had a serious side. It might prove dangerous for the seer if his oracle turned out to be wrong. The giant fellows seated around the fire were no doubt not easy to manage when irritated. My companion and I are both short of stature, and we looked amongst them like "Tom Thumb" of the nursery tales, in the ogre's den. But in this case the ogres numbered fourteen, and although we could almost feel confident that they did not eat the flesh of lost travellers, they could certainly not be fooled with impunity.

The lama asked them many questions about the roads which the *pönpo's* messenger might have followed in order to leave the country, and thus I secured a good deal of geographical information. We also learned that a man had been dispatched toward the Aigni *la,* but had turned back, and this explained the faint jingling of a horse's bell that I had heard before daybreak. The man had deemed it useless to proceed farther, realizing by the quantity of snow already heaped up at that level that the pass must be completely blocked. Therefore the astonishment of the Popas had been all the greater when they had seen us coming from the other side of the range. They enquired again and again if we had seen nobody or no traces of steps. But we had truly seen neither, and certainly the *pönpo's* messenger had not taken that road.

After a good deal of muttering and gesticulation which were watched with deep attention by the interested spectators, the lama declared something to this effect: "If your men run faster than the *pönpo's* messenger they will catch him." But of course this was said in oracular style, wrapped in a quantity of solemn words and was really very impressive.

What prompted me, then? . . . I could not say. The romance of that political intrigue of the wilds, these William Tells of an unexplored land, plotting in the heart of the forest against a Gessler from Lhasa, may have tempted me and awakened the desire to play a part in the drama. Be that as it may, in the silence which followed the prophecy of Yongden, I pronounced, as if speaking for myself:

"No harm will be done. All will end well."

The fourteen conspirators and my astonished companion gazed at me dumfounded.

"What? . . . what? . . . What does she say?" they asked after a while. "Is she a *pamo?*" [1]

"Not exactly," answered Yongden. "My father was a black *nagspa,* [2] and she was his initiated consort."

"Indeed! . . . indeed! . . ." replied some of the Popas. Then, huddling themselves closer together, to give me room near the fire, they invited me to approach.

"Do not stay in that corner, *Sangs Yum.* [3] You must feel cold. . . . We are sorry that you have come too late to share our meal. . . . So, truly, all that trouble will end well for us?"

"*Yakpo chung yong* [Good will arise]," I answered, then gazed into the fire, apparently sunk in profound thought.

The Popas did not feel very comfortable. I could see it. They rejoiced over the favourable oracles, but the company of the black *nagspa's yum* in the middle of a forest after sunset seemed to them rather disturbing. So they took leave, requesting the lama to say that they had all gone home, if some one should come and ask about them.

The men had told us that we were not far from a village called Cholog, but what appeared a short distance to these sturdy hillmen might be a long one for tired, lame, and exhausted people like ourselves. We had drunk a quantity of buttered tea and had received a small piece of butter and a handful of tea, and these secured us a liquid breakfast for the morrow. It was better to spend the night under shelter.

We may be certain, I told Yongden, that these Popas will

---

[1] A woman who, during mediumistic trances, is possessed by a god or a demon who speaks through her mouth. If the medium is male he is called *pawo.*

[2] *Nagspa:* A knower of the secret spell, a dreaded kind of sorcerer.

[3] Literally, "secret mother." A polite title to address the mystic consort and helper of a magician or any lama belonging to a Tantric sect.

not come back to rob us. They are too busy with their own business, and, moreover, they fear me.

The young man agreed, but he did not think that the hut was a safe place in which to spend the night. The followers of the *pönpo* may have learned, he said, that his enemies have met here, and come at night to take them by surprise and kill them. They could mistake us for those who had stoned their master. We risked getting bullets through the door or being dragged before an official to explain who we were, or having to answer countless other embarrassing questions.

I could not deny that he was right to a great extent. But it was already dark beneath the trees, and, not being acquainted with the path, we could easily have met with an accident of the same kind as that from which Yongden was still suffering. As for being fired at or arrested, this could as well happen to us when tramping at night in the forest as in the hut. I would stay!

Once we had decided to stop there, Yongden went into the forest to cut wood. I gathered as much as was lying about near the cabin, and when I had finished I sat near the fire.

All of a sudden, without any noise, a head appeared over the top of the door, which closed only about three-quarters of the entrance.

A man looked hurriedly into the hut and pronounced a few words which I did not understand. He did not give me time to ask him to repeat them, and disappeared while I shouted, so that he might hear it, what the lama had been requested to say: "They are all gone!"

Those could not be, it seemed to me, very compromising words, and if some one were looking for the conspiring Popas they would not come to trouble us.

Anyhow, the romance was to continue at the expense of our repose. A little later we heard a noise in the bushes, steps on the fallen leaves, dry twigs broken under the feet of an invisible wanderer.

Yongden called from the door: "Arau! Arau! [comrade] you may come."

But no one appeared. I felt inclined to believe that wild animals were roaming about, and we threw some stones in the direction where the noise was coming from, but this did not stop it in the least. This confirmed Yongden in his opinion that human beings and not beasts were there.

However, as they did not attack us, we left them to their business and went back into the hut. We barricaded ourselves as well as we could, covered the fire, and lay in a corner where we could not be easily seen or fired at through the gap in the top of the door. That was all that we could do; and in whatever case, when one has done one's best, worries of any kind are superfluous and unwise.

Thus reflecting, we fell asleep and slept so soundly that the sun was already high in the heavens when we awakened.

We drank a bowl of tea with pleasure, but my tired body cried out for some solid food. This was the sixth day of our fast, and, without appearing too gluttonous, I can confess that we were hungry!

Cholog, the first village we were to come upon, was not so near to the hut as the conspirators had told us the day before. We reached it at noon.

We had at last arrived amongst these Popas, heroes of so many strange tales, about whom Yongden and I had spoken for years. Up till now all had gone well, and we were full of confidence in the future.

The village was situated in a narrow valley surrounded by alpine scenery and partly covered with snow. Neither its wooden cottages nor the few people visible had anything especially threatening about them.

I felt really safe as to my disguise, after having passed these huge mountain ranges. No one would ever think that a foreign woman had dared to venture on that road. No one would ever suspect the pilgrim tramping over these distant tracks on which a white traveller was never seen. This feeling of security was a great comfort and allowed me to enjoy the charm of my adventure more freely.

We could not begin our wanderings in the land of Po in a better way than by going round a-begging. It was in accordance both with our programme and our present needs. We therefore knocked at the door of the first cottage we found on our road.

When we answered the usual question, "Whence have you come?" by saying that we had just crossed the Aigni *la*, the woman who had interrogated us burst into loud exclamations which attracted a few neighbours. How could we have come through the snow? It was a real wonder! And again the unquestionable protection of our *Po lha* and *Mo lha* came forward.

We were invited to sit down and produce our bowls, which were filled with hot soup.

Was it good, was it bad? I could not say. I only felt the inner animal joy of the starving man at his first contact with food, after a long fast. It seemed to me that beings rushed up from the depth of my body toward my mouth to feed upon the thick mixture of *tsampa*, water, curd, and turnips that I swallowed eagerly. Other good people gave us *tsampa* and a little butter, and taking our bags in hand we went through the village to continue our begging. We quickly gathered a quantity of *tsampa* sufficient for two days. As we were now in an inhabited country, we could renew our supplies, and did not need to load ourselves with heavy bags. Thus we left Cholog and followed the river downwards.

We had left the village, when a strange idea took root in my brain. That soup which we had eaten—the woman had taken it out of a pot standing in a corner behind an open door. . . . Why had that earthen pot been put in such a place? . . . Could it be? . . . No. I revolted at the mere thought of it. And yet . . . in a corner . . . behind the door. . . .

I turned toward my companion.

"*Gelong lags,*"[1] I said, very politely. "Methinks we have eaten the dog's soup."

[1] Honourable monk.

The lama, who was enjoying the pleasant sensation of excellent digestion, started:

"What do you say? . . . What, dog's soup?"

I explained to him calmly the particulars on which my suspicion was grounded. He turned pale, the expression of his face reminding me of those one sees among the passengers on a steamer's decks in rough weather.

Then, amongst the details of our meal, I remembered that to fill our bowls our benefactress had dipped in the soup a ladle which was hanging near the hearth, with the kitchen utensils. A Thibetan would never touch the dog's soup with a ladle used in cooking. I could therefore be certain that the soup was men's food, and I reassured the trembling lama.

"What a fright you have given me!" he said, laughing.

"What a fool you are!" I answered. "Men's or dog's, the soup refreshed you. Why make yourself unhappy and sick over a mere idea?"

"I fear," replied Yongden, "that under your hermit masters' guidance you have made too much progress in the *thul shugs*.[1] In the future I shall carefully examine the contents of our pot when you make our broth."

"I hope I shall not have to fill it again with boot-leather broth as you have done."

The good soup that I had so unjustly calumniated kept us jolly.

We were proceeding in that gay mood when we saw three well-dressed and handsome men coming toward us across the fields. Long hair falling freely on their shoulders, fur robes, cloth vests in shades of warm green and dark red, beautiful swords with jewelled sheaths stuck in their belts, they looked vaguely like those knights of yore one sees in old paintings. The mystic landscape of fir trees in the background, the clear river, and the narrow path that wound through the fields added still more to the impression. It made me think of the Memling paintings I had seen in my youth in Belgian galleries.

---

[1] An ascetic and philosophic doctrine whose adepts practise complete indifference in all respects.

They politely requested the lama to make some *mos* about the very same affair on which he had already been consulted the day before, in the forest. The men sent after the Governor's messenger had not yet come back. Had they caught him, or not? It appeared that the whole country felt greatly concerned about the matter. Yongden told them that the gods had already been consulted and that it was neither fit nor prudent to trouble them again. Still, he could say that, according to his previous *mo*, all things would end well. The two knights seemed satisfied, and with a most graceful dignity, went back to their houses near by.

A few minutes later a villager passed us and stopped my companion to ask a *mo* about some private business; and, as the latter satisfied him, a lama rode by on a horse and, having alighted, requested the same kind offices from his humble pedestrian colleague.

Human credulity, be it in the East or in the West, has no limits. In India, the Brahmins have for centuries kept their countrymen to the opinion that offering presents to those belonging to their caste, and feeding them, was a highly meritorious religious work. Nowadays this cunning old device has taken in its snare the very ones who invented it, and on various occasions Brahmins are compelled by the custom to give gifts to other Brahmins. In the same way, a Thibetan lama, adept in ritual, cannot perform the magic rites for his own benefit and must rely on the well-remunerated services of a colleague.

Hermits (*Gompchen*) alone can escape. Some of them have completely renounced all religious ceremonies, whereas others condescend to oblige the believers who beg their help, but never perform any rites on their own behalf, or ask anyone else to do so.

The views of these lonely ascetics and the teachings they impart to those whom they take as disciples are interesting in many respects, and may be a revelation to those who consider Thibet a land of benighted savages. But to return to Yongden, I must say that although they are more numerous and more powerful, as members of the State Church, the lamas who belong to the "Yellow Cap" sects acknowledge the superiority of their brethren in the various "Red Cap" sects in all questions more or less connected with magic and occult science. Humble and dirty as it was, my companion's red hat enjoyed much success.

A contribution of *tsampa* and butter entered our bags as a result of the delivery of these various oracles. Truly the beginning of our adventure in the country of the dreaded Popas was quite encouraging.

We soon entered a narrow, dark gorge, and being tempted by the provisions we carried, we thought of taking a rest for a while, and eating some barley flour and butter. We were already seated on the trunk of a fallen tree when a man passed and advised us to proceed quickly because we were still a long way from the nearest village and the road was anything but safe. Robbers, he said, roamed in the region even during the day and were much more to be feared after dark.

The news agreed with what we had been told about Po *yul*. We started immediately, our revolvers in readiness under our dresses.

The sun had set when we reached the end of the gorge.

There three wide valleys opened and their very large intersection was entirely cultivated. Farms were seen here and there, and a cluster of houses forming a hamlet. The valley on the opposite side of the river led to Chös Zong, where there is an important lamasery, the very place where the Lhasa mandate had been stoned.

We crossed a bridge, well-built, although it had no breastwork, and were allowed to spend the night in the mill room of a small isolated farm which was extremely clean. As a rule, the place where grain is ground is the cleanest in a Thibetan house, and very often only the inmates are allowed to enter it, for fear lest it be defiled by strangers.[1]

---

[1] Professional beggars are more or less considered as impure, although the system of castes does not really exist in Thibet. As for travellers, they may, so think the Thibetans, have come into touch with impure objects or be accompanied by evil spirits.

Our hosts sent us a few pieces of dry cow dung to light a fire, but refused to give or even to sell us enough fuel to cook a meal. I went outside, along the river and in the fields, gathering whatever branches I could find. When I came back, Yongden had some visitors, and the question of the Governor, his messenger, the men sent after him, etc., was once more the topic.

Other people appeared later on, and requested from our host a contribution in grain to feed a party of armed Popas who were mustering to go somewhere—we were not admitted into confidence as to their destination. It looked as if the country were rising. The next morning some more armed fellows came to the lama for *mos* about the Governor, who had succeeded in fleeing from Chös Zong and had taken refuge in another lamasery at Sung Zong.

Spies of both parties were certainly wandering through the country, such being the Thibetan custom. We might be taken for spies ourselves, and get into trouble. We therefore re-crossed the river, and strode away, endeavouring to put Sung Zong behind us as soon as possible.

Pilgrims returning from the holy Pemakoichen mountains called us to drink tea on the road and made us a little present. We again crossed the Polung tsangpo and proceeding now on its right bank, we entered a narrow gorge where I met with a peculiar accident. I merely knocked my toes against a stone sticking out of the ground and did not hurt them, but felt such terrible pain in the bowels that I nearly fainted. I remained lying on the ground for quite a long time, incapable of standing, and as a comical element was never absent in even our most unpleasant adventures, Yongden did not dare to throw water on my face when he saw that I was fainting, lest it should remove the accumulated dirt and special "make-up" that constituted a part of my disguise.

The enthusiastic opinion which we formed of the Popas, after our first meeting with them, did not last more than a single day.

That evening on emerging from a gorge we saw the valley suddenly widen. A number of farms were scattered over the fields, and near the road we noticed two or three half-ruined and abandoned houses. I proposed to Yongden that we stay for the night in one of these tumble-down habitations, but he objected, with reason, that the fire which we should light would attract the attention of the villagers, and that undesirable visitors might call on us.

As we thought it imprudent to spend the night alone in the vicinity of the village, we had to beg shelter somewhere, and we thus made a real acquaintance with the Popas' hospitality.

At the first farm a young shepherd left his flocks as soon as he caught sight of us, and ran as for his life, to inform the inmates of the house that *arjopas* were coming. Instantly doors and windows were closed and no one answered when we called and shouted outside. All had been done so quickly and so artlessly that it was really amusing. I nearly laughed aloud, but as such gaiety would not have fitted my disguise, I endeavoured to appear sad whilst proceeding to another farm.

"We were wrong," said Yongden, "to go to such a small cottage. Poor people have none too much for themselves, and fear the beggars because they have nothing to give. On the other hand, they do not like to refuse alms to a lama pilgrim, for it is a bad deed, so they cleverly manage to avoid seeing him. Did you not notice that they fastened the door and the blinds without looking outside? They may even have made a pretence of not hearing me when I shouted at them, or they may have said amongst themselves: 'Here is one of those rascals who imitate the lama's way of begging to deceive householders.' So the cunning ones are blameless, since they pretend not to know that a lama was at their door. What a wonderful trick! . . .

"Let us go to a rich farm!"

At the *chukpo's* (rich man) house no one shut the doors, but five big dogs were allowed to attack us freely. While I worked hard with my iron-spiked staff to keep the beasts away,

Yongden endeavoured to express his request loudly enough to be heard above the furious barking of animals. Nobody answered at first. Then a young woman appeared on the flat roof and asked us many questions, without ordering the dogs to leave us. Yongden answered with angelic patience, while I continued the fight around him. Her curiosity satified, the woman retired inside the upper-story apartment to report to the *nepo* about us and our request. This lasted another good ten minutes, and finally she came back bringing a negative answer. We were not allowed to enter the house!

Thibetans, like many other people, are very much like sheep. The traveller may be certain that if he is refused hospitality by one farmer, all the other villagers who may happen to know it will close their doors to him. We had not the least chance of success in the vicinity of the owner of the ferocious dogs.

We went away, already resigned to walking a few more hours, and if we did not come to any village on our way, to sleep hidden in the woods. But the last house at the end of the cultivated area happened to present a good appearance. Just as we passed, a woman opened the door of the cattle pen to let the cows in. Yongden begged that we might be allowed to stay inside the farm until the next morning. As he was speaking with her, another woman appeared at a window, and he repeated his request.

The answer was that the permission of the master of the house was needed, and that she would ask him.

After a while, the same woman came down with a plate of *tsampa*, sent by the *nepo*, who did not wish to receive us.

"We do not ask *tsampa*," explained Yongden. "We only want *netsang*.[1] We will eat our own food and trouble nobody for alms. Let us only come inside."

The woman returned upstairs with the flour, and very probably the fact that we had refused it inclined the *nepo* to believe in our respectability. We were admitted into an exceedingly clean and well-built room such as I have seen only in the dwellings of quite upper-class Thibetans. A servant lighted

[1] Hospitality, a place in which to sleep.

184

the fire and gave us a plentiful supply of wood. Our opinion of the Popas, which had fallen very low after the experiences at the other farms, rose a little. We cooked some soup, and while eating it we had an interesting talk about the economical and political conditions of the country with a man who belonged to another part of Thibet, but who had settled in Po *yul*. The *nepo* came also with several women, and Yongden had to comply with the usual requests for *mos*.

One of the women noticed a turquoise which the lama had hung to the rosary he wore around his neck. Like coral and pearl, turquoise is a very prized part of Thibetan jewellery. But what goes under the name of *yu* (turquoise) in Thibet is seldom genuine. It is mostly polished malachite, or even some gross imitation made in China. The stone in Yongden's rosary was of a pretty colour. It greatly pleased the women, who examined it again and again. Finally one of them wished to buy it, but with the cunning of peasants in every country, she tried to take advantage of our apparent needy condition to acquire it practically for nothing, and her friends did their utmost to help her.

It was quite amusing to hear them talking about imaginary dangers, thieves along the road which we were to follow, and how food would be more useful to poor travellers than a useless precious stone. There was no one amongst them who did not recognise the spiritual superiority of an ordained lama. They would not have failed to ask his services in case of illness, death, or epidemic among the cattle. They would have called on him to bless the harvest or the house, and to make *mos*, but, nevertheless, they endeavoured, with all the cleverness they possessed, to cheat the poor holy one delivered by Fate— as they believed—into their hands.

The lama refused to accept the price offered, and as I knew that he had inherited some really fine turquoises on his father's death, I thought that this was one of them which he was carrying with him.

Was it the talk about robbers, or the many *mos* he had made, or other causes that troubled Yongden's sleep?

I was suddenly awakened in the night by a rather loud exclamation.

"Where is the gun?" said the lama. "They have taken my gun!" and some incomprehensible muttering followed.

At first I did not realise that he was dreaming aloud. I quickly extended my hand toward the two revolvers which we had, as usual, hidden with our money under the tent spread over us as a blanket in Thibetan fashion. (I have already said that poor Thibetan travellers do not undress to sleep.) The covering allowed us to part with our heavy belts containing the money. When we thought it unsafe to use it for fear that so much cloth might awake our hosts' cupidity and thus endanger our safety, we were compelled to keep these belts, as well as our arms, under our dresses. Their weight on the breast during a whole night was, I need scarcely say, most tiring and unpleasant. It often prevented me from sleeping.

Our revolvers and belts were there, but the young man continued to speak aloud.

There were two people beside ourselves in the room: the strange man and his Po wife. Our companions might awake, throw a piece of resinous wood on the fire to get a light to see what was the matter. Even if convinced that the lama was dreaming, they might persuade themselves that his dream had roots in something real and that we were really hiding a gun. Knowing the passion of all Thibetans for firearms, I was afraid that anything might happen if our hosts happened to suspect that we owned one. To what extreme means would they not go to secure it?

I gently pushed the dreamer. But it was no use; he continued to twaddle about the gun. I then crawled close to him and shook him, whispering in his ear to be quiet. The poor fellow was tired and enjoyed the sound sleep of youth. He did not awake, although he opened his eyes. I gave him a slap. I blew on his face. I did not known what to do to silence him! At last he turned on one side and ceased his muttering. Already our companions moved in their corner. I took our belts and the revolvers, and buckled them all hastily under my dress, so that no sign of them could be seen if some one made a light and came over to us to enquire about the meaning of the noise.

I did not dare to sleep again, and watched Yongden till a little before daybreak, when he awakened.

While we were drinking our morning tea, two women came again to try to buy the turquoise, and after we had taken leave and were proceeding on our way, the one who wanted it ran after the lama with a small piece of butter and some *tsampa*. Still thinking that the *yu* was one of his genuine stones, I scoffed at the silly female who believed that she could acquire a beautiful stone at such small expense. But in order to prevent any of her male relatives or friends from following us with the desire of getting the precious jewel still cheaper, I added: "My son is a pure *gelong*. He forgets too often that his father was a *nagspa*, as his elder brother still is in our country. That *yu* has been hung on his father's *tötreng*,[1] and anyone who is not connected with the *ngags* will find to his cost the result of wearing it. All but an initiated *nagspa*, or a *nagspa's* near relative, is *na mi thet*[2] to it, and would die if he became its owner."

This was sufficient to cool the coquettish person. She understood that the turquoise was definitely out of her reach. Perhaps she considered herself lucky to have been informed of the danger of wearing it. Perhaps, at the bottom of her heart, she regretted the niggardliness which had prevented her from acquiring it, when she could have hung the sky-blue stone at her ear or on her neck without suspecting its origin.

She went silently away, carrying back with her the butter and the *tsampa*.

"Why should you sell your turquoise?" I asked Yongden. "We do not need money. It is better to keep it and give it, later on, to one of your relatives."

[1] A rosary made of 108 small disks of bones taken from 108 different human skulls.

[2] A peculiar expression meaning that one is not worthy of the object of which he makes use, and that he cannot bear its special power or dignity.

"They do not care for such *yu*," he answered, laughingly.

"What? . . . They do not like turquoise?"

"Yes, they do . . . genuine ones."

"But this . . . ?"

"It is an imitation from China. The *tsampa* and butter would have been a good price for it."

And I had taken it as genuine, as, of course, had the woman at the farm! Anyhow, that kind of fun was not to be repeated. It would have been too absurd to get into trouble with robbers, and be killed for a supposed precious stone of which one could purchase about a pound for less than twenty cents. The turquoise was therefore removed from the rosary.

CHAPTER VI

HAVING crossed a dense forest, we reached the neighbourhood of Sung Zong a few days later.

A reading of the whole Khagyur had taken place in a village, at the conclusion of which the 108 big volumes, loaded on yaks, were taken back to the monastery by a few country folk. Amongst these an old woman ambled leisurely, walking at a slack pace before her hairy bullock, which enjoyed an occasional graze. The good grandmother chatted with us, and seeing that I was eating dry *tsampa* as I went along, she produced a piece of bread out of her *amphag* [1] and gave it to me.

Who could tell in what strange and dirty places that bread had been? Of course, I could not refuse it, and I was even compelled to make a pretence of eating it. But the first morsel was far from being unpalatable—quite the contrary. I quickly overcame my disgust, and with the solid appetite of a wayfarer I ate the last crumb of it.

We came upon Sung Zong as I was finishing this rustic delicacy. Groups of houses forming hamlets were scattered hither and thither. The lamasery itself stood isolated on a small hillock, between the Po and Nagong rivers. The latter emerges from a valley that opens behind the lamasery, and the ranges which bound it. This provides a commanding background for the insignificant buildings of the large monastery.

Although Sung Zong is one of the most important places of the Po country, and is of considerable geographical interest, being at the junction of two large rivers, it has not yet been charted on the maps. The whole region is still *terra*

[1] *Amphag* is the pocket formed on the breast by the large Thibetan dress tied at the waist with a belt. Thibetans have no other, and the quantity and variety of things they carry in it, often next the skin (for poor people do not wear underclothing), is really astonishing, and makes the leanest of them appear big-bellied.

incognita to geographers, and I could not but deeply regret that the odd disguise I had been compelled to assume prevented me from gathering the few observations that my modest ability would have allowed me to make.

In all my travels, including this last journey, I have been uncommonly successful in my search for documents pertaining to the field of my own studies, and I should have been glad to do something that would prove of interest to others in different fields of knowledge. If I have failed, the fault is not mine. During the whole period of my stay in Chinese Thibet my movements were closely watched by the spies of the border posts. The Lhasa officials in charge of them had received strict orders to prevent me from entering the part of Thibet under British influence. My small baggage, containing some instruments and requisites for plain scientific work, which I had once tried to smuggle into the country, led to my detection, and I was stopped on my way.[1] Under such circumstances it only remained for me to start as I did, empty-handed.

I enjoyed too much these months of free life to entertain unkind feelings toward those who forced upon me the hardships and dangerous risks of my pilgrimage as a beggar. I feel rather grateful to them for having led me to that wonderful experience. Yet one cannot but lament the fact that such efforts are hindered and not allowed to bear their full fruit.

It is beyond the scope of the present book to deal with geographical matters. Nevertheless a few words may be of interest.

I have already mentioned that the region around the upper course of the river Po is unsurveyed. Maps mistake the Nagong for it, but the former has its source farther to the southeast.

No one is to be blamed for this error, as no white traveller has ever gone up the river higher than Showa, which is situated far from Sung Zong, downstream. If I am not mistaken, only one English officer has visited the former place.

The Nagong springs from the foot of a small pass, near **a**

[1] See Introduction.

monastery called Dugang, in the range that divides the basin of the Salween from that of the Brahmaputra. On the opposite side of the pass flows the Daishin River, which joins the Salween.

As the Nagong is an important stream, some might like to discuss the question as to which of the two rivers that unite at Sung Zong is the main one, and which is the tributary. But the natives have answered this definitely. The river formed by the three streams which I discovered on my way to Po *yul* they call the Po. One of these three comes, as I have said, from the Po Gotza pass.

Above Sung Zong, the river Po receives two important tributaries emerging from wide valleys, the upper one leading to Chös Zong and the second in the direction of Chundo, where is situated the parent monastery of the two large lamaseries of Chös Zong and Sung Zong.

The maps of that region, which have been drawn from reports and not actual surveys, indulge in many fancies which are faithfully copied in successive editions. Amongst them is the invention of a town called Pozong. In reality Po Zong means "the fortress of the Po country." It is a title rather than a name, almost like our own word "Capital." But the Popas do not agree as to which of their towns is entitled to bear it. While the people of Pomed (the lower Po) declare that Pozong is Showa, where the King of Po has his residence, the inhabitants of Potöd (the upper region, extending downstream along the river Po as far as Dashin) affirm that the Pozong is Chundo.

This is not the only peculiarity offered by the maps of Thibet. In fact, in most parts of the north and the east they are of but little use to travellers, if indeed they are of any use at all. The names written on them seldom correspond to those one hears from the natives. The rivers and mountain ranges are not really in the places they are shown to be, and a number of them are completely ignored, as are also the roads with the exception of a few main tracks.

Geographers are wanted on that side of the globe—geographers and other scientists. For I doubt if any land is more wonderful than that unknown and still forbidden Thibet!

The most annoying but unavoidable necessity of revictualing delayed us at Sung Zong.

The environs of the monastery were full of animation. Country people could be seen moving hither and thither, leading yaks or horses loaded with wood, meat, or grain. Petty chiefs rode amongst them giving orders with an important and busy mien. *Trapas* also ran to and fro, in and out of the gate of the *gompa*. From the distant spot from which I witnessed this agitation, the lamasery with its unwhitened mud houses seemed an anthill occupied by diligently working insects.

The fugitive official had taken refuge at Sung Zong, and wherever a chief stays, the inhabitants of the region are not only compelled to feed him, his retainers, servants and beasts, but also to offer him daily presents. This explained the procession of poor ants going to fill the storerooms of the *pönpo's* household.

The prophecy with which I had surprised and gratified the conspirators in the forest cabin, was nearing its fulfilment. Several great lamas had intervened as peacemakers between the offended Governor and the braves of Chös Zong. One of them had passed by us while we were eating, seated near a stream.

Looking at the pretty procession of riders clad in gold brocade and bright-yellow satin, with their dark-red travelling coats and *zens*,[1] we had entirely forgotten that humble folk such as ourselves ought at least to stand up to show our respect. The great lama, who was a young man, did not appear offended, and smiled at his less fortunate brother in the Order, who had become indescribably ragged by this time. The Thibetan servants, always more arrogant than their masters, looked at us angrily. But the *Tulku*[2] had smiled and

---

[1] A long shawl of dark-red colour—it is sometimes yellow amongst some hermits of Amdo—worn by the members of the religious order.

[2] Literally, illusory body created by magic. A *Tulku*, according to popular belief, is the reincarnation of some powerful-minded being, man

they had to refrain from beating us, as they would have enjoyed doing.

Yongden remained about three hours at the *gompa*. He met some nice obliging *trapas* who gave him goods in addition to the provisions he had purchased, such as a liberal amount of bread, and dried apricots. Such kind treatment gave him no chance of shunning the long chat which Thibetans enjoy so much, or of refusing to drink the tea so cordially offered. Thus time passed quickly (and rather pleasantly) for my companion, but rather dully for me, who remained seated with our baggage in a wild and barren spot swept by a piercingly cold wind.

For company I had first a few children minding cattle, who came to sit near me. I learned a few things worth knowing from their candid mouths! After them came a well-to-do traveller, accompanied by several servants. He stopped to ask for whom I was waiting, as he saw my two loads and so understood that I had a companion.

I told him that my son, a *gelong,* had gone to the monastery. This looked quite respectable, and the man dismounted to ask me more questions about my native land and other topics.

At that time I had again adopted a new mother country— the far-off Ngari. The traveller had only heard about it, but he had once been to Shigatze, the capital of the Tsang province. As I had stayed there some years before, I was quite at ease in discussing it, and the man having seated himself on the ground, we had a pleasant chat together, in which the servants joined. He was coming from the Kongbu province and carried some cakes of dried molasses, of which he gave me two. When the lama returned proudly with his provisions, and boasted of the presents he had received, I enjoyed puzzling him with my two sugar cakes, which I said that a *lhamo* (goddess) had given me.

The country which we entered soon after leaving Sung Zong must without doubt be admirable in all seasons, but winter had

---

or god. Very improperly foreigners call these lamas "Living Buddhas." That name, as well as the idea which it conveys, is unknown to Thibetans.

now transformed it into a bewitching fairyland. For miles we proceeded under cover of gloomy, silent, and mysterious forests. Then, an unexpected clearing suddenly revealed, behind the dark line of tall fir trees, extraordinary landscapes of shining snow-clad mountains, towering high in the blue sky, frozen torrents and glittering waterfalls hanging like gigantic and immaculate curtains from the rugged rocks. We looked at them, speechless and enraptured, wondering if we had not reached the confines of the human world and were confronted with the abode of some genii. But as we continued on our way the forest again surrounded us, and the vision disappeared. Yet to-morrow or the day after a new fantastic apparition would rise before us in the same instantaneous way!

I tarried long in that beautiful region, making long deviations from the direct road, walking leisurely during the day, sleeping generally in the open, at the foot of a tree or in a cave when lucky enough to discover one on my road at the time of camping. But the beauty of nature was not the only object of interest offered by Po *yul*.

We did not always spend the night in the forest. On reaching hamlets, isolated farms, or monasteries, we often begged hospitality. Sometimes it happened that we were forbidden to enter. More than once we had to defend ourselves against dogs left loose to keep us away; and with utmost gravity we sometimes discussed the degree of ferocity of the canine watchers of the different places we passed. We had been given enough opportunities to make a study of it! Other selfish people answered our request by saying that there was a sick person in the house, and this was equivalent to a strict prohibition to approach it.

A superstition, having nothing to do with the desire to avoid the propagation of diseases, is at the bottom of this custom. Thibetans, as I have already mentioned, never believe that any illness or accident has a natural cause. These are considered as the work of evil spirits, which are hunting for the vital principles of the beings to enslave them or feed upon them. A strong and healthy person is supposed to be more difficult to catch and kill than one already debilitated by sickness, just as a swift deer is a harder match for the hunter than a lame or already wounded one.

Now, Thibetans suspect all travellers coming from afar of being accompanied by devils,[1] so that, if introduced in the house where a man is ailing, undesirable and invisible visitors could enter it in their train.

Needless to say, the cunning Thibetans often take advantage of this superstition to shut their doors even when all the inmates enjoy perfect health. I once terribly frightened a woman who used this excuse to send us away. Before she closed the blinds of her only window I had had time to peep inside and to see that no one was lying down. Then, assuming an inspired air, I exposed her lie and prophesied that, as she had falsely told saintly pilgrims that one of her family was ill, real sickness would indeed come on her house. This declaration was accompanied by brief choregraphic exercises in which I shook the lap of my large dress as if I were liberating a host of devils who had been sheltered in it. The comedy ended with a present of butter which the selfish housewife, who was now weeping, offered us. She also begged us to spend the night under her roof, but we refused. Still, to console her, Yongden blessed the small farm from outside to charm away the sickness I had foreseen. It may be that my performance has benefited, in the course of time, some tired and hungry *arjopa* to whom the woman has not dared to refuse hospitality.

But all doors were not closed to us. Far from it! This gave me most interesting opportunities of witnessing from the inside, as we had done along the upper Salween Valley, the life and customs of the inhabitants. Familiar talks allowed me to study their peculiar mentality, their views and beliefs. I heard witty stories and terrifying legends. Thanks to the time I had allowed for slow progress and wandering at random, I

---

[1] Explanations of that peculiar view would be too long to be given here. I shall discuss the subject in a special book devoted to the study of Thibetan religion and superstitions.

was also quite unexpectedly favoured with two unforgettable meetings, most valuable for my observations on Thibetan mysticism. However, for the present, I must confine myself to the brief outline of my adventures of travel, putting aside the more special topics which will find their place elsewhere.

The first important place we reached after Sung Zong was called Dashin. It is the seat of a large monastery.

The day before we arrived there, we met on the road two villagers, husband and wife, who had bought a cow somewhere and were leading it to their house at Dashin. As was nearly always the case when coming in touch with people, Yongden was requested to make *mos* about some land business. We walked several hours with the pair, and as we stopped to drink tea, they went on ahead, promising a hearty welcome in their home. However, toward the end of the afternoon, while crossing a village, we saw the cow tied before a door, and its owner shouted at us from the threshold, "Go slowly. We will join you soon!" But evening came and the peasants did not appear. We understood they were spending the night at their friends' house. It was too late to beg hospitality at the first village we reached. People were certainly asleep and would not open their doors. The incident did not trouble us in the least, for by that time we had become quite accustomed to remaining at night in the open. We found a pit in the forest and lay in it with our baggage; and, as patches of snow were to be seen here and there, we spread our tent over us in the old way. The sky generously came to our assistance and sprinkled real snow on our sham snow during our sleep. We were therefore really well hidden, and kept warm all the night.

The next day, after having passed a village, we stopped to take our breakfast on the bank of a wide mountain stream. We were just finishing when the couple appeared with their cow. They explained that they had been delayed and had slept at their friends' house, and pressed us to proceed with them to their house. We went together, and very likely out of the desire to get payment of their hospitality beforehand, they asked Yongden to make *mos* again, about various affairs, even while walking. One of the *mos* concerned the health of a man very seriously ill. Would he still be alive, or not, when the two villagers reached Dashin?

Although he was, as a rule, a seer full of prudence, Yongden was bored by the importunity of the peasants, and said bluntly, "He is dead!"

I could not tell whether the news brought them sorrow or pleasure. We did not know if they were the anxious heirs of the supposed departed one, or his loving relatives. At any rate, they spoke together in a low tone, and then kept silent.

About half an hour later, a man passed us, coming from Dashin. Our companions at once asked about the fate of the sufferer.

"He is much better," was the answer.

The prestige of the lama fell immediately, and when the golden roof of the Dashin monastery emerged from the forest, those who were to be our hosts went their way without taking any more notice of us.

We did not attempt to follow them or try in any way to claim the hospitality which they had promised us. We really cared very little for it. It was indeed a happy time in my life when the many nights spent in the open had freed me from concern about shelter and the like!

The place where we had been abandoned was a pretty one, half smiling, half austere. The lamas of Dashin had evidently felt, as I did, the peculiar beauty of the spot, for they had built several *Tsam Khang*[1] there, high above the road, against a rocky cliff. The small white houses of the recluses appeared as if hung on the black rock, while a few daring fir trees, which had taken root in some crevices, framed the whole cluster of ascetic dwellings.

Anchoritic life is held in great honour in Thibet. Nearly every monastery erects in some remote place in its neighbourhood some habitations for the use of those of its monks who wish to retire for a time—or forever—from all worldly activity.

[1] *Tsam* means boundary, line of demarcation; and *Khang* means house.

These houses are called *Tsam Khang* because the recluses remain isolated behind their closed doors as if a barrier had been erected around them, to be crossed by no one.

Any lama who is above the common lot is expected to spend, at least once in his life, a period of a little over three years in such a retreat, and, in addition, one month or more yearly. These periods of retreat are called *Tsam,* and the recluse *Tsam-pa.* There are many varieties of *Tsam,* more or less severe as to the strictness and length of the reclusion. Between the lama, who merely shuts himself in a *Tsam Khang* or even in his own apartment, and who, although he does not receive visitors, sees freely a number of attendants who wait upon him, and the one who dwells in complete darkness and silence, receiving his food through a double wicket, there exist many degrees.

Besides *Tsam Khangs* there exist in Thibet *riteus,* which are a more remote kind of hermitage, to which the still stricter ascetics resort. Details about them cannot be given in the present book. I must leave them for a future publication. Indeed, this world of the Thibetan mystics is a mystery in the mystery of Thibet, a strange wonder in a wonderland country. Very possibly Thibet will soon cease to be forbidden ground, but one may doubt if the secret of its *Tsam Khang* and *riteus,* the aims of their dwellers and the results they achieve, will ever be disclosed to the many.

I sat in the meadow near a huge erratic boulder, and enjoyed weaving fancies about the men hidden from me behind the white walls of their miniature dwellings. During this time a large party of *neskorpas* passed me. They had visited Lhasa on a pilgrimage, and were on their way to their homes in the Nu valley. Yongden and I endeavoured to get information about the road and the country they had crossed, but we got very few interesting details. These poor villagers or members of the low clergy do not take the least interest in what they see on their way. They walk like cattle, without even noticing the road which they follow. Most of them are certainly not bright-minded, but it may be said in their defence that the fatigue caused by the long daily tramps with a heavy load on the back and scanty food tends to benumb the mental faculties. I have experienced this myself and once had to struggle with all my might against a kind of overpowering dullness, which would have made me walk in as bovine a fashion as these poor pilgrims.

On nearing the monastery I remarked, standing at some distance, the man and the woman whom we had met on the road. They looked at us shyly, though intently.

"They are not bad fellows, after all," I said, pointing them out to Yongden. "I am certain that they repent having abandoned us, and now wish to keep their promise."

The lama cast a glance at the couple.

"The sick man has died," he declared.

"How do you know?" I asked, with astonishment.

"It is not difficult to understand," replied my companion. "Have you not noticed how humble their attitude is and how different from their manner on the road? They fear to have offended a great prophet, and dread the evil consequences of their rudeness. That means that they have found the man dead on their arrival."

Perhaps this pessimistic opinion was, after all, justified. I never knew.

Yongden walked with a dignified gait toward the monastery, without giving as much as a glance at the anguished pair, and I sat on the stones bordering the avenue which passed along the river below the *gompa*.

Although it was not built on a summit, the deep river winding at its feet and the rocky headland which confronts it from across the green water, surround the lamasery with a pretty and romantic landscape to which the gilded dome, emerging above the old walls of the enclosure, adds a peculiar character. Behind the monastery, a wide cultivated valley opens out. A track follows it, and leads to southern Thibet, across several passes. This trail has branches, some of which reach the borders of India in Assam, on the banks of the Brahmaputra, while others take the traveller to China or to Burma. On the opposite shore of the Polung Tsangpo, a short distance from Dashin, yet another track runs northward through the hills, touching the main road from Chiamdo to Lhasa. This gives access to several roads leading to the "Land of Grass," to Jakyendo, the market town situated on the route of the tea caravans. Then, proceeding still farther north, one can reach the great Sino-Thibetan markets of Sining and Dankar, in Kansu. Continuing the journey, one arrives in Mongolia. All the northern part of this track, beyond the Chiamdo road, is familiar to me. In any other country, a place situated in such a favourable geographical location would have become an important centre. The divers roads which converge there would have been duly improved, if not as cart roads, at least as good mule paths. But in Thibet no one gives a thought to such questions, and Dashin is but a village.

As I was seated by the side of the river, several people passed, and amongst them were some women going to cut wood in the forest which we had crossed on our way. They stopped to question me. I told them I was waiting for my son, who had gone to the monastery, and we enjoyed a short chat together.

Yongden remained very long at the *gompa*. He had by chance met a monk coming from the same land where his great-grandfather had been a "Red Cap" married lama of rank. He knew a number of people there, if not all personally, at least by name; and although he had not heard about them for years, he satisfied the eager curiosity of his brother in the Order and gave him news of everybody and of everything. Such a lucky meeting could not pass in Thibet without eating and drinking. While her "son" enjoyed the clerical company behind the wall where women were forbidden,[1] the "old mother," after the sun had set began to feel rather cold, seated on the stones telling her beads.

[1] Women are only allowed to enter the monasteries of the "Yellow Cap" sect on certain religious festival days, and even then must retire outside of the walls after sunset. My situation at Kum-Bum was quite exceptional. I never heard of a woman to whom a house had been granted there.

The women returned, each one carrying a load of wood. They were most astonished to see me still in the same place. This gave them the opportunity for another chat, and the eldest one kindly invited me to her house for the night, explaining to me minutely where it was situated. They then went away, but had only gone a few steps when Yongden appeared, accompanied by a young novice lama. Both were loaded with provisions, and we were invited to pass the night somewhere in the village. But I preferred to go with the good woman with whom I had had a talk, and so it was she whom we followed.

The master of the house into which we were shown, although only a villager, was remarkably intelligent. He had travelled much and had lived long at Lhasa. We took great pleasure in listening to him, though we were rather afraid that he might penetrate my disguise. So I performed all the menial work, leaving the lama seated on the carpet that had been spread for him near the fire in an entrance room, for we were not invited to enter the family kitchen. I noticed, since my arrival in the Po country, that the inhabitants of that region were rather particular in that respect. In the Nu valley, and often in that of the Giamo nu chu, we were allowed to sleep with the people of the house in the kitchen; but the Popas seemed decidedly against it.

We started at daybreak. The weather was cold and the wind blew hard, sweeping along the large open valley toward the south, but we soon entered the forest again, and felt warmer.

The Po valley, from its source, at the foot of the range which we had crossed, down to the Brahmaputra, offers a variety of climates. We had found it amongst deep snows, and now it was flowing between barley fields, in January.

The virgin soil of the valley seems to be very fertile. Attracted by the hope of better harvests, a number of new settlers coming from the adjacent provinces had cleared small parts of the forest, and built rustic farms of logs, very like Russian "isbas." The fir trees which sometimes surround them

201

add to this likeness, and give a decidedly Russian or Siberian aspect to the landscape.

Many of these primitive homes are no more than cabins, of which some are not larger than eighty to a hundred feet square.

In one of these we found an idyllic pair of lovers. Youth had long since passed for both, though they were not yet old. The man had a wen on his neck, and his spouse herself was no beauty. In the hut, together with the couple, slept a cow, her suckling calf, two other youngsters of the same species, and a few baby black pigs . . . a true nursery of four-footed young brothers, having, alas! no attentive nurse to lead the little ones outside when their needs required open air. In these surroundings we heard a most touching love story, though of the kind Western moralists call "sinful." For the housewife of the Noah's Ark had been mistress of another, better and larger dwelling, and had run away into the wilds, penniless, with a penniless Romeo. They had no children, and—a thing rare in Thibet—did not desire any. Their love for each other, though of long standing, filled their hearts to the brim.

These poor people treated us well. We shared a turnip soup with them, and they then insisted on presenting us with some *tsampa* to eat on the road.

Yongden was requested to make *mos*. He ended cleverly enough by saying that in order to please the *Lu*[1] they ought to clean their house carefully, and to offer milk[2] to the snake deities.

We four then lay down to sleep, our hosts on one side of the hearth, Yongden and I on the other side, the cow near the door, the calves at our feet, and the lively little pigs running to and fro over us, as there was not much room left for them in the hut.

When we heard the lovers snoring, Yongden muttered in my ear:

[1] Known in Sanskrit literature as *nâga*, or serpent demigods, owning fabulous riches and granting wealth to their devotees.

[2] The customary offering to these deities, who feed only on pure things such as water and milk. They are offended by the mere smell of meat or bad odours.

"I will put five rupees in a pot on the shelf. They will find them when they clean the house and will think that the *Lus* have brought them. . . . May I?"

It was a wonderful joke; but I advised him to give them Indian rupees. This was a little precaution for safety's sake. Had we been suspected of being the donors, these rupees would have proved almost certainly that we had gone from Lhasa (where these coins are available), to eastern Thibet, and were on our way back home. As the Indian money was in a separate bag, even in the dark it was easy to get at it.

I should like to have been able to witness the finding of the five rupees. How great an opinion the two good people must have formed of the holy, learned lama whose blessing had attracted to them the bounty of the *Lus!* But as there are countless popular stories about *Lus* wandering about in human shape, perhaps our hosts would believe that we were ourselves *Lus* in disguise.

That visit of gods to faithful lovers reminded me of the fable of Philemon and Baucis and I related it to my companion.

New Year in the Po *yul*, as well as in some parts of Kham, does not come at the same date as at Lhasa, where people follow the Chinese calendar. This peculiarity caused us to arrive at Showa, the humble capital of Pomed, on the very day of the Popas' New Year. The King was at Lhasa with his wife, a sister of the present general-in-chief of the Thibetan army. We already knew this before reaching Showa, but a servant of the palace whom we met on the road repeated it to us. Nevertheless, as everybody would rejoice and be merry on that day, we wanted to get our own little private fun and the profit thereof. So we boldly began a loud recitation at the gate of the royal dwelling. Blessings on each and all flowed freely from our eloquent lips. I doubt that even in that country of noisy beggars they have often seen our equals. Heads appeared at the windows, people swarmed down the steep staircases. They were bewildered, bewitched. Our triumph made us bold, and our boldness increased the strength of Yongden's deep voice, trained in the choir in the lamasery.

203

The dogs which had begun to bark were finally silenced, and disappeared as if terrorised, or fled to the farthest corners of the courtyard.

I guess that, however uncommon our performance may have been, the men themselves must have felt anxious to see the end of it, for servants brought out a pot of spirits, tea, and *tsampa*, and we were invited to sit down in the courtyard and feast. We declined the offer of *chang* (spirits), saying that as Buddhists we never drank any. This increased the esteem of the palace stewards still further, and they showed it by ordering dried meat to be placed before us. But when we again declared that as Buddhists we respected the life of all things and did not approve of the slaughter of animals—a view which necessarily meant vegetarianism—and that, above all, we would not begin the year with a cruel action, their admiration became extreme.

Regarding the flesh diet, it is against the spirit of Buddhism, though one cannot find in the Scriptures a text which forbids it expressly, as is the case with intoxicating beverages. But the restrictions mentioned in connection with the partaking of flesh amount to a formal prohibition, for there is no way to avoid transgressing them. A Buddhist is allowed to eat meat under the following restrictions: He must not have killed the beast himself, he must not have ordered anyone else to kill it, it must not have been killed by somebody with the intention of supplying it to him, he must not suspect that the animal has been killed.

If the two first restrictions may be easily turned, the third one is already a trifle more embarrassing; but some get around it by saying that the butchers slaughter for the public at large and not to supply the requirements of any particular person. As for the fourth, it must be difficult indeed to eat a piece of meat without "suspecting" that the animal from which it has been taken had been killed! But in all countries there are able sophists. The band of jovial monks, in the mediæval tales, who in Lent baptized a chicken "carp" so as to eat it lawfully, is a case in point. And the subtleties of the Oriental mind can easily provide many arguments in favour of gluttony!

As I am on that subject, I should like to point out a striking difference between Lamaism and the self-styled primitive orthodox Buddhism of the Southern school. The discussion, being connected with Thibetan custom, is not out of place.

Meat-eaters amongst the Buddhists of Ceylon, Burma and Siam, try, as I have said, to justify their flesh diet by various sophistic interpretations of the above-mentioned restrictions. When they belong to the religious order, they declare also that they are not allowed to choose the food begged by them, and must accept whatever they get from charitable people. This is altogether wrong. The genuine round of the Bhikshus[1] of yore has become nowadays a mere pretence, a ceremonial walk to appointed places to fetch a meal specially cooked for the monks. Moreover, they would not fail to withdraw if bad, dirty, or unhealthy food was poured into the ritualistic bowls they carry themselves, or into the various vessels that are brought behind them by their attendant boys.

In Thibet, the situation is quite different. Certainly, many are those who repeat: "I have not killed the animal myself," but they do it with complete scepticism as to the value of the excuse. In fact, there is not one Thibetan who is not convinced that eating flesh is more or less wrong. The usual practice of the lamas—I do not say the *trapas,* or common clergy—is to abstain from animal food on the eighth, fifteenth, and thirtieth days of the moon, and during the whole of the first month of the year, thus showing their regard for the right way of living which they have not the strength to follow continually.

Men and women, either "lay" or in the Order, who are strict vegetarians—who feed on "white diet," as it is called in Thibetan—are not exceedingly rare in Thibet, and they are greatly praised for it.

[1] Original name of the Buddhist monks, which means mendicants. It has been translated exactly in Thibetan as *Gelongs:* that is to say, virtuous mendicants.

The "Tantrik" sects hold special views about killing. These are interesting in many respects, but it would take too much space to examine them here. They will find place, in due course, in a study on the philosophic and mystic doctrines of Thibet.

However, before continuing our story, I must add that, although at first sight the habit of eating meat causes the premature death of many animals and appears more important than spirit drinking or than the actual fact of being drunk, Thibetans are justified in their opinion [1] that sobriety is the most important factor in mental and spiritual progress. A sinner who knows what may come of his bad actions is likely to change his ways, but the drunkard is helpless, owing to the collapse of his reasoning faculty. They illustrate it by an amusing story:

A Buddhist monk was made by an evil spirit to choose any of the following three sins: to kill a sheep, to break his vow of celibacy, or to drink strong drink.

The poor monk, after having pondered the matter, shrank from the first two and thought that the last would bear the lightest consequences. Once drunk, excited, and having lost all control over himself, he took a woman, and this second kind of intoxication led him to kill the sheep to give a feast to his mistress!

But enough! Thibetan stories about monks and the lamaist church are a rich mine of fine humour, and if we are once sunk in it we shall never get to the end of the chapter.

After being entertained with tea, *tsampa*, and different kinds of cakes, we received a full supply of provisions and went away, followed by many admiring eyes.

At Showa, the main track of the Po valley crosses the river. The covered bridge, with its small watch-towers, is large and well built, all of wood. The gates can be shut on both sides when required. A considerable number of posters, on which

---

[1] Unfortunately, a mere academic opinion held only by the *literati*, for the laity and even a part of the lowest clergy are rather fond of alcohol.

are printed magic or mystic formulæ, cover it, and bundles of miniature paper flags, fluttering in the breeze, are hung in quantities on all its sides. The stream is supposed to carry with it the words of praise or blessing that are printed on them.

The Thibetans, as well as the Chinese, are fond of decorating the bridges, the roads, and the peculiarly beautiful sites of their country with inscriptions of a religious, philosophical, or poetic character. Some travellers have thought proper to ridicule that custom. I find it impossible to follow them. A few lines of delicate poetry, a page of a philosophical treatise such as one sees engraved on certain rocks in Thibet, the meditative image of a Buddha painted in a natural cave, or even a strip of paper hung above a river or swinging in the air at the top of a pass, bearing the old Sanskrit wish "*Sarva mangalam*" (Joy to all), seem to me greatly preferable to the advertisements of whiskey or ham which "decorate" the roads of Western countries.

I beg my readers' pardon. I am but a savage!

At the end of the bridge there is a large *mani lha khang* with engraved stones, revolving *mani* wheels and a number of flags. From there one gets a general view of the Po king's palace, merely a square squat building whose upper story is lighted by small windows and whose architecture has nothing especially striking.

Our big meal and the time spent in inspecting the place had delayed us long. Nevertheless, as we were only at the beginning of the afternoon, we preferred to continue our way rather than remain all night at Showa.

The evening brought us to a village where we feasted again with some country folk. On the morrow we feasted in yet another one.

If our Christmas had been somewhat dramatic, that first Thibetan New Year proved really merry. Yet how much merrier was to be the real New Year at Lhasa! But at that time the enjoyments which we were to find in the sacred city lay still shrouded in the mystery of the future.

In the second village we were the guests of a large family of new settlers who treated us most cordially. While we were seated with the family around the hearth, I watched one of the girls kneading a big ball of dough. She worked at it for several hours. Yongden, as usual, had made *mos* several times, and we began to feel sleepy, yet she still kneaded her flour. I was rather puzzled as to what would become of it, and I would very likely have continued to chat with the housewife in the hope of seeing the end of the girl's work and its outcome; but Yongden asked permission to sleep, saying that I was tired and that we wished to start early the next morning. I could not say anything to the contrary, so we retired to a corner of the kitchen-dormitory, and lay down under our tent-blanket.

Asiatics do not feel, as we do, the need of privacy and silence in sleep. Even sick people, unless they belong to the upper classes, lie amongst others who do not in the least refrain from noisy talk and loud laughter. I once saw an old, dying man, stretched on the counter of a shop while commercial transactions went on as usual between his son and the customers. And this man was not a pauper but a well-to-do-trader, but neither he nor his son had ever thought it necessary to make special arrangements for sleeping.

I know that even in Western lands one can find families whose dwelling is composed of but one room, but it is utter poverty which leads them to such a way of living. In Thibet, amongst country folk, the farm always includes a number of rooms, but none of them has really a special purpose. Wool, grain, provisions, ploughs, and so on fill the different parts of the house, and, for the most part, the family's general living and sleeping room is the kitchen.

Our hosts had not to stay their New Year revels on account of tramps such as we, and so the merriment continued. We were supposed to sleep undisturbed by the noise, as true *arjo-pas* would have done. But I naturally remained awake, and long continued to watch the Thibetans and to listen to their talk. Still fatigue prevailed, and I was dozing when a smell of frying dough aroused me to the reality of the situation. The girl had ceased to knead and was now frying New Year cakes in that sweet oil made with the kernel of the apricot stone, which is a peculiar product of Pomed. What a pity! Had we stayed longer, we would have had our share of them! And now . . . they would, perhaps, eat them all and we would only get the smell of them!

I am not particularly gluttonous, but the daily dish of *tsampa* and scarcely anything else was rather austere. . . . This smell of fresh, warm, crisp cakes. . . . I was enraged with the lama. What was he doing? Perhaps he slept. . . . That was too bad! I did not want to be tantalized alone. I extended my arm as far as I could, but it was too short to reach my hateful son. I managed to crawl toward him under our cover and discovered that his eyes were wide open.

"They are eating cakes," I whispered in his ear.

"Oh, I can see," he answered in a subdued, desolate voice.

"Do you think they will give us some?"

"No hope. They believe we are sleeping."

What a disheartening answer! So I remained watching the happy ones. But they could not keep pace with the girl and eat as many cakes as she fried. Those which were left over were heaped in a large basket and my hopes were concentrated on them. . . . To-morrow the cakes would be cold, but still they would be different from our everlasting *tsampa*. . . . Should we get some to-morrow?

The family lay down in its turn, on the floor under blankets; the hearth fire burned low; darkness spread in the room. I fell asleep.

In the morning there still remained some raw dough and we ate fresh, crisp, New Year cakes, and carried away a good number of the cold ones in our provision bag.

Until then our journey through the Po country had been perfectly peaceful, and I began to think that there must be much exaggeration in the stories which are current about the Popas.

Popas—so Thibetans say—are born robbers. Each year gangs, sometimes to the number of a hundred, fall unexpectedly on their neighbours of the Kong-bu or Dainshi provinces and loot their villages. Beside these organized expeditions, most Popas—traders, pilgrims, or mere villagers—find it difficult to let any traveller they may happen to meet on their way pass without trying to levy an undue tax on his baggage, however miserable it may be. A few handfuls of barley flour, a worn-out blanket, two or three copper coins—all is good to them. But if, as a rule, they let the poor folk who meekly submit to their demands go unmolested, they are quick to turn murderers when resistance is offered or a valuable booty expected.

Truly, no wealthy travellers venture to go through the forests of Po. Only the poorest of the poor—the beggar pilgrims made bold by the fact of their utter destitution—are to be met along the tracks which cross the Popas' hill.

As for us, we had not met any outsider, either rich or poor, on our way. The few people whom we had seen on the solitary roads were all natives of the country, or settlers who had practically become Popas.

Events were now to take another turn, and that gay New Year marked the end of a period of quietness.

The very afternoon after we had left the hospitable house where such good cakes were baked, we passed by an isolated farm just as a number of people were emerging from it. The New Year festivities were still going on; some of the men who had enjoyed themselves were decidedly drunk, and the remainder were not very sober. All of them carried guns across their shoulders, and some made a pretence of shooting at us. As for us, we proceeded as if we had noticed nothing.

In the evening I discovered a roomy cave in which we slept comfortably. We slept much too long, and delayed still further over some soup at breakfast. As we did so, a man appeared and asked us if we had nothing to sell. He regarded the contents of our bags, which were still open.

Our two common spoons especially attracted his attention. Then he seated himself, and taking a piece of dried, fermented cheese out of his dress he began to eat it.

That kind of cheese is very much like French Roquefort. Thinking it would improve our menus, Yongden asked the man if he had some to sell. He answered in the affirmative; he had some at home, not far from the cave, and would barter one against needles, if we had any. We had a few which we had carried for this purpose. So the man went to fetch his cheese.

We had not yet finished our packing when he came back with a cheese and followed by another man. The newcomer was much bolder than the first with whom we had dealt. He fingered the cloth of our tent and told us that he would purchase it. He then took the spoons and examined them, while his companion cast glances in the direction from which they had come, as if expecting other arrivals.

We had no doubt about the intentions of the two Popas. The bolder one had already put the two coveted spoons in his *amphag* and refused to give them back, while the other one endeavoured to take the tent out of the lama's hands.

I realized that others had been summoned and were to assist in the robbery.

The matter would soon become serious. We must frighten these two away and start in haste. Perhaps we would be able to reach the next village, and the thieves would not dare to follow us.

I endeavoured to appeal to the good feelings of the men, but it was of no avail. Time was of importance; we must put an end to the business, and show the others that we were not timid and defenceless folk.

"Let that tent alone at once!" I commanded. "And give the spoons back!"

In the meantime I had my revolver in readiness under my dress. The boldest of the thieves only laughed and, turning his back on me, he bent to pick up some other object. I shot, from close behind him, turning my revolver away from him. But his companion saw me and, being too terrified to warn his friend, he could do nothing but stare wildly at me. Whether or not the other fellow saw him, I cannot tell, but he threw

211

himself backwards just as I shot, and the bullet passed close to his head, grazing his hair.

Flinging the spoons and the tent on the ground, the two ran like hunted hares across the thicket.

The situation was not entirely pleasant. The ruffians might have gone to fetch some of their kindred, the men whom they seemed to expect. I told Yongden to tie the loads in haste and be off as quickly as possible.

What would have happened, had we remained alone, I cannot say, for a party of about thirty pilgrims—the first foreign travellers we met in Po *yul,* and the only ones we were ever to meet—suddenly appeared. They had heard the shot, and enquired as to its cause.

It was annoying to be identified as carrying a revolver, for only chiefs and rich traders own these. Of course they thought that it was Yongden who had fired; and later on when they asked to see the weapon, we produced an old-pattern small one, instead of the automatic pistol that had nearly sent the Popa on to another world.

We joined the party, and perhaps we owe our lives to this most unexpected meeting.

We learned from our new companions that the Popas truly deserved their bad name, and we were soon to confirm this from our own experience.

The party which we had joined was mostly composed of people from Zogong in the Nu valley, the place that we had avoided by crossing the river and cutting through several ranges.

The very day after we arrived at the *dokpas'* camp where we had taken a guide and a horse to climb to the Aigni *la,* they had reached another cowmen's encampment at the foot of the pass leading into the Nagong valley.

Before crossing the mountain a number of the *trapas* wished to sew new soles on their boots, and so the larger part of the band decided to remain one day more near the *dokpas'* encampment to get this done. A few laymen and nearly all the women preferred to ascend the pass slowly, instead of lingering at the *dokpas'* place. They set out and slept somewhere under the trees, lower down on the other side of the range. At daybreak a number of Popas appeared, proceeding, with loaded yaks, toward the Daishin province to exchange dried apricots, chillies, etc., for barley. When they saw the poor pilgrims they rushed at them and took away all their blankets and the few coins they had hidden under their clothes. Then, learning that others were expected, they ordered them to proceed, without loitering on the road. They unloaded their yaks, drove them on the hills, and seating themselves near the top of the pass waited for the remainder of the party to appear.

The *trapas* found them there, on the watch, like demoniacal spirits of the mountain, ready to prey upon travellers. The Popas asked them for some present, which is a polite way common to robbers of China and of Thibet. But many of the monks were armed with spear or sword, and preferred to do battle. The Popas had swords, too, but the pilgrims were more numerous, and the valiant sons of Po *yul* were defeated. The lamas joined their unfortunate vanguard the following day.

Some of these, acting as guides to their companions, had already travelled to Po *yul* through the Gotza *la*. When they heard that we had been able to force our way through the ranges, they very much regretted that fear of the snow had prevented them from following the summer road across the solitudes, where we had had a hard time but avoided robbers. Of the three passes on that side, they knew only the Gotza *la*.

Like most Kampus of the Nu and upper Giamo nu chu valleys, these people were exceedingly pleasant. We greatly enjoyed their company, and accompanied them for several days. But then, in order to make up the time they had lost in the highlands of Po, they began to race with such speed that I left them to their sport, and fell back.

On the second day that we spent with that gay party we left the banks of the Po lung river, which we had followed from its source in the snow-buried highlands. It was now a beautiful, large blue stream, about to lose itself in the Yeru Tsangpo.

213

But before this merging of its personality it had still to
receive a tributary as big as itself, the Yigong Tsangpo. We
had to cross this river in the same way as we crossed the
Giamo nu chu, and before it the Mekong, that is to say, by
hanging to a rope and being hauled from the opposite side.

Our good luck had again brought us companions at that
moment when they were so sorely needed. The *tupas*[1] who
make a trade of hauling the travellers across would never have
taken the trouble for two lone beggars. We should, perhaps,
have waited for days, camped on the bank of the river, until
a number of passengers had collected.

An insolent lot they seemed, these ferrymen whose ferry
was a woefully sagging leather cable spanning a river at least
twice as wide as the Giamo nu chu where we had crossed it.
Their chief seemed to be an old grandmother, who looked like
a witch. She received the money paid for the passage and
directed operations.

At first the Popas told us to wait until the morning, but
after repeated entreaties, and because we were a large party,
they condescended to do the work that afternoon. Truly
it was a difficult business. The *tupas* were at least a dozen
strong. To begin with, some of them passed the towing rope
across—a real acrobatic feat that requires an uncommon
strength in the wrists and a complete absence of giddiness.
These men were not towed, as we, the passengers, would be.
They scrambled unaided over that sagging and swaying rope
at a considerable distance above the rushing waters. When
they had reached the opposite bank, the passage of the luggage began, during which the old woman required from us all
three needles or a little money as a supplement to the price
already paid. Needles are in great demand in the interior of
Thibet, and are very difficult to get. The mother *tupa* certainly made a profitable trade with those she exacted from
the travellers.

Most of the men in our party belonged to the lamaist order
and to the great state monasteries of Lhasa: Sera, Depung,

[1] Ferrymen.

or Galden. The old woman did not show any regard for them, but she approached Yongden and asked him to make *mos*, telling him a quantity of things about her private concerns. She also let us go without any needle tax. My turn to cross came long before that of the lama. Passengers were sent two together, and I was tied at the hook with a woman in exactly the same way as at the Salween. No accident happened this time, but on account of the greater length of the cable the jolting over the river was much more lively and unpleasant. From the middle of the river the wonderful snowy peak of the Gyalwa Pal Ri (the victorious and noble mountain) [1] appeared in all its splendour. Enclosed in the narrow frame of the river gorge, it had a peculiarly mysterious beauty which I had never seen in the wide snowy ranges.

I hastened to find a shelter for the night, and came across a cave amongst the huge rocks which form the river banks.

When Yongden arrived, I had already collected the necessary fuel. We had our food and went to sleep. The temperature was mild, and it was hard to realise that we were in the middle of winter.

In the morning light the Gyalwa Pal Ri appeared still more glorious than on the day before. It was a perfect jewel; one might have fancied it to be the immaculate abode of some radiant god, feeding upon pure light. Our companions, who thought much more of the gifts which the Lhasa government grants to the monks of the three state monasteries who attend the solemn New Year gathering, than of any God, were now in a great hurry to reach the capital, and did not lose any time in contemplating the "victorious" peak. When we started they had already all gone, and we found the large cave in which they had slept quite empty. This looked like an annoying complication, for the right trail to follow was hard to find in the dense jungle which now reminded me of the lower slopes of the Himalayas. I noticed a large number of plants and creepers which I was accustomed to find in the Sikkin forest between 3,000 and 4,000 feet level. The air had also entirely

[1] Which is also styled, "the victorious lotus mountain," Gyalwa Ped Ri.

215

lost that peculiarly strong and invigorating savour of the dry tablelands. It never freezes in that region. The ground was muddy, the sky cloudy, and the people on the other bank of the river Ygong had told us that we must expect rain.

A number of trails crossed near the river. One led north toward the upper country of Potöd where it joined tracks that allowed one to reach the grassy northern solitudes. Another went down toward the Brahmaputra, and a third one led to the Kongbu province.

We started off correctly on the Kongbu track, but hesitated when it branched into a short cut and a main path. We decided in favour of the former, following mere intuition, without suspecting that the two would join later on. This short trail was a true masterpiece of the "Public Works" engineers of Po *yul*. It was cut by perpendicular rocks against which ladders of a peculiar pattern had been placed to enable one to climb up and down. At other places it ran like a balcony on branches thrust horizontally into the ground, and the whole device was built for tall Popas, with much longer legs than ours. Our feet were left waving in the air on the primitive staircases, whose steps were shaky stones or the notched trunks of trees. What we could not do with our feet we had to perform with the help of our hands, hanging in the air until we touched a point of support, and relying on our strength to raise ourselves when climbing. Had we not carried baggage on our backs, we should have enjoyed the sport, but we were heavily laden. Knowing that no food would be available on our way, which lay through uninhabited forests, we had provided ourselves with a full supply of *tsampa*, which weighed heavily on our backs and put our acrobatic feats of equilibrium in jeopardy.

But worst of all, we feared missing our road. Such a trail might lead to some forest village, but it could scarcely be the main highway from Kongbu to Po *yul*, followed, as we knew by loaded horses and mules. We also failed to discover any trace of the party of pilgrims. Thirty men would have left the imprint of their feet in the soft mud. It was most certain that our former companions had not passed this way. Yet, as we were proceeding in the right direction, I ventured to continue. After all, we were again alone. We had no gift to expect from the Lhasa government, nor was our presence requested to read the Scriptures. It would be enough for our own enjoyment if we reached the Lamaist Rome in time to witness the various New Year festivities. We therefore had time to loiter over the country. Fresh meetings with robbers were the only serious annoyance we had to fear. The Popas villagers themselves had told us to be careful on this forest track, which they call the Po southern road (*Po lho lam*), for robbers haunted it and people ventured on this side only in large parties. But as we were now in that ill-famed region, being willingly or unwillingly compelled to cross it, it was useless to torment ourselves with the possibility of future danger, which could not be averted.

This most uneven trail, on which we had expended so much exertion, ended near a beautiful, huge tree dedicated to some sylvan deity. And here, also, it joined the main track. Happily, we had not missed our way.

This spot broke the monotony of the jungle in a pleasant way. The giant tree, from the lowest branches of which hung countless tiny paper flags bearing spells meant to protect travellers, appeared to be a mighty guardian against the dangers that lie in the gloomy forest. Around it spread that queer psychic atmosphere peculiar to places consecrated to Nature's gods, which tells of times long past when mankind's heart was still young and naïve.

Our progress became more rapid now that we were trading a tolerably good path, and I regretted having taken the difficult short cut. I ought rather to have blessed the very friendly sylvan deity of that road who had perhaps suggested the choice to me.

A little farther on I found in the middle of the road a long shoot of wild orchids in full bloom and quite fresh, as if it had just been plucked. I relate the fact because, as we were then in January, it shows that the whole of Thibet is far from being an icy-cold, bleak country, like the region which extends from the south of Lhasa to the Himalayas.

At the end of the afternoon we overtook the party of pilgrims, who were camped in a pretty clearing near the junction of the Po river and one of its tributaries.

Our arrival caused some commotion, and our new friends rushed toward us to ask us if we had met any robbers. We were astonished, and replied that we had not seen a single human being on our road. They could not understand how this could be, for they had met a gang of about thirty men who had tried to extract some presents from them. As they refused to give the least thing, a fight followed in which the robbers had been defeated and some of them wounded. Two of the travellers had been wounded with swords and had lost a quantity of blood. Another, who had been pushed violently and had fallen on a rock, complained of internal pains.

At last, when we had explained that we had come by the narrow short cut, our new friends congratulated us on having escaped the robbers on the main path. For, angered as they must have been after their defeat, they would certainly have stripped us of all our belongings.

After having heard this news I ceased completely to regret my tiring exertion on the short cut. Once more I had been uncommonly lucky.

Encounters with brigands are common enough in Thibet, and fail to impress travellers deeply, unless they are extraordinarily bloody. In spite of the three who lay suffering near a fire, the others did not feel in the least sorrowful or depressed. On the contrary, it seemed as if this little adventure had relieved the monotony of their journey, and had joyfully excited them! We spent a very pleasant evening. The Lhasa *trapas* related a lot of stories told in the capital, and the latest gossip about the lamaist court, the high officials and the *philings* rulers of India. We heard, also, interesting details about the economic situation of the country and the political opinions of the clergy. Lastly, they took us into their confidence as to a number of private affairs in which some of

218

their companions were concerned. Thanks to them, my store of observation was further enriched.

The big fires which the party had lit, and the noise made in the forest by cutting wood, attracted the notice of a few Popas villagers living on the bank of the river. Several men, who did not look perfectly sober, came, inspected our camp, and chatted with some of us. I suspected that they were scouting to ascertain our strength and would inform their friends of the chance they might have of successfully looting us.

They came to Yongden and asked him to remain one day with them to bless their houses and properties. The lama, of course, declined the invitation, mentioning the necessity of making haste in order to reach Lhasa in time for the great New Year *mönlam*.[1] They understood his excuse and did not press him, but added that they would send him their wives and children to be blessed the next morning.

In spite of these soft speeches, watchmen were posted at night around our camp, but the hours passed peacefully—so calmly and silently, indeed, that, having pitched our tent apart from the others, we did not hear our companions starting. I then insisted on drinking our early hot tea, a custom that I seldom neglected and which, I am certain, had much to do with the good health that not only myself, but Yongden and all our servants during previous journeys, have always enjoyed; whereas so many Thibetan travellers whose habit it is to start before dawn without any breakfast, even during the winter and in the coldest regions, often suffer from severe attacks of fever and other ailments.

But this most excellent and agreeable custom detained us, and Yongden felt very uneasy at remaining behind in that unsafe country. We were finishing our packing and I was bending over some pieces of luggage when he suddenly announced the arrival of robbers. I glanced in the direction he pointed out, and saw a number of people coming toward

[1] The gathering to send good wishes, including the festivals taking place at that time.

us; but when they arrived we discovered that they were women and children.

In spite of the spirits they had drunk, our visitors of the previous evening had not forgotten to send their womenfolk and youngsters to be blessed. The latter brought with them a very acceptable present of chillies, which are a valuable article of exchange at Lhasa, and also some butter and dried fruits. So the dreaded robbers became in fact our benefactors. The ceremony of blessing, packing our gifts, and some unavoidable gossip delayed us still further, and when we started we had but little hope left of being able to rejoin our companions.

It was wonderful indeed to have escaped so many dangers of various kinds and to be there, just as I had planned it, in Po *yul, en route* for Lhasa. Nevertheless, it is always presumptuous to rejoice too soon about one's good luck or success. I had not finished with the Popas. But they, too, were to see more of the first foreign woman who walked through their beautiful country, and while their acts were to be quite commonplace and not in the least surprising, mine will probably live long in the memory of those who witnessed them. Maybe a legend will arise out of it all; and who knows if, in the future, a learned student of folklore will not offer some interesting commentary on the story, being far from suspecting the truth of it.

At dusk that very evening, weary after a long tramp and having definitely abandoned the hope of joining the travellers, at least that same night, we were following the rising course of the Tongyuk river which, hidden by the thick foliage, roared far beneath our narrow trail. I was walking ahead, looking for a camping-place, when I saw seven men coming toward me. A sudden foreboding seized me. I did not expect any good from this meeting. Nevertheless, as *sang froid* is the best of weapons, and as many years' experience of adventurous life had accustomed me to situations of this kind, I continued to walk calmly, with the indifferent air of a tired woman pilgrim. One of the band stood in the middle of the narrow track and asked me where I was coming from and where I was going to. I muttered the names of some holy places, and passed between him and the bushes. He did not attempt to stop me. I was already rejoicing inwardly at the thought that this time, once more, nothing would happen, when looking back, I saw that my son had stopped and was leaning against a rock and speaking with the men. However, the talk seemed friendly and the voices did not rise above the normal pitch. But I could not hear what was said.

Then I noticed that one of the tall fellows was taking something from the handkerchief of the lama. I knew that he had a few coins in it. But I did not realize what was happening, and I thought that the Popas were selling us something.

I only understood the truth when Yongden shouted to me, "They have taken my two rupees!"

The amount was not worth a thought, but I saw that some of the robbers had laid their hands on the load he carried on his back and were about to open it.

The situation was growing serious. Fighting was out of the question. Had I shot one of the men, the others would have immediately stabbed my defenceless companion with the long swords they carried thrust in their belts.

On the other hand, to let them examine the contents of our bags would be dangerous. In them were a few foreign objects, unfamiliar to these savages, that would have appeared strange in the possession of ragged pilgrims and would have awakened suspicion as to our identity. And once on the track, the robbers might perhaps search us and discover the gold hidden under our clothes. What would follow? They might kill us on the spot, or take us before one of their chiefs, who would inform the nearest Lhasa government official if I confessed to be a foreigner in disguise, or would treat us as thieves if I persisted in my incognito. In a word, he would appropriate our gold and beat us both mercilessly.

Most of all, I feared being recognised, and thus prevented from proceeding. At any rate, the robbers must be left with the quickly forgotten impression that they had but met a poor lama pilgrim with his aged and beggar mother.

In much less time than I have taken to write it, all these thoughts passed through my mind. I found the plot of the drama to be played on that rustic stage and I began my part.

Screaming at the top of my voice, howling in utter despair, with tears rolling on my cheeks, I lamented the loss of the two rupees; the *only, only* money we had got. What was to become of us? How would we feed ourselves during the long trip to Lhasa? . . .

And these two rupees were sacred money indeed, the offering of a pious householder whose father had died and for whom my son, the lama, had performed the funeral rites, dispatching him to the "Land of Bliss, the Western Paradise." Now these miscreants had dared to steal it! But revenge would come! . . .

Here I ceased to weep and rose to imprecation. The task was not very difficult, well acquainted as I am with the various deities of the Thibetan pantheon.

I called upon the most dreaded ones, uttering their most terrible names and titles.

There was Palden Dorjee Lhamo, who rides a wild horse on a saddle made of a bloody human skin; there were the Angry Ones who devour the flesh of men and feast on the fresh brains served in their skulls; and the giant Frightful Ones, companions of the King of Death, crowned with bones and dancing on corpses. I conjured them all and implored them to avenge us.

Verily, I was the initiated and ordained wife of a black *nag spa*. His tutelar demons would not fail to avenge the harm done to his innocent son, who had taken to the pure saintly path of the *gelong*.

I am a tiny woman with nothing dramatic in my appearance; but at that moment I felt myself rising to the height of a powerful tragedienne.

The forest had become darker and a light breeze had arisen which caused a distant murmur to run under the foliage. Lugubrious and mysterious voices seemed to spring out of the unseen torrent below, climbing toward us and filling the air with threatening words in an unknown language.

I was cool and did not fear the thieves—I had seen more than seven together on other occasions—yet I could not suppress a thrill born of the occult atmosphere I myself had created.

I was not alone in this. The seven robbers looked petrified, some standing in one line against a rock behind my son, and others lower down on the path—an awe-struck group which tempted my photographic inclinations. But the hour was not ripe for snapshots.

Then one of the Popas cautiously moved toward me and from a little distance uttered words of peace:

"Do not be angry, old mother. Here are your two rupees. Do not weep. Do not curse us any more! We only want to go peacefully back to our village."

So I allowed my anger and my despair to be cooled, and I took the two coins with the air of one who recovers a unique treasure.

My young companion had rejoined me. The thieves reverently requested his blessing, which he gave them, adding some good wishes. We then parted.

There was no fear that the same band would retrace its steps to rob us. But this new adventure was a warning, not to be overlooked, to leave that specially dangerous area as soon as possible.

That night we made a prolonged march in the forest, which seemed still alive with the phantoms of the deities I had summoned.

A slow rain, mixed with half-melted snow, began to fall, and a melancholy waning moon rose late amongst the clouds. About two o'clock in the morning we came to a place near the river where there was a small level clearing. We were too tired to proceed farther, and discussed the question of how to camp there. Would we dare to pitch our miserable tent, or did prudence command that we should sleep unsheltered on the wet moss, hidden under the trees?

Supper was, once more, not to be thought of, although we had neither eaten nor drunk since early morning, nearly twenty-four hours before. No dry fuel could be found to boil our Thibetan tea, and the dim light was not sufficient to find a place amongst the rocks where we could safely fetch water from the foaming torrent.

I thought we could at least give ourselves the comfort of a shelter. It was very doubtful that anybody would be traveling at night in that bad weather. We therefore pitched the small tent, and lay down in our wet damp clothes and muddy boots on the damp ground.

The moon, which appeared and disappeared between the clouds, cast fantastic moving shadows of branches and rocks on the white cloth above our heads. The river talked loudly with the many voices of a crowd. Invisible beings seemed to surround us. I was thinking of those I had invoked . . . and, after all, I did not altogether disbelieve in that mysterious world that is so near to those who have lived long in the wilds. My heavy head resting on a small bag of *tsampa,* I smiled to unknown friends, and departed for dreamland.

It was not the first time, in the course of my peregrinations in Thibet, that sham magic and robbers combined in the same adventure. I may perhaps be allowed to relate here a rather amusing incident which happened in the Desert of Grass some eighteen months before my meeting with the Popas brigands.

I had lingered that day far behind my men to collect plants which I meant to send to the Botanical Society of France. It was the rainy season. The grassy desert had become a sea of mud. Under a dull sky low clouds rolled heavily, hiding the summits, filling the valleys, and wrapping the steppes in a grayish, melancholy shroud. I did not recognize the luminous solitudes, the scenes of so many of my joyful rides some years before, and I should easily have been overpowered by the depressing influence of that region of dampness, rain, and fog across which we had wandered, shivering and feverish, for weeks, had I not had many reasons to prevent me from giving way to lassitude and discouragement.

MY JOURNEY TO LHASA

My present party numbered seven, including myself. The six were Yongden, three servants, and a Chinese Musselman soldier, going back to his country with his Thibetan wife and their little boy, whom I do not reckon in the number.

Yongden and the woman had remained with me, helping me to gather the plants, and the other men were far ahead of us. The weather had now cleared. One could see, between the clouds, the sun almost setting. It was time to proceed to the camp, so we set out, riding slowly in full enjoyment of the peaceful evening.

We had left the plain, and having turned the spur of a range, entered a narrow valley, when I saw on my left three men carrying guns slung over their shoulders, who silently disappeared in a recess of the mountains. Who they were was clear enough. Thibetan travellers, in that country, never fail to salute one another with the customary greeting: *"Oghiai! Oghiai."* [1] Then they habitually exchange questions about the country whence they came and toward which they go. The silence of these men looked very suspicious, not to mention the fact that they hid themselves, instead of walking along the trail.

I went my way, pretending to pay no attention to them, but feeling under my dress to see if my revolver was handy. I whispered to the woman who rode near me, "Did you see them?" "Yes," she answered. "They are robbers. Perhaps they are the scouts of a gang."

I looked at a flower that grew on a rock, as if deeply interested in it, and pointing it out to Yongden, I called him to me. To show any sign of agitation which the brigands, who were perhaps watching us, might interpret as fear, would endanger our lives. The members of the special Order of Lamas, whose dress I wore, are believed to be fearless and to possess occult powers, and this was our best safeguard.

[1] This means: "You have undergone hardship," and the answer is: *"Lags, ma Kaa; kiai la oghiai!* I have suffered no hardship but you have had a hard time!"

225

"Have you seen the men in the ravine?" I asked my young companion.

"No."

"Three men carrying guns—thieves, no doubt. The woman has seen them. Have your revolver ready. As soon as we reach the turning of the trail, and are out of sight, we will ride on fast. We must reach the camp quickly and inform the servants." As I had spoken in English, I did not fear being overheard.

We had good beasts, and proceeded quickly. But what was this? We heard a shot in the direction of our people. We rode faster and soon discovered our four tents pitched in the high grass near a stream.

"Have you seen three men on your road?" I immediately asked the servants who came to hold our horses. No, nobody had seen any human being for the last ten days.

"I heard a shot."

They all hung their heads. "I have killed a hare," confessed the soldier. "We have no more meat, and my wife feels weak."

I always strictly forbid my servants to hunt, but the soldier was not my servant. I dropped the subject.

"This woman and I have seen three armed men who appeared to hide from us," I said. "We must take special precautions to-night for the safety of the camp. It may be that these three have companions in the vicinity."

"There they are!" exclaimed my head servant, Tsering, pointing out two men who stood on the crest of the hill above the camp.

I looked at them with my glasses. They were the very men that we had seen on our way. Where was the third one? Had he been dispatched to call still other ruffians in order to attack us? The two remained watching us.

"Let us take no more notice of them," I said. "We will devise a plan while drinking tea. Put the guns and revolvers in such places that they may be seen by the robbers, if there

are any besides these two. It is good to let them know that
we are able to defend ourselves."

The tea was ready. One of the servants dipped a ladle into
the cauldron and threw a few drops of the liquid toward the
six quarters (including zenith and nadir), shouting "Drink tea,
O Gods!" Then our bowls were filled, and, seated around the
fire, we began to discuss the situation.

The servants suggested that they might climb the neighbouring hills and from there try to discover if any gang was in the
vicinity. I did not like this idea. The robbers might arrive
while they were roaming far from the camp, taking that opportunity to steal some beasts or other things. Yongden and I
alone would have a hard time to defend our belongings, even
if the three men whom we had seen, and who had good guns,
were the only ones to attack us.

"I know a better way," said the soldier. "Let night come,
and when darkness hides us, I and two of the men will ambush
ourselves separately outside the camp at three different points.
Another will remain here as watchman, and he will, according
to the Chinese custom, beat a drum or make some such noise
all night. The robbers will think that we are all in our tents,
and if they appear, one or another of those who are hidden
outside the camp will see them and shoot at them when they
are between him and the tents. They will thus be surprised
and fired upon from behind and in front at the same time!"

This appeared to be the best plan for a small party like
ours, and I decided to follow it. We tied the beasts as fast
as we could, for when they do not dare to fight openly, Thibetan
brigands fire volleys at short range to frighten the animals. If
some of these break their cords and escape, they chase them
away and seldom miss capturing a few.

Yongden insisted on erecting a barricade with the bags and
boxes containing our provisions. He meant it, of course, as a
shelter for us, but, as distinguished a *literatus* as my adopted
son may be, his knowledge does not extend to the art of war.
As it was built, it appeared to me that we should rather protect the barricade with our bodies than be protected by it,

but I am myself far from being an expert in these matters, and no great general happened to be there to enlighten us.

Seldom have I spent such a delightful night as that one, when at each minute we expected an attack! But it was not this prospect which lent charm to my vigil.

Seated at the entrance of his tent, a bowl of tea near him, Tsering sang ballads of the land of Kham, thousands of years old. He marked the cadence by striking with a small rod on a Thibetan cauldron in which we boiled tea or soup over our camp fire. The songs extol the high deeds of rustic knights and the primeval forests in which arise shining peaks clad with eternal snows. Robbers these heroes are, like those whose presence in our neighbourhood compelled us to keep a watch, like the watchman himself, who—I was aware—had played his part in more than one hot encounter, like the three others who are now acting as sentinels, like everyone in that land of primitive braves who know of no field in which to show their prowess other than the trails followed by rich caravans.

Tsering had a fine voice. His accents were now heroic, now mystic. The songs told not only of warriors, but of merciful goddesses and holy lamas. Some of the stanzas finished with ardent aspirations toward the spiritual awakening that puts an end to fear and all sorrow. The vulgar cauldron itself had risen to the level of that poetry; its metal sounded solemn as a bell. Tsering was indefatigable; he went on with his bewitching recital until dawn.

The sentinels came back benumbed by their prolonged stay on the damp grass, and ran to revive the fire and make tea. Tsering's song had ceased, and the harmonious cauldron, fallen back to its utilitarian rôle, stood already filled with water, among the flames. As for Yongden, he was fast asleep with his head resting against his barricade.

The robbers had not dared to attack us, but they had spent the night near our camp. As we were finishing eating our breakfast the three men appeared, each one leading a horse. My boys leaped to their feet and ran to them.

"Who are you?" they asked. "We saw you yesterday. What are you doing here?"

"We are hunters," answered the newcomers.

"Indeed! That is good luck for us. We have no meat left. We will buy some game from you."

The self-styled hunters looked embarrassed. "We have not yet killed anything," they said.

My servants did not need to hear more.

"Do you know," asked Tsering of the three Thibetans, "who is the noble, reverend lady who travels with such a beautiful tent and wears a *töga* (kind of vest worn by lamas) of golden brocade?"

"Would she be the *philing* Jetsunma who lived in Jakyendo? We have heard about her."

"Yes, she is. And you understand that she does not fear robbers any more than wild beasts or any other thing. One who stole the least of her belongings would immediately be discovered and caught.

"In that case, she has only to look in a bowl full of water, and at once she sees in it the likeness of the thief, together with the stolen articles and the place where both are to be found."

"So it is really true," said the men. "All the *dokpas* say white foreigners have this power."

"Nothing is more certain," confirmed my head servant.

Tsering was well acquainted with the story which was repeated among the cowmen, and he had cleverly taken advantage of it to frighten the robbers and to dissuade them from going to bring their friends to rob us a few days later.

About ten days after that incident, we stopped for the night in front of an encampment of *dokpas*. I retired to my tent before night had fallen, and I heard many visitors in the camp. They were bringing presents of milk and butter, and Yongden told them that the lama lady had shut herself up for religious meditation and could not be disturbed, but that she would see them the following morning. Then some whispering took place, and a servant having called the *dokpas* to drink tea near the kitchen fire, they all moved away and I heard no more of what was said.

At dawn Yongden asked permission to enter my tent.

"I must," he said, "inform you, before the *dokpas* call again, about the request they made yesterday. They say that some of their horses have been stolen, they do not know by whom, and they wish you to look in a bowl of water in order to describe to them the thieves and the place where they are keeping the stolen animals."

"What did you tell them?" I asked.

"I think," answered Yongden, "that maybe these men have bad intentions. Perhaps they have not suffered any loss and they only wish to know if what is said about that bowl of water and the magic power of the 'white foreigner' is really true or not. Who knows whether they have not an eye on our fine Chinese mules and would not be delighted to steal them if they were convinced that you could not trace the thieves, especially if the robbery happened at a few days' march from their own encampment, at a place where the tribe to which the brigands belong could not be located? If you tell them that you have seen their horses, and that none have been stolen, they will be convinced that you have not been able to detect their lie, and that, therefore, as you are powerless in magic, they may loot us with impunity. I accordingly explained to them that you could indeed see all that they want to know in a bowl of water, but that the water needed is somewhat different from the ordinary water just drawn from the stream. This water must be prepared by ceremonies and the recitation of a ritual that lasts for three days. They understood this at once. I then said that it was doubtful if you would stay here three days, because you were called to Amdo for an important meeting with a great lama. Also, as I know how much they shrink from the idea of killing in cold blood a man who has only stolen property, I added that as soon as you had discovered the thieves you would hand them over to the Chinese magistrate to be put to death. It would be, I said, in the power of no one to spare their lives. The *Towo* [Wrathful Deity] by whose power this divinatory rite is performed would claim them as victims and, if they were not sacrificed, he would turn his anger against those who had requested the rite to be performed, and he would take their lives instead.

"On hearing this, they all became terrified. They declared that they feared to irritate the *Towo,* and preferred to look after their horses in their own way, trying to get a good compensation from the thieves."

I smiled at his ruse, and when the *dokpas* came with some more presents, I repeated to them the very things Yongden had told them the day before, so that they definitely gave up all idea of requesting the celebration of the too tragic rite.

The head servant, Tsering, had travelled in his early youth as far as Tachienlu, and had been in the service of foreigners. As a result of these associations he had acquired a skepticism which he liked to display before his more credulous companions. During the next few days, he did not cease making the incident a subject of his jokes, and laughing at the simpletons who had been so easily fooled.

By that time we had reached the shore of the large blue lake, the most holy Koko-nor, worshipped by thousands of Thibetans and Mongolians. The rains were over. I could again see that wonderful inland sea, bathed in bright sunshine, and its rocky islands, the largest of which has been for centuries the dwelling of a few anchorites.

Once when I was coming back to the camp after having bathed in the lake, I saw Tsering leaving Yongden's tent and hastily putting something in his breast pocket. He looked a little agitated and proceeded quickly toward the kitchen place without noticing me. The same evening Yongden told me that, having been called away on some business while counting money, he had left his purse on a box in his tent and had forgotten about it. When he returned, three rupees were missing.

I did not tell him about Tsering. I only scolded him for his carelessness, and the thing ended there.

Three days later I arranged on my camp table a few blades of grass and some rice. I lighted several incense sticks, and in the middle I placed a bowl full of water. Then I waited until I knew that the servants were in their tent, undressed and lying down, if not yet asleep. At that time, according to their custom, all their most precious belongings, and especially their money, would be hidden beneath whatever they used as a pillow.

For a while I rang the small bell and beat the tambourine used by lamas in their religious ceremonies. Then I called Tsering.

"Tsering," I said with a stern voice, when he appeared, "three rupees are missing from Lama Yongden's purse. I have seen them under your head when you were lying down. Go and fetch them!"

The skeptic dropped his manner of sneering incredulity. He turned pale, his teeth were chattering. He bowed down three times at my feet and without a word went to the servants' tent and brought back the money.

"*Jetsun Kusho rimpoche,*" he asked, trembling, "will the *Towo* kill me!"

"No," I answered, gravely. "I shall do what is needed to spare your life."

He bowed down again and went away.

Then, alone in my small tent, open to the silent desert and the bright starry sky, I took once more the lamaist bell and the drum of mystic rites and, led by their archaic music, I meditated on the strength of ancestral faiths in the human mind and on the deep and mysterious side of the farce that had just been enacted.

In Thibet, adventures with robbers have always a certain picturesqueness, of the kind, however, that one does not want in too large a quantity, so that I was glad to meet no more ruffians on my way during the days that followed my dramatic performance in the forest.

We were now nearing Tongyuk, where a *zong* has been cunningly placed at the intersection of two roads for the examination of travellers proceeding to Lhasa. Like many things in Thibet, this cleverness is a little childish, and a pedestrian can dodge it without making extraordinary efforts.

From Tongyuk one can reach Giamda, the capital of the Kongbu province, by a much more direct track than that which winds far to the south touching the Brahmaputra. I have been told that it crosses uninhabited regions, and for that reason travellers prefer the long bend on the south. Time has but little value in the East, and the safety and convenience of a road are the main concern of all Thibetan travellers. It is also possible to travel northwards from Tongyuk toward the grassy solitudes.

Although only a few of them are shown on the maps, Thibet is crossed by a large number of tracks, some easy, some rough; and, save in exceptional circumstances, the future explorers of the unsurveyed regions need not fear the necessity of cutting their way with axes through impassable jungles. What I say applies, of course, only to people who can travel according to the native fashion, as I have done on all my journeys. If one needs large tents, tables, chairs, tinned Western food, an oven to bake the bread, and a gramophone which some explorers carried in their luggage, then perhaps he will get into trouble with the rustic Thibetan paths, and also, perhaps, with the sturdy hillmen who have made them.

The toll bridge of Tongyuk spans a narrow but rather deep mountain stream, which throws itself into the river Tongyuk a little farther on. It is cleared by a gate, and near by is the house of the bridge-keeper. When we knocked at the gate, the latter set it just ajar to look at us. Without leaving him the time to put any question, we asked, hurriedly, as if in great anxiety:

"Are our friends there?"

"Which friends?" enquired the man.

"That large party of Sera and Depung monks."

"They left this morning."

"What a pity!" we both lamented.

The keeper had opened the door a little more. We took

233

immediate advantage of this to step in, continuing the while to make the poor fellow giddy with our questions. We wished to know if the *trapas* had not left a message for us, and also a bag containing some dried meat which belonged to us. Yongden eyed the Thibetan in a suspicious way, and the latter endeavoured to convince him that no one of the party had handed him anything, protesting that he was too honest to keep the property of a lama!

My companion, intent upon the question of the dried meat, seemed to have forgotten everything else, especially the fact that travellers had to apply at the *zong* to get permission to proceed. His pretence was played in a masterly fashion. Yet I thought that the keeper, although he looked bewildered, might still bear his duty in mind and remind us of the permission we had to secure before proceeding farther. I asked in a whining voice: "Has the *pönpo* given some *sölra* [alms] to our friends?"

"I do not know," was the answer.

"Well," I replied, "I shall try to get some. My son, the lama, has hurt his foot. We have fallen back and have no food left, now that this bag of dried meat is not here."

"About the bag I will know through a *mo*," said Yongden, sternly. "My *mos* never fail to be true."

"Yes, yes," the suspected innocent gladly agreed, "*mo gyab*, lama. You can see the *pönpa* afterwards."

"I am going at once," I declared. "Maybe he will be kind to me."

This was a matter of indifference to the keeper.

I went, and on nearing the official's residence I met a rather well-dressed man. I saluted him most politely, and enquired if I could be shown the way to the *pönpo*.

"What do you want?" he asked.

I explained that my son, a *trapa* from Sera monastery, belonged to the party which had crossed Tongyuk the day before, and that, owing to his bad foot, we had lingered behind, and were now making haste to join our companions, since we had no food. I then produced with affected shyness two *trankas*, to be offered, I said, to the *pönpo* when my son, the lama, came, which would be very soon. At present he was enquiring at the gate-keeper's about a bag that our friends should have left behind for us, and in the meantime I wished to beg a *sölra*.

The man snatched the two silver coins—I expected this!—and told me to wait. Then he went away. A few minutes later a servant brought me a small bowl full of *tsampa* and, from a distance, I heard the voice of the one who had taken my money commanding: "Take her down. It is useless for the *trapa* to come here."

So the servant went ahead. What he said to the gate-keeper I do not know. I found the latter rejoicing proudly because Yongden, whose *mos* were infallible, had discovered that our friends had not handed our dried meat to him! I deemed it wiser not to remain to investigate the identity of the man whom I had seen near the *zong*.

Once more we had escaped. We made haste to be off, which did not appear strange, since we were supposed to be anxious to overtake our party, and that evening we camped in a beautiful forest. Only the toll bridge of Giamda now remained on our way. But this was still a long distance ahead, and we had time enough before us to devise some plan.

I was heartily thankful for our lucky meeting with the party of travellers. In the first place, they had prevented the Popas from robbing and perhaps injuring us. In the second place they had made our crossing over the river Ygong both easy and speedy. And lastly, although we were no longer with them, we had been able to make use of them to get smoothly through the Tongyuk Post. May they be justly rewarded for their aid!

We were now nearing the end of the track which is called the "Po Southern Road" ("*Po lho lam*"), a borderland region that joins the "Kongbu Southern Road" ("*Kongbu lho lam*"). It is mostly covered by forest, and villages are scarce. Although the inhabitants of that zone have no better name than those of the upper country, we passed through it without any trouble.

The women of this part of Thibet wear, as do those of Po *yul* a fur dress over which they slip a kind of large chasuble, made of bearskin for the rich, and of dark goatskin for the common lot. Both garments are worn, like all fur in Thibet, with the hair inside. Men also wear a scapular, but it does not reach farther than the waist, while those of the women fall nearly to the knees.

What struck me was the sight of the women with black round felt hats of a Western-like shape. Had these been trimmed with a ribbon, a feather, or a bunch of flowers, they could have been shown in the window of any millinery shop.

More remarkable still were the mournful and pathetic tunes which I heard along my way. At first I was led to think that they belonged to some peculiar religious rites performed in the depth of the forest. But circumstances disclosed a less poetic truth.

Hearing from a distance a slow, poignant, and really impressive dirge, I walked across the jungle in the direction of the invisible choir. As I progressed, my imagination already pictured a funeral or some still more dreadful spectacle. Slightly excited, as the traveller may well be on nearing an interesting situation, I strode through the thicket and reached the border of a clearing. There were the mournful singers—about thirty women clad in goatskin, wearing the national black felt hat. The work in which they were engaged had nothing of a dramatic character. They were merely carrying logs of wood which the males of their tribe had felled higher upon the hill, and the dirge helped them to keep step when the heavy loads were borne by several of them together. The words of the song were not especially melancholy. Where could that strange tune have originated? I never heard anything like it in other parts of Thibet.

The women rested in the clearing, and a loud prattling took the place of the singing. Their gossip occupied the wood-carriers enough to prevent them from noticing me through the foliage. I remained hidden, for had I shown myself I could not have avoided having to talk. Also I should have heard no more of the song.

After a while, the black-capped village girls and housewives got up, loaded their logs, and the melodious lament of their deep contralto voices spread again through the forest.

I followed them at a distance as far as the path where I joined Yongden. While I was away, two travellers who were returning to the Ygong district had asked him to make *mos*. He had just finished with these and had received his honorarium, some *tsampa* and two handfuls of dried apricots.

When we emerged from the Po forests, we reached an open country formed by the wide intersection of several valleys. A number of important villages were scattered in this large area, which is partly cultivated and partly left as pasture land. The scenery is exceedingly beautiful and looks a little—but on a much larger scale—like some landscapes in the French or Swiss Alps.

The region extending to the north is still unexplored. I felt very much tempted to undertake a scouting tour over the ranges which rose between the Tongyuk river and the Giamda river.

Time, unfortunately, was short. I should have to make haste if I wanted to be in Lhasa to witness the New Year festivals. I also feared to attract the attention of the villagers if I was seen wandering out of the main paths. What could I answer, in that case, when asked where I was going? In Thibet, no one roams for pleasure. Thibetans deem it absurd to walk if not compelled to do so by some definite business.

When the people of the borderland hear about foreigners climbing the hills, travelling through distant lands or merely taking photographs, they cannot believe that this is done for personal satisfaction only. According to their opinion, explorers and tourists are all working for a salary paid by their governments. What sensible man, think the Thibetans, would take the trouble to move when he could remain seated at home? Only the necessity of earning money, or the desire to acquire religious merit, could induce them to do such a thing.

Had I know the name of a monastery or of a *zong* situated in that direction, I could have used it to explain my journey. But I did not even know where to find the track which led to the opposite side of the range. I was not even certain that such a track existed; I only suspected it.

Nevertheless, I started, but at night, in order to be out of sight when the villagers went to work in their fields the next morning.

I reached a wooded ridge, descended it, and, having climbed another one, I came in sight of snowy crests. I had walked for two days, and could be nearly certain that I was about to reach the Giamda river. On the other hand, I desired to see the Brahmaputra, and as I have just said, time was short—too short to allow me to turn back south toward the Brahmaputra, after reaching the Giamda river, and then having to retrace my steps to reach Lhasa *via* Giamda Zong.

On the evening of the second day, while Yongden boiled the tea, I was still pondering over the itinerary I should choose, when suddenly, like a ghost in an olden tale, a lama appeared on the scene. We had not heard him coming. In fact, he did not seem to have come. One would almost have believed that he had just sprung out of the ground in front of us. Thibetans who wear *dokpas* boots with soft flexible soles do not make any noise in walking, yet there was something so unexpected, so instantaneous in the apparition of the lama, that Yongden and I looked at him in wonder.

He was dressed in the very plain garb of the *gompchens*, which is somewhat different in shape from that worn by the inmates of the monasteries. The *ten-treng* was hung round his neck, and the long iron-tipped staff which he carried was surmounted by a trident.

He sat down near the fire without uttering a word, and did not even answer our polite greeting, *"Kale jou den jags."* [1] Yongden tried, but without success, to engage him in conversation. We then concluded that, according to a custom often followed by ascetics, he had made a vow of silence.

[1] Thibetan equivalent of "Be seated, please."

This mute stranger, who looked at me fixedly, proved embarrassing. I should have liked to see him get up and go away, or do something that was natural to travellers—eat or drink. But he had no baggage with him, not even a bag of *tsampa,* which was an extraordinary thing in this country devoid of inns. What did he feed on? Seated cross-legged beside his trident, which he had stuck in the ground, he looked like a statue with only the eyes alive. Night had fallen. Was he going to stay?

The tea was ready; the enigmatic wayfarer drew from beneath his robe a skull fashioned to serve as a bowl, and held it out to Yongden. As a rule, into these lugubrious cups used only by followers of the *tantrik* sects, no beverages except spirits are poured. My young companion made a gesture of excuse, saying, "*Gompchen,* we have no *chang.*[1] We never drink any."

"Give me what you have," replied the lama, opening his mouth for the first time. "It is all the same to me."

Sunk again in silence, he drank and ate a little *tsampa.* He did not seem to be going away, neither did he appear to want to sleep by the fire.

Suddenly, without departing from his immobility, he addressed me:

"Jetsunma," he said, "what have you done with your *tentreng,* your *zen,* and with your 'rings of the initiate'?"

My heart stopped beating. This man knew me! He had seen me dressed as a *gompchenma,* either in Kham, in the northern solitudes, in Amdo, or in Tsang—where, I did not know. But his words showed clearly that I was not a stranger to him.

Yongden tried to prevaricate. He did not know, he stammered, what the lama meant . . . his mother and he. . . . But the strange traveller did not give him time to invent a story.

"Go away!" he commanded in an imperious tone.

[1] Beer or barley spirits.

I had recovered my *sang-froid*. Deception was useless. I could not recall this man's features or anything else about him, but as it was evident that I had been detected, it was better to brave the situation out, for this lama probably would have no interest in denouncing me.

"Go," I told Yongden, "light a fire for yourself a little further off." He took a handful of wood, a blazing ember, and went away.

"Do not try to remember, Jetsunma," said the ascetic to me when we were alone. "I have as many faces as I desire, and you have never seen this one."

The conversation which followed was a long one on subjects pertaining to Thibetan philosophy and mysticism. Finally he arose and, staff in hand, vanished like a phantom, as he had come. His footsteps made no sound upon the stony path. He entered the jungle, and seemed to melt away in it.

I called Yongden and put an end to his questions by saying laconically: "This *gompchen* knows us, though I cannot remember having seen him, but he will not denounce us."

Then I lay down, making a pretence of sleeping so that I might be left undisturbed with the thoughts that my talk with the lama had aroused. Soon a rosy light spread in the sky and day broke. I had been listening to the mysterious traveller the whole night long without noticing how time passed. We revived the fire and prepared our humble breakfast.

The nature of my conversation with the lama should have completely reassured me as to the possibility of denunciation by a man of his character. But my mind was overtired by months of painful watching and anxiety, and I could not entirely prevent fear from creeping back into it. I did not feel any longer inclined to continue toward the Giamda valley. By going forward in that direction, the strange *gompchen* had more or less answered my enquiry about the existence of a way across the range. Unless he was going to some anchoritic dwelling hidden in the recesses of the mountain, he would most probably descend the slopes of the Giamda basin. Moreover, though I had been deeply interested in our nocturnal talk, I preferred to avoid following in the steps of anyone who knew me.

"Let us turn back," I said to Yongden. "We will cross the Temo pass and see the large Temo monastery. You may be able to purchase there the warm dress which you need so badly."

We went down again into the broad valley, followed it toward the head, skirting several villages, and finally reached the foot of the Temo pass. I preferred it to the Nyima pass situated to the southeastward, because the road to the latter has been surveyed, which is not the case with the track crossing the Temo.

At dusk we reached a large well-built house that stood alone in the pastures near the river. In spite of its comfortable appearance this massive building of grey stone looked rather disquieting. Perhaps its surroundings of densely wooded black ranges were responsible for that impression, or it was perhaps its greyish colour. Be this as it may, hospitality was immediately granted to us and we were led upstairs to a large and comfortable but dim room. Yongden and I boiled some soup and we had begun to eat it when a lama entered, followed by the mistress of the house, who carried his few packages. We understood that we were to be given a companion for the night. This did not please us, but there was no way of avoiding it. The apartment in which we had been allowed to stay was the best after the host's private quarters. Traders returning from Lhasa occupied the other rooms, and in putting two lamas together the housewife had shown courtesy to both.

The traveller appeared to be a polite and quiet man. He spread out his carpet at the end of the room opposite to us. He then approached the fire to boil his tea. Politely Yongden told him that he could dispense with that trouble, for soup was ready and we would make tea afterward. The lama accepted the invitation, at the same time producing some bread and other provisions which he placed at Yongden's disposal to add

241

to the meal he was to share with us. Having done this, he sat down and began to eat.

Thibetan custom required me to remain humbly at some distance, and I took advantage of this to observe from my dark corner the lama taking his meal near the blazing fire.

A *gomthag*[1] slung across the shoulders of his Chinese travelling robe, some other details of his dress, and the staff mounted with a trident which he had thrust upright between two boards of the floor on entering the room, revealed to me that he belonged to one of the "Red Cap" sects, most likely the *Zogs chen*.

The mystic *dung khatang*[2] lighted by the flames leaping from the hearth, cast moving shadows on the red wall. It brought to that commonplace country house something of the fascinating occult atmosphere of the Thibetan ascetic dwellings and reminded me of other anchorites with whom I had sojourned or whom I had visited on my way. It would have especially recalled the *gompchen* to whom I had, a few days before, listened a whole night through, had I forgotten him, which was far from being the case.

But aside from that symbolic implement, common to all Tantrik lamas, our new companion had nothing of the silent mystery of the one who had so unexpectedly joined us in the forest. He turned out to be a most pleasant and well-read *literatus* of the Kham province, quite ready to converse.

At first I listened to him from a distance, as my disguise compelled me to do, but after a while, seeing that Yongden could not follow his really very erudite and highly philosophical colleague, and that I should thus miss hearing the latter's view on a question which interested me, I forgot prudence and intruded upon the lama's talk. The stranger did not appear

[1] A kind of sash used as a binding and support by the lamas, belonging to mystic sects, who spend hours in meditation and who often remain the whole night in the peculiar sitting posture, cross-legged like the images of the Buddha. When travelling this sash is worn across the shoulders.

[2] A staff surmounted by a trident. Sivaite ascetics of India likewise carry a trident, but the Thibetan shape is somewhat different.

astonished at the knowledge—quite uncommon for one of her kind—showed by the poorly dressed lay woman who seated herself before him. Deeply absorbed in his subject, he perhaps did not pay much attention to his questioners.

We remained far into the night, quoting from the old books, offering explanations, referring to the commentaries of famous authors. I was delighted.

But when I awoke, before the daybreak, the fear which had tormented me so much at the beginning of my journey made me tremble again. It was not enough that I had been recognized by the mysterious *gompchen*. I had now imprudently shown myself well acquainted with Buddhist and Tantrik philosophies. Perhaps I had made the lama who spent the night with us suspicious! What a fool I had been! What would come of it? . . . Should I reach Lhasa? . . .

It was in this cheerless mood that I began the climb toward the Tempo pass, after having left the philosopher traveller still asleep in the grey stone house.

We crossed the pass without difficulty, though the snow was rather deep near the summit. The road lay through woods all the way. It was good, but it is a long tramp from the top of the pass to the foot of the hill, on the slope looking towards the Brahmaputra. Temo, an important place with several *gompas* and *lhakangs*, besides the large monastery, was reached at dusk.

We pitched our tent in an out-of-the-way spot in the fields, when we felt confident that village people were shut indoors and asleep. The moon was full, the sky was wonderfully clear, and at the same time a bank of mist, about ten or twelve feet from the ground, extended all over the valley and created the bizarre illusion of an immense veil shrouding the earth.

After a peaceful rest I awoke early, or rather I thought that I awoke, for, most probably, it was only a dream born of my anxieties and of the recent meetings. The day had just dawned: I saw a lama standing before me. He did not resemble the *gompchen* nor the *literatus* I had left on the other side of the range. He was clothed in the white habit of the *resky-*

243

angs,[1] his head was bare, and a long tress of hair fell to his heels.

"Jetsunma," he said to me, "this dress of a poor laywoman, and the rôle of old mother which you have adopted, do not suit you at all. You have taken on the mentality proper to the part. You were braver when you wore your *zen* and your *ten-treng*. You must put them on again later, when you have been to Lhasa. . . . You will get there. Do not fear. . . ."

He smiled with a sort of benevolent sarcasm: "*Jigs med naljorma nga* [I, a fearless yôginî]," he quoted, from a poem I was very fond of reciting.

I wanted to answer him, but now I really began to wake. The first rays of the rising sun gleamed upon my forehead, the space before me was empty, and through the open curtain of the small tent I only saw, far away, the shining golden roofs of the Temo *gompa*.

Most luckily, Yongden found, at the very first place of call, all that he needed for provisions and clothing. It was quite time! His monastic dress was in rags, and now that we were out of the cover of the forests he felt the cold at night. He got an old lama travelling robe, which fitted him well enough; the material was of good quality, so that, clothed in it, my companion looked like a well-to-do pilgrim whose dress had been worn out during the journey. A kind man presented him with a goatskin for a carpet to sleep on, a luxury which he much appreciated.

At Temo I heard for the first time some news which caused me great anxiety. The Penchen lama of Tashilhumpo had fled from his residence. Soldiers had been sent to capture him . . . and what had happened afterward was not known by those who told us the story.

The Penchen Tashi lama, as I have explained in the introduction of this book, had been my host, and a very kind one. For years I corresponded with his mother, who never failed

---

[1] A peculiar kind of Thibetan ascetics, who are adepts in the art of generating internal heat, as I have mentioned before.

to send me, at the beginning of each winter, a pair of felt boots and a bonnet of yellow brocade which she had embroidered and sewn herself.

How could it be that the mighty spiritual lord of Shigatze had become a fugitive? Truly, I did not altogether forget that he was far from being in good odour at the court of Lhasa. His avowed sympathy for China and his aversion to the military expenditures had greatly displeased the Thibetan king. I knew that on several occasions heavy contributions had been exacted from him, but I had never thought that he might be forced to fly from Thibet, where he is worshipped as the incarnation of a most high spiritual entity. Later on, I got some details about that truly Oriental political drama. The story may be of interest.

As years elapsed, the hatred of the Dalai lama and of the Court party, won over to the British influence, had increased against the Tashi lama. He had been ordered to levy more money in his Province and hand it over to the Lhasa government. People from whom I got these details said that the officials dispatched to collect it could not gather the amount required, and that the Tashi lama proposed to the Dalai lama to go himself on a collecting round in Mongolia, where his personal prestige might achieve the result which had not been attained by his envoys in the already impoverished villages of Tsang.[1] This permission had been refused, and the Penchen Tashi lama was asked to go to Lhasa.

A new house was built for him in the park of Norbu ling, the habitual residence of the Dalai lama. (I saw it, apparently unfinished, in a rather remote part of the estate.) It was said that a jail was attached to the house, and that it was on learning of the imminent danger which threatened him that the Tashi lama had run for his life with a few followers across the northern wilds.

Did the Court of Lhasa really mean to imprison the Grand

---

[1] Tsang, a large Thibetan province situated to the west of the Ü province whose capital is Lhasa. The capital of Tsang is Shigatze, where stands the great monastery of Tashilhumpo.

Lama of Tashilhumpo? None but the few who are in its political secrets can say for certain, but the story has nothing absolutely improbable about it.

The revenge of the Court party on those who had sided with the Chinese after the latter had been driven out from Thibet seems to have been sometimes cruel. I have been told of a Grand Lama who, on account of his dignity as a "tulku,"[1] could not be openly executed. The poor man was imprisoned, and allowed to die of starvation. But the members of his ecclesiastic household, dignitaries of his monastery, were tortured, iron nails being trust in their bodies day after day until death came.

Is there any exaggeration in such stories? I do not know.

At about the same time, a member of the high Thibetan nobility who as a state minister had supported the Chinese was killed at the Potala. It is said that he was summoned before the ruler, who had just returned to the capital. There he was first stripped of his silken robes, beaten mercilessly, then bound, and thrown down the long flight of steps which go from the top of the Potala to the foot of the hill. He was still alive when he reached the bottom and was there executed on the post. His son, having heard about the dreadful execution, and foreseeing his own fate, attempted to flee, but was shot as he rode away.

As a peculiar specimen of the Thibetan mentality I will add that the widow of the unfortunate minister, his daughter, and his daughter-in-law, were all three given as wives to a favourite of the ruler who, being ennobled, received the title and the estate of the late minister.

I deem it useless to give any name. The man who has taken the succession of the late Thibetan lord is perhaps quite innocent of his tragic end.

I can state that, even now, more than twelve years after the victorious revolt against China, three high ecclesiastical dignitaries are still detained as state prisoners at Lhasa. One of

---

[1] One of those lamaist dignitaries whom foreign writers call improperly "incarnated lamas" and "living Buddhas."

them has been given as ward to the commander-in-chief. Another was sent to Ngaböd shapé, and the third to Lön chen shatag—since the latter's death his son has taken his place as warden. These three lamas, who are *gyarongpas*—that is to say, natives of the tribes established in China—have worn the *cangue* ever since they were sentenced: and unless another revolution frees them, will die with their necks in these heavy wooden collars.

In such circumstances, the Tashi lama could find abundant reason for fearing the hospitality that his high lamaist colleague offered him. But his apprehensions were still more justified if town talk at Lhasa was true. It was said that three or four noblemen of the Tsang province were then imprisoned in the part of the Potala prison that is reserved for "quality," in connection with the tax-levy affair.

But to return to the Tashi lama. Whether entirely true, or even only partly true in its detail, the account of his flight, as I heard it, was really dramatic.

For nearly two years, one of his faithful friends with whom I am personally acquainted had scoured the country disguised as a pilgrim in order to discover the roads that offered the greatest safety for a speedy flight. He had not yet come back from his last tour when the Tashi lama, deeming that things had now grown too threatening to admit of further delay, left Shigatze hurriedly. His friend, the lama Lobzang, arrived there the following day. He ran after his master, but was compelled to turn back because of a fresh fall of snow which completely blocked the pass.

Thibet was no longer safe for him. He crossed the Indian border, but his movements were known. Telegrams were sent in all directions, giving orders to arrest him. Nevertheless, he succeeded in sailing for China a few hours before the order to seize him had reached the harbour.

As for the Tashi lama, a Thibetan official in charge of a small *zon* (that of Reading or another in the same region) had detected him amongst a party passing near his residence. Fearing to make a mistake, afraid also to lay his hands on the exalted person of *Öd pa med*, before whom all Thibetans, Mongolians, Manchurians, all lamaists of Siberia and even of the far away shores of the Volga, prostrate themselves with utmost reverence, he dispatched a messenger to Lhasa to inform the ruler.

At Lhasa, everybody believed the Tashi lama was at Shigatze, and the inhabitants of that town, as well as the monks of the Tashilhumpo monastery, were not aware of his flight.

When the official dispatched by the Dalai lama had ascertained that the Tashi lama was truly gone, three hundred soldiers were mustered under a *depung*,[1] and were ordered to bring back the fugitive. But much time had been lost. The Tashi lama and his companions had doubtless excellent horses. I remembered the large stable full of fine beasts which I visited at Shigatze, and could easily understand that the regiment reached the Chinese border after the Tashi lama was safe on the other side.

No need to add that the simple account of a political drama could not satisfy the mind of Oriental masses. The flight of the Tashi lama was only a few months old when I reached Lhasa, only to find that it had already become a legend. After he had fled from Shigatze, said some, the lama had left there a perfect likeness of himself, a phantom who acted exactly as he used to do, and thus all those who were not in the secret were deceived. It was only when the Tashi lama was safely in China that the phantom vanished. But others told the tale in a different way. According to them (and they were many) it was the phantom which had fled to China, and the real *Penchen Rimpoche* was still at Shigatze, invisible to his enemies, but visible to his faithful subjects and the pilgrim devotees.

I was to learn all these details later on, but the first vague news received at Temo made me fear that my host was not yet safe. I thought of his good mother, my friend. What had become of her in that storm? This also I did not know,

[1] Depung: a Thibetan colonel or general.

namely, that before her beloved son had fled, death had liberated the kind lady from all her earthly troubles.

As I proceeded toward the Brahmaputra, brooding sadly over this strange event, a sudden memory came back to me.

A little more than two years before, while I was staying at Jakyendo, a bard from Kham chanted for me the famous Thibetan Iliad, the poem of "King Gesar of Link." In the course of his recital the man related to me some old prophecies connected with the coming of the northern warrior Messiah, expected by the Thibetans. One of them actually announced that the Tashi lama would leave Thibet, proceeding to the north.

I listened with the utmost incredulity, and jokingly asked him in how many centuries the event would take place. My bard, who was a rather enigmatic person, seriously declared that I should see the fulfilment of the prophecy, and that the Tashi lama would leave Shigatze before two and a half years had gone by.

This seemed to me still more improbable, even absurd, and yet there I was, in the heart of Thibet, hearing about the flight into the northern solitudes of the mystic lord of Tashilhumpo,[1] which actually happened just two years and one month after the prophecy.

Strange coincidence? But what next? Would the other prophecies also prove true? Would a hero arise in the mythical Shambala, which modern Thibetans identify with Siberia, surround himself with an army of stern, invincible soldiers and unite all Asia under one rule? . . . A dream, maybe, but thousands, nay, millions, dream it in the East.

From Temo, we reached the sandy banks of the Brahmaputra. The large majestic river, in its setting of high hills,

---

[1] The Thibetans of Tsang, alluding to these prophecies, were singing at that time:

Da tsoi Lama ting red	Our Lama is a cloud
Lamai chipa lung red	His horse is the wind
Lung gi tengla chip nes	Riding on the wind
Thurgöd yul la pheb song.	He is gone to the land of Thurgöd
	(The Chinese Turkestan).

breathes a spirit of calm and peace which takes a firm hold of one's inner consciousness. Landscapes have a language of their own, expressing the soul of the things, lofty or humble, which constitute them, from the mighty peaks to the smallest of the tiny flowers hidden in the meadow's grass. The Brahmaputra spoke of serenity, and in this serenity all our preoccupations, fears, and cares were drowned.

Amongst the interesting sights on our road, before we turned northward, following the Giamda river upstream, were parties numbering hundreds of Bön pilgrims who circumambulated the Kongbu Bön hill,[1] one of the most sacred of the holy places of their religion.

The Böns are followers of the faith that prevailed in Thibet before the introduction of Buddhism. Their beliefs may originally have been much like those of the shamanists of Siberia, but it is most difficult to be certain of this, for at the time when primitive Bön doctrines existed in Thibet, writing was probably not known in the country. Consequently, there is no hope of finding any genuine Bön scriptures. The Böns themselves affirm that they possess books of a high antiquity, written before Buddhism entered Thibet. There may be something true in these affirmations, but up to the present no authentic proofs have come to light. Nowadays Böns resemble, in so far as their religious practices are concerned, the old "Red Caps" sect, called *ñingma-ñingma* ("the most ancient of the ancients"), with the difference that they slaughter animals for sacrifices. As for their monasteries, they have copied those of the lamas; their clergy wear a habit identical with that of the lamaists and they style themselves lamas as well.

In brief, the White Böns are merely lamaists who have kept a part of the old religious practices, just as the lamaists have incorporated in Buddhism an almost equal part of the same. The Black Böns are more original and nearer the primitive shamanism. Most of them are only ignorant, vulgar sorcerers, but a few interesting and intelligent men may be found here and there in their midst who hold peculiarly bold philosophical

[1] Kongbu Bön ri.

views, and some of them are believed to be powerful magicians.

However, the common run of the Böns distinguish themselves from the lamaists only by keeping their sacred edifices on the left when circumambulating these, whereas the lamaists keep them on the right. One may add that, instead of the formula *"Aum Mani Padme hum"* recited by the lamaists, the Böns repeat *"Aum Matriyé salendu,"* which some travellers have understood as *"Matri Matris da dzu."* Space forbids treating the subject in fuller detail.

Many of the pilgrims went round the mountain, prostrating themselves at each step, that is to say that, stretching their arms as they lay on the ground, and marking with their fingers the length they had covered with their bodies, they would then get up and stand at the exact place which their fingers had touched, after which they would again prostrate themselves and measures their length once more, and so on, all the way.[1]

Lamaists perform these repeated prostrations around the monasteries containing especially holy relics, such as the grave of Tsong Khapa. During my stay at Lhasa I saw men circumambulating the sacred city in this fashion. One even hears of people who come thus from distant Mongolia to Lhasa, passing years on the road.

The Bön pilgrims were mostly tall, athletic fellows with bold energetic faces. To see them stretched head downwards when descending steep, rocky slopes was indeed a striking sight. A large number of women also walked around the hill, and some accomplished the exhausting and endless prostrations with remarkable courage.

We left the Brahmaputra, continuing upstream along the river Giamda. We visited on our way the Pu chung ser kyi Lhakhang, a small golden-roofed temple with a golden altar.

Then, as I made my way along the valley, I noticed the air of abandon, of ruin, which prevailed all over the country. Deserted villages had fallen in ruins, the jungle triumphed, reconquering the lands which had been cleared and cultivated.

[1] It is called *"Kora la Kyang chag ches pa."*

Chinese posts had existed on the road—at that time the main road—which follows the left bank of the river. One could see, here and there, high watch towers crumbling into ruins. Around them a Chinese population had settled and cultivated the country. The track along which they stood was now haunted by daring robbers from the mountains I had thought of crossing before my meeting with the strange *gompchen*. People of the neighbouring villages had strongly advised me to cross the river and proceed on its right bank, although it was a longer way round, because the country was a little more populated and safer on that side. Yet even this bank was sparsely populated. Indeed, after Chimazong, we saw little but solitary forests.

On that road I twice met lonely pilgrims, like the man I had seen at the beginning of my journey dying near the Kha Karpo, but in this case both were women. One of them, in spite of our pressing advice and the little money we had given her, did not appear inclined to ask hospitality in a village house. We left her behind, but she overtook us by walking at night, though this time she appeared to be at the end of her tether. We offered to lead her to a hamlet near by, but she refused. She wanted to light a fire under the trees on the border of the road; Yongden collected some wood which he placed near her, and then we went away. The last sight I had of her showed me the abandoned devotee seated next to the fire that was beginning to burn. A thin bluish spiral of smoke rose straight before her and dissolved in space—a symbol, it seemed, of the life which was about to depart.

The second wanderer I met lay under a thin shelter made of branches by some half-compassionate villagers whose kindness was strong enough to help the sick and lone pilgrim, but did not go so far as to give her a corner in their homes. With the woman remained her little dog, which barked ferociously and tried its best to frighten away those who approached its mistress. The poor faithful thing was really touching. Here again I could do no more than give her a little money and pass on my way. Is there a more cruel torture than to have continually to pass on one's way, powerless to relieve the countless sorrows which lie along all the roads of the world!

Giamda, which is considered all over Thibet to be an important town, is little more than a village, but its situation at the intersection of the main road from Lhasa to Chiamdo and the road to the Brahmaputra gives it perhaps a strategic and trading interest. Although the town is situated at a height of nearly 11,000 feet, the climate of the valley is warm and, during the day, when the sun shines, equals even in January that of summer in such European countries as Belgium.

Travellers on their way to Lhasa, after having crossed a toll bridge, must appear before an official to get permission to proceed.

How often I had discussed with Yongden the best way in which to surmount this obstacle! As a rule things appear much more difficult and terrifying in the course of such discussions than when the moment of action has arrived.

To pass through Giamda was an easy matter. We crossed the bridge, paid the toll, and were led by a boy to the official's house. I sent Yongden in and sat down on a stone in the dust, at the door. Many people passed through the narrow street, and no one took any special notice of me.

Yongden saluted the gentleman of the *zong,* or perhaps he saw only his secretary or some pretty clerk of the place. After a few minutes he came out, and we took up our loads . . . the dreaded Giamda was left behind.

We were now on the post road,[1] the only one which crosses Thibet. The progress of civilization along it is seen in the shape of small buildings like shrines which mark the miles. Indeed I took the first one I saw to be a rustic village chapel, or *tsa tsa* house.[2] What added to the illusion was that on some of them lay carved stones bearing the usual *Aum mani padme hum,* or other such formulæ, and that I could see around them

---

[1] The old post road, on which, at the time of the Chinese suzerainty, the mail ran from Peking to Lhasa, but which now stops at Chiamdo and does not cross China.

[2] See Chap. iv, p. 136.

the trace of circumambulation in the little path made by the feet of the devotees. It was one of these which helped me to discover my mistake. Seeing an old man walking round with a pious mien, I wished to see the picture of the deity enclosed in the little shrine. To my astonishment I was confronted with a piece of reddish stone, on which some figures—135, I think—were inscribed. Strange! . . . All my notions concerning lamaism were disturbed. It took a few minutes of reflection before the mystery of that uncommon cult was revealed to me. Never should I have thought that my Oriental researches would lead me to discover the worship of the milestone!

Many were the sights, the talks and the observations, all well worthy of being related, which filled the last part of my journey to Lhasa. But I must omit them to make room for the account of my stay in the capital itself.

Our crossing of the Kongbu Ba Pass was saddened by a painful spectacle. A party of pilgrims, mostly women, had been robbed there of all their belongings by some of their travelling companions who had suddenly turned brigands, a thing not so rare in Thibet. Some of the unlucky women had not been able to continue their journey and had sheltered themselves in a mountain cave. One of them had a gash in her head; another had a terrible wound in the breast; the arm of a third one was broken; others were more or less injured. Their vile and wretched countrymen, though hailing from the same district, almost the same village, had attacked them with spears. At a short distance from the cave the corpses of two men were lying. All this happened within a hundred miles of Lhasa, on the main route. Horse soldiers could easily have overtaken the murderers, but what official would trouble himself about such a common occurrence in that lawless country?

CHAPTER VII

AT last, after four months of tramping, filled with adventures and observations of which I have been able to relate but a very small part, I left Dechen one morning at dawn, and set out upon the last stage to Lhasa.

The weather was clear, dry, and cold, the sky luminous. In the rosy light of the rising sun, we sighted the Potala, the huge palace of the lamaist ruler, still far away, yet already majestic and impressive.

"This time we have won," I said to my young friend.

He silenced me.

"Hush! Do not speak too soon! Do not rejoice yet. We have still to cross the river Kyi. Who knows if there is not a post of watchmen there?"

So near were we to our goal that I refused to believe failure to be still possible. Anyhow, I dropped the subject.

As we advanced, the Potala grew larger and larger. Now we could discern the elegant outlines of its many golden roofs. They glittered in the blue sky, sparks seeming to spring from their sharp upturned corners, as if the whole castle, the glory of Thibet, had been crowned with flames.

Our eyes fastened upon it. We walked at a good speed, for success was near and gave us wings.

The valley which we followed since leaving the Bala had become quite open. The slopes which border it may, in days of yore, have been covered with forests, but not a single tree was now to be seen there, except a few that had been planted in certain gardens.

Villages stood closer as we proceeded toward the capital, but I felt very astonished to meet so few people on the highway. I was told by countryfolk that a much larger traffic used to pass during the Chinese suzerainty. Their remarks reminded me of what I had observed in the Kongbu province—abandoned and ruined villages at the feet of crumbling watch towers, and large tracts of formerly cultivated land on which the forest had again encroached.

The Lhasa valley did not present so desolate a spectacle in the part that I was crossing. But how much ground remained uncultivated on which barley could have been grown for the town near by, where the cost of living is so high!

Thibetans have lost much in parting with China. Their sham independence profits only a clique of court officials. Most of those who rebelled against the far-off and relaxed Chinese rule regret it nowadays, when taxes, statute labour, and the arrogant plundering of the national soldierly greatly exceed the extortions of their former masters.

Arrived at the river, which in the winter is but a narrow stream, we embarked on a rustic ferry adorned with the head of an animal, which the artist probably intended to be a horse. A mixed crowd of men and beasts was packed on the boat. A few minutes later we landed on the opposite bank. Neither the busy ferrymen nor any of the passengers had given us so much as a glance. Hundreds of ragged pilgrims cross the Kyi chu each year, and nothing distinguished us from our fellow *arjopas*.

We were now in Lhasa territory, but still far from the city itself. Yongden once more repressed my desire to rejoice, even in a whisper. What could he still fear? Had we not reached our goal? And now, nature itself gave us a token of her maternal complicity.

As on the night of our starting, when we disappeared in the Kha Karpo forests, "the gods lulled the men to sleep and silenced the dogs." A miracle seemed to protect our entrance into Lhasa.

No sooner had we landed than the air, till then so calm, became agitated. All of a sudden a furious storm arose, lifting clouds of dust high into the sky. I have seen the simoon in the Sahara, but was it worse than this? No doubt it was.

Yet, that terrible, dry lashing rain of dust gave me the impression of being once more in the great desert.

Indistinct forms passed us, men bent in two, hiding their faces in the laps of their dresses, or whatever piece of cloth they might happen to have with them.

Who could see us coming? Who could know us? An immense yellow curtain of whirling sand was spread before the Potala, blinding its guests, hiding from them Lhasa, the roads leading to it, and those who walked upon them. I interpreted it as a symbol promising me complete security, and the future justified my interpretation. For two months I was to wander freely in the lamaist Rome, with none to suspect that, for the first time in history, a foreign woman was beholding the Forbidden City.

"The gods threw a veil over the eyes of his adversaries and they did not recognise him." So went an old Thibetan tale which I had heard long ago in the Land of Grass.

At that time of the year, a large number of people from all the provinces of Thibet congregate in the capital to enjoy the various festivals and merry-makings, which take place there. The inns are full. All those who can vacate a room or any shelter rent them. Travellers sleep in the stables and camp in the courtyards.

I could have gone from door to door for hours, in quest of a lodging, without any other result than showing myself to a number of householders of both sexes and being compelled to answer a lot of questions. Fortunately, I was spared the trouble and danger of this.

The storm abated as suddenly as it had arisen. Newcomers, unacquainted with the city, we stood a little at a loss amid the crowd without knowing where to go. Unexpected help came again to me in the shape of a young woman.

"You want a room, Mother?" she said. "You come from very far. You must be exceedingly tired. Follow me. I know a place where you will be all right."

I only smiled at her, uttering thanks. I felt rather astonished. Obliging people are many in Thibet, and the kindness of the unknown woman was not altogether extraordinary, but how did she know that "I had come from very far"? This puzzled me a little, but no doubt she had gained that idea from the sight of my pilgrim staff, and I was lean enough, after so many fasts and so much fatigue, to inspire compassion.

Our guide was not communicative. We followed her like sheep, a little bewildered by the noise and the traffic after months spent in the solitudes, and perhaps still more bewildered by our good luck. She led us outside the town to a place from which one enjoyed an extended view of most beautiful scenery, including the Potala. This detail struck me particularly; for all along the road I had wanted to get a lodging from which I could see it.

I was granted the use of a narrow cell, in a ramshackle cottage occupied by beggarly people. This was indeed the best hostelry one could have wished for the security of my incognito. The idea of looking there for a foreign lady traveller would not have occurred to anybody; and the poor beggars who frequented the place never suspected my identity.

The woman went away smiling after a brief farewell. All had happened so quickly that it seemed a dream. We never saw our guide again.

In our hovel that evening, lying on the ground amongst our miserable luggage, I said to my faithful companion: "Do you allow me now to say that we have won the game?"

"Yes," he said, and he shouted in a suppressed, yet most triumphant tone: "*Lha gyalo. De tamche pam!* We are at Lhasa!"

I was in Lhasa. No doubt I could be proud of my victory, but the struggle, with cunning and trickery as weapons, was not yet over. I was in Lhasa, and now the problem was to stay there. Although I had endeavoured to reach the Thibetan capital rather because I had been challenged than out of any real desire to visit it, now that I stood on the forbidden ground at the cost of so much hardship and danger, I meant to enjoy myself in all possible ways. I should really have felt ashamed of myself had I been caught, locked up somewhere, and taken back to the border, having only had a superficial and brief glance at the exterior of the palaces and temples. This should not be! No! I would climb to the top of the Potala itself; I would visit the most famous shrines, the large historical monasteries in the vicinity of Lhasa, and I would witness the religious ceremonies, the races, and the pageants of the New Year festival. All sights, all things which are Lhasa's own beauty and peculiarity, would have to be seen by the lone woman explorer who had had the nerve to come to them from afar, the first of her sex. It was my well-won reward after the trials on the road and the vexations by which for several years various officials had endeavoured to prevent my wanderings in Thibet. This time I intended that nobody should deprive me of it.

Lhasa, the largest town of Thibet, its capital and the Rome of the lamaist world, is by no means a big city. It is prettily situated at a little distance from the bank of the river Kyi, in a large valley with a commanding horizon of high barren mountain ranges. Still, in a country of wonderful landscapes, as Thibet is, the scenery of Lhasa would be quite ordinary, but for the huge palace of the Dalai lama erected on the *Dsi Potala,* one of the two summits of a small, isolated ridge that shoots up in the middle of the valley. The other summit is called *Chog bu ri* and is crowned by the buildings of the Clerical Medical College. Better than any description, pictures can give some idea of the gigantic edifice, but even the best photograph will fail to convey a true idea of its imposing appearance, as it stands, a red palace capped with golden roofs, uplifted high in the blue sky, on a shining pedestal of dazzling white buildings. With the riches contained in that enormous cluster of habitations, rising one above another, without any order or plan, on the slope of the Tsi Potala, there could have been built a real wonder-palace, but Thibetan architects never were artists. The most precious materials, when handled by their rough hands, succeed only in expressing might and wealth and fail to reach beauty. Yet that barbaric treatment of silver, gold, and precious gems gives the temples and palaces of

259

Thibet a peculiar character, in harmony with the rough scenery in which they stand. And this, in itself, makes a powerful impression.

Chinese painters or students of Chinese art are responsible for a great part of the Potala's decoration, as well as that of the Jo Khang, the holiest temple of Thibet. One could spend weeks in the many galleries and corridors of the Dalai lama palace, reading in pictures on the walls the legends of gods and the lives of saintly men, gracefully and wittily rendered in millions of tiny figures full of lifelike animation.

Here and there amongst the apartments are scattered a large number of *Lha Khang* (God's Houses), in which may be seen a variety of images of all the symbolic and mystic deities of Mahâyâna Buddhism. Most of them are sumptuously decked with golden ornaments inlaid with turquoise, coral, and precious stones. A special room contains the images of the previous Dalai lamas, and the present one is seated amongst them, but in miniature only.

Darker recesses are devoted to some of the aboriginal gods and demons of the pre-Buddhistic religion, which Thibetans have never been able to forsake. A few words about them may perhaps not be out of place here.

The story of the admission of these personages into the lamaist Pantheon, as told in the old books, is always the same. It depicts the struggle of the Indian missionaries, or the first Thibetan members of the Buddhist Order, against beings who opposed their preaching and harmed their converts. These holy men were always endowed with magic powers, and when they succeeded to a certain extent in conquering their malignant enemy, they took advantage of his momentary defeat to extort from him the oath to renounce his hostile state of mind and to become a protector of the Buddhist doctrine. In exchange, the title of *Chöskyong* (protector of the religion) was bestowed upon the god or the demon, and a place was granted to him in the temples.

Lamaism does not stop there. Even worse creatures are symbolically fed in special buildings, and the offerings placed there stand as a substitute for the more realistic and bloodier sacrifices of the pre-Buddhistic cult. It is only—so Thibetans believe—strict attendance to their needs, and a due reverence, that keep human beings and animals safe from their ferocity. Other dread Malevolent and Invisible Ones are chained by the power of magic charms, and a perpetual watch has to be kept in order that the spells and other occult devices, whose strength prevents the dangerous beings from escaping, shall be recited and performed at the right time.

Needless to say, all these rites have nothing to do with true Buddhism, which does not admit of any rite at all. But in Thibet they are favoured even by the *literati;* for, so these say, such performances suit their country and the mental level of its masses. Be that as it may, all kinds of worship are practiced in Lhasa, even in the palace of its king, as well as all over Thibet.

The Potala contains sumptuous suites of apartments, and the upper terrace, on which stand Chinese pavilions, could be made into an ideal roof garden, such as the world has never seen; but the desire, or even the idea, of creating such a thing has probably never entered the minds of any of the Dalai lamas who have successively sat upon the throne of the Potala.

From the top of the palace, the view embraces, in front, the whole of the valley, with Lhasa outspread in the plain. Behind it a desert extends for a long distance, until a high range rises suddenly like a Cyclopean wall. Seated at its foot, the large monastery of Sera (the hail), snowy white, rears its red temples and golden roofs like the Potala itself. Its monks are a formidable power in the state, which even the master of the Potala must reckon with.

The comic element which had been to me the breath of life, even in the midst of the most trying circumstances, did not desert me at the gates of the Potala. The story of my visit to the Thibetan Vatican may well be worth the telling.

As the future was uncertain and my incognito precarious, prudence advised me to hurry on with my sight-seeing tour, and to begin with the most important places of interest. I therefore decided that, before anything else, I would visit the Potala.

As I was on my way with Yongden, I thought it would be safer for me either to join some pilgrims or somehow to manager to enter the Palace with a group of people. The unquestionable authenticity of real Thibetan companions would save me from suspicion. Unfortunately, we did not meet any *dokpas* or other border folk, and I was already resigned to proceeding with Yongden alone when I noticed two men, clad in the plain white dress of coarse serge worn by countryfolk, strolling at a little distance from the first gate.

"Let us take those men with us," I said to Yongden.

"How could we ask them such a thing?" he replied. "Perhaps they do not wish to go to the Potala."

"Let us try," I continued. "They look just the dear, good, stupid fellows we need."

In a few words I instructed Yongden in the part he was to play.

At that moment a group of workmen came along, carrying huge trunks of trees. People threw themselves hurriedly aside to get out of their way, and Yongden took the opportunity to give one of the peasants a push in the back.

"*Atsi!*" he exclaimed, politely. "I did not see you."

"No harm, Lama," answered the man.

"Where are you from?" enquired my companion, in the patronising tone of a full-fledged denizen of the capital speaking to countryfolk.

They gave the name of their village and informed us that they had come to Lhasa to sell barley. They had finished their business and now thought only of enjoying themselves a little in the big city, before leaving on the morrow.

"You are going to meet[1] the Potala," said Yongden, as if quite sure of what he was saying.

The men confessed they did not intend to do so, as they had "met" it on several occasions already. Then Yongden, speaking with the authority of one of the monks of the Potala, told them

[1] This is a respectful way of speaking of a visit to a holy place.

of the religious merit that such a visit produced and said that
the New Year was the proper time to perform meritorious
deeds. Rather than loitering in the streets, drinking spirits in
the public houses, they ought to pay reverence to the Potala
shrines. Assuming an air of profound compassion and kindness, he added that, as they had been brought together, he
was willing to lead them around the shrines and tell them the
names and stories of the deities. This was, of course, a wonderful opportunity. The faces of the two simpletons were
beaming and they followed the lama, rejoicing and thankful.
Like all Thibetans, they were very religious-minded.

Behind them, full of confidence, I climbed the long flight
of steps and reached an upper gate. The three men walked
in first, strong in the superiority of their sex. I was about to
follow humbly, when a boy, ten or twelve years old, a novice
lama, short and fat, with a red face, flat nose, and large ears,
looking like a gnome in a clerical robe twice too large for him,
stopped me. He was acting as doorkeeper, and he ordered me
rudely to take off my fur-lined bonnet, such headgear not being
allowed inside the Potala.

What a calamity! I had forgotten that these bonnets were
not allowed there. I had worn mine a long time, in fact ever
since it had been *sent*, by some friends from an invisible world,
to provide me with a most useful piece of disguise. It screened
my face and I felt protected against detection when I had it
on my head. What now?

My hair had resumed its natural brown shade. The Chinese
ink I used as a dye had worn away before I reached Lhasa,
and in my present dwelling, with the cracks in its doors, and
walls, through which my neighbours could peep at any time, I
had not dared to darken it afresh. It no longer matched the
braids of jet black yak hair that I wore, and the latter had
gradually lost a large part of their substance, until they had
become as thin as rats' tails. They were all right, however,
with the bonnet on. They shadowed my forehead enough to
reproduce vaguely the hairdress of some *dokpa* tribes. But now
that I had to obey that horrid little toad and take my bonnet

off, I knew that I should look funnier than any clown in any circus in the world.

However, escape was impossible. I had my bonnet under my dress, as I was ordered to do, and rejoined my companions. Yongden had lingered a little, waiting for me. At the first glance, stricken with terror, he opened his mouth wide and hardly suppressed an exclamation.

"What have you done?" he said, in dismay. "Who took your bonnet away?"

"I am not allowed to proceed with it on," I answered hurriedly.

"You look like a demon," he continued, trembling. "I never saw such a face in my life! Everybody will stare at you. . . ."

A little more, and I should have cried. However, I derived some comfort from the complete indifference of the two villagers, who did not appear to notice anything wrong or peculiar in my appearance and listened eagerly to their guide, as he related stories about gods, holy men and Dalai lamas of yore. Others joined them, commenting on the profound learning of the kind lama. I followed with the crowd, jostling along the corridors, in the steep staircases and narrow shrine doors, and none of them looked at my extraordinary head. I was the only one to feel it, and I began to enjoy the fun myself. As for Yongden, a little reassured now, he did not dare to look at me too often, lest he should laugh aloud.

At last I reached the upper terrace, which is occupied by the Chinese pavilions, whose elegant and glittering roofs had appeared to me the day I arrived from China, announcing that the goal was near.

After a few hours I went down, and only then a pilgrim seemed to realise that there was something unusual in my appearance. I heard him saying to his friends: "Where do you think she came from?"

But he at once found the answer himself.

"She must be a Ladki," [1] he concluded.

[1] Ladak, a region in Western Thibet.

So we went on, having reached the top of the dominating Potala, and enjoyed the beautiful sight of Lhasa, its temples and monasteries, lying at our feet like a white, red, and gold carpet spread in the valley.

The two countrymen were delighted. They thanked the good lama profusely, and offered him a few copper coins as a token of gratitude and reverence.

"All is well," said Yongden as we went away. "I have prevented them from drinking and they have served us." He put the coins into the hand of a blind beggar, and thus some one else rejoiced also!

In spite of the splendour of the Potala, the present Dalai lama does not seem to find much charm in it. He goes there only occasionally, at the time of certain festivals. His habitual residence, Norbu ling,[1] is situated outside of the town in a large park which, owing to the lack of capable gardeners, is not much more than a wooded tract of land cut by a few avenues and paths.

A miniature zoo is one of the attractions of the place. This includes a strange poultry yard where only cocks are admitted. The celibate birds number at least three hundred, and the absence of any ladies of their species appears to have softened their combative instincts. They peck their grain peacefully side by side, and battles are rare. The animals live near one of the gates opening on the high road and even wander on the road in the hope of being fed by people as they pass. Pilgrims, and even inhabitants of Lhasa, go on purpose to throw grain to them, for they belong to the Dalai lama, and such offering is considered to be meritorious!

Several houses reserved for the use of the Thibetan Lama-King are scattered in the grounds of the Norbu ling.

The rooms of one of them are furnished in different styles, or at least what Thibetans believe to be different styles. One room they call the English room, another the Indian, another, again, the Chinese room, and, as on the flat roof of the building

[1] Norbu ling, the "Jewel Island" or the "Jewel Place or Quarter."

stand the gilded ornaments called *gyaltsen*, emblematic of power and victory, the courtiers of the Dalai lama repeat to satiety before him: "All these various rooms, English, Chinese, Indian, and so on, are under the Thibetan roof whereon stand the Thibetan *gyaltsen*, and so Thibet is above all nations, and you are the highest among all rulers."

I have been told that this clerical King of Thibet smiles and takes pleasure in these flatteries. One may well doubt his taking them seriously. He has been twice in exile, first in China and then in India, and hence must have learned many things about the world outside Thibet. But if the ruler is perhaps aware of his true situation, it is not the same with the common folk, to whom most extraordinary stories are told about the greatness of the Dalai lama and the position in which he stands before Great Britain. Very likely the court of Lhasa spreads these absurdities in order to increase the prestige of the Dalai lama, with which its own is bound up. I will venture to relate one of these stories, as it is rather amusing.

At the time when the Dalai lama was in India, he happened to be the guest of the Viceroy. Once, being seated with the latter and many distinguished guests in a large drawing-room he stretched out his two arms. And behold! On each of his upturned palms appeared one of the hills of Lhasa. On one hand one could see the Potala, on the other the great Medical College of Chog bu ri (the tent-shaped hill). At the sight of this marvel the Englishmen were all awe struck. With the Viceroy at their head, they all fell on their knees and bowed down at the feet of the Thibetan pontiff, begging his protection. The King of England was immediately informed of the miracle. He, of course, shared the feelings of his eminent subjects and entreated the Dalai lama to become the patron of his kingdom, and to grant him his help if he were ever attacked by enemies. The compassionate lama promised graciously to send him his army should the security of England become endangered.

Relying on stories of this kind and misunderstanding some facts the details of which are beyond my present subject, most

Thibetans are convinced that they have in some way become suzerains of Great Britain. Thus are explained to them the temporary stays at Lhasa of a British political agent. He comes, they think, to ask respectfully the orders of the Dalai lama, and to convey them to His British Majesty!

This is, of course, funny, but there is to fun of this kind a side fraught with danger for white residents all over Asia, which only those who have lived long in out-of-way regions of the East are able to detect clearly.

In Lhasa, one does not see the quaint shops and bazaars that offer such an exciting hunting-ground to the collector in China. Nowadays, the most conspicuous articles in the Lhasa market are aluminum wares. For the rest, the display is exclusively composed of inferior goods exported from India, England, Japan, or a few other European countries. I have never seen elsewhere uglier cotton cloth, more hideous crockery than that which one finds on the stalls of the Lhasa merchants. The trade with China, formerly very prosperous, has been so greatly hindered in favor of the goods imported from India that it hardly exists any longer. The importation of tea and manufactured silk still continues, but efforts are being made to drive Chinese products entirely out of the Thibetan market.

Coming from China, where silver was plentiful, both in coins and in bullion, a surprise awaited me at Lhasa. There is no more silver in central Thibet. The national money, the *tranka*, a small thin coin of very low standard, quantities of which were circulating when I was at Shigatze, has nearly disappeared, and the few which remain can only be had at a premium. As for the "silver shoes" of fifty taels, the tamigma,[1] as the people of Lhasa call them, which were current money when the Chinese occupied the Thibetan capital, they have completely disappeared.

The Lhasa government has cast an ugly copper coinage

---

[1] *Tamigma*, "horseshoe shaped," also called *Ngagchuma*, "the fifteen one," which is current money in northwestern China.

which is now in general use, in Lhasa and the neighbourhood, but at a distance of less than one hundred miles from the Potala it is no longer accepted, since it cannot be taken at its face value in any transaction with people who have no business at Lhasa. The Lhasa government has also issued some notes, but they remain an object of curiosity and the traders refuse them. There exists a place near Norbu ling where golden coins are stamped, but they do not circulate.

I have enquired of many people concerning the cause of this strange disappearance of the silver from central Thibet, seeing that it continues to be plentiful in Chinese Thibet. The answers I have gathered differ according to the social condition and the special turn of mind of those to whom I put the question. Some only smiled when asked where the silver had gone. Others declared: "The government hoards it." But a number of more outspoken fellows told me brutally: "Our government gives it to the *philing* masters of India (Englishmen) to pay for the old guns, no longer good for their own soldiers, which they sell us. We can fight badly armed Chinese with them, but they would be of no use against a *philing* army." The same idea was several times expressed before me in a more original and superstitious way. Before being dispatched to Lhasa, said some Thibetans, the guns sold to their country were deprived of the power of harming the white foreigners or their servants by the magic practice of the *philing* priests.

In the part of Kham conquered by the Lhasa troops, when the country people lament about the considerable rise of the taxes, the Lhasa-appointed officials answer that their most kind protector, the Dalai lama, is not responsible for these hardships, but that the *philings* tell him to collect money. Why he obeys them, what he receives in exchange for his silver, and many other things, are not of course explained to the simple-minded ones whose brains are not those of a logician. They only remember and bear in mind that these hated "white-eyed" (*mig kar* [1]) foreigners are the cause of their ruin. Thus the hatred

---

[1] *Mig Kar:* "white eyes," the blue or grey eyes are called "white" by Thibetans, who deem them most unsightly.

of the white men is sown and cultivated in the remotest corners of Asia, where it will thrive and spread.

A very famous festival takes place each year at Lhasa on the evening of the full moon of the first month. Light wooden structures of a large size are entirely covered with ornaments and images of gods, men, and animals, all made of butter and dyed in different colours. These frail frameworks are called *tormas*. About one hundred of them are erected along the *par kor*—that is to say, the streets that form the middle circle of religious circumambulation around the *Jo khang*,[1] and in front of each one, a large number of butter lamps burn on a small altar. That nocturnal feast is meant to entertain the gods, just as are certain concerts on the roofs of the temples.

The butter *tormas* festival at Lhasa is famous all over Thibet, and even in Mongolia and China. It is no doubt truly glorious, yet, I think the feast is much more beautiful in its sumptuous surrounding at the great Kum Bum lamasery, where I have seen it several times during the years I lived in that monastery. However, I very much enjoyed that part of the New Year merry-making at Lhasa.

As soon as darkness had come and the lamps were lighted, Yongden and I went to the Par Kor. A dense crowd was there, waiting for the Dalai lama, who was to go round to inspect the *tormas*. I had more than once seen big Thibetan gatherings, but I had gone through them with servants and other attendants who made a way for me. This was my first experience of being part of the crowd myself.

Groups of sturdy giants, cowmen clad in sheepskin, holding on to one another, ran for joy in the deepest of the throng. Their big fists belaboured the ribs of those whom bad luck had placed in their way. Policemen, armed with long sticks and whips, growing more and more excited as the time of the Dalai lama's coming approached, used their weapons indiscriminately

---

[1] There are three circles of devotional circumambulation: the *nangkoe*, inner circle near the great temple of the Jowo; the *parkor*, at some distance from it; and the *chikor*, which includes the whole town of Lhasa as well as the Potala, in its circle.

against anybody. In the midst of this tumult, trying our best to guard ourselves against hustling and blows, we spent some lively moments.

At last the arrival of the Lama-King was announced. Then more policemen appeared, followed by soldiers. The knocking, beating, boxing increased. Some women screamed, others laughed. Finally there remained along the walls of the houses that confronted the *tormas* only a few rows of people, more tightly pressed against one another than tinned sardines. I was amongst them. From time to time a man seated at a ground-floor window, whose view I was blocking, gave me a strong push in the back, but it was of no use whatever. Even had I wished it I could not have moved a single step. Finally he understood this, or my insensibility disarmed him. Anyway, he ceased from using unnecessary violence.

The whole Lhasa garrison was under arms. Infantry and cavalry marched past the dazzling butter edifices, lighted up by thousands of lamps. In a sedan chair covered with yellow brocade, the Dalai lama passed in his turn, attended by the commander-in-chief of the Thibetan army and other high officials. Soldiers marched in the rear. The band struck up an English music-hall tune. Crackers were fired and meagre Bengal lights coloured the procession red and green for a few minutes.

That was all. And the lamaist ruler had gone.

For a long time after the regal cortège had passed, private processions followed: people of rank surrounded by attendants holding Chinese lanterns, high ecclesiastics with clerical followers, the representatives of the Nepal Maharaja, and many others; clergy, nobility, wealthy traders, and their womenfolk all dressed in their best, laughing—all more or less drunk and happy. Their gaiety was contagious. Yongden and I went with the crowd, running, jostling, and pushing like everybody else, enjoying as youngsters might have done the fun of being there in Lhasa, feasting the New Year with the Thibetans.

When at last the time came to go back to our hovel, we noticed on our way that the streets which ought to have been well lighted by the full moon were growing darker and darker. What did it mean? We are teetotalers, and could not have the same reason as most citizens on that night, for clouded vision. We reached a square, and noticed a black shadow in a corner of the moon. It was the beginning of an eclipse, and soon we heard a noise of drums made by the good people to frighten away the dragon which was trying to swallow the nocturnal luminary! The eclipse was total. I observed it during the night, and it was the most interesting one that I had ever witnessed.

"This is still better than the curtain of sand before the Potala, on the day of our arrival," said Yongden, jocularly. "Now your gods are screening the moon so that we shall not be seen too distinctly. I think you had better ask them to stop their kind protection of our incognito. They might put out the sun!"

Whatever may have been the protection with which I was favoured, the day came when the safety of my disguise was again endangered and I had to defend myself in my own way.

I was wandering in the market when a policeman stopped and gazed at me intently. Why? Perhaps he only wondered from what part of Thibet I might hail, but it was better to be prepared for the worst. A new battle was to be fought, and I began it, my heart beating rather quickly, but brave as usual. I chose, amongst the things for sale, an aluminum saucepan, and began to bargain for it with that ridiculous obstinacy shown by the people of the half-wild tribes of the borderland. I offered an absurd price and talked nonsense in a loud voice, hardly stopping to breathe. People around the booths began to laugh and exchange jokes about me. The cowmen and women of the northern solitudes are a habitual subject of mockery for the more civilized people of Lhasa.

"Ah!" said the merchant, laughing, and yet irritated by my continuous twaddle, "you are a true *dokpa*, there can be no doubt of that!" And all present ridiculed the stupid woman who knew nothing beside her cattle and the grass of the desert. The policeman passed on, amused like everybody else.

271

I bought the saucepan, and, as I feared being followed, I compelled myself to loiter about the market, playing a comedy of admiration and stupidity before the ugliest and cheapest goods. Then my good luck caused me to fall in with a group of true *dokpas*. I began to talk with them in their own dialect. I had lived in their country some years ago. I spoke of places and men known to them, and they were convinced that I was born in a neighbouring tribe. I have no doubt that, with the quickness of imagination that is peculiar to them, they would, next day, have sworn in all sincerity that they had known me for a long time.

A second incident happened a few days later. A kind of special constable tried to extort money from me; but I managed the affair cleverly enough to give him nothing without disclosing my identity.

Still another policeman hit me with his truncheon because I had trespassed in a place where "quality" only were admitted, and truly I had to make a great effort to prevent myself from giving a gratuity to that man, so delighted was I with the fun. "What a wonderful incognito is mine!" I confided to Yongden. "Now I am even beaten in the street!" And after that I felt completely secure.

Lhasa is divided into several quarters: Yu thog, Lubu, Ramoche, Lhasahöl, Tsemoling, Tengyailing, Tsecholing, Banajong, Parkor, Norbu ling. The city boasts of a bridge and an obelisk. The bridge is of Chinese shape, painted red and roofed with green tiles. Its name, "Turquoise-roofed Bridge," is derived from a noble Thibetan family whose dwelling is in the vicinity. An ancestor of that family having received from the Chinese Emperor the distinction of the "turquoise knob" (in Thibetan: *Yu thog*), his descendants were, from that time, known as the Yu thog gentlemen, whence the name of the bridge, further justified by its blue-green roof (*thog*). The obelisk is much shorter than that which one sees in the Place de la Concorde at Paris. Yet, even though it has no hieroglyphics, it makes quite a respectable appearance. In front of it, on the highway, at the foot of the Potala, a tablet bearing Chinese and Thibetan writing is sheltered by a small building.

That highway, humble as may be its appearance, is one of the great arteries of the world. Starting from India, it crosses central Asia, enters Mongolia, and ends in Siberia—a long track which cuts through high ranges of mountains, but does not offer great difficulties to a good horseman. During the winter, when the temperature allows one to carry provisions of ice for drinking purposes, travellers can follow the road nearly in a straight line across a waterless region. In the summer, they follow the devious route, passing to the east of the Blue Lake, the Koko Nor of which I have already spoken.

One day, perhaps not far distant, "Transasiatic Expresses" will carry there parties of tourists, seated in comfortable sleeping and salon cars, but then the charm of the journey will be greatly diminished. As for me, I am glad to have travelled from Ceylon to Mongolia before this happens.

The capital of Thibet is a town full of animation, inhabited by jolly people whose greatest pleasure is to loiter and chat out-of-doors. Although the population is far from being considerable, the streets are crowded from sunrise to sunset, but it is not deemed prudent to go out after dusk. The citizens say that the establishment of a national police and army have much increased the insecurity, for the official protectors of the public safety often turn robbers when darkness has come.

With the exception of a small part of the town, the streets of Lhasa are large, with broad squares at their points of intersection, and relatively clean. Unfortunately, there is no sanitary accommodation in many houses some empty plots of ground being reserved for this purpose in different quarters of the town.

Several important monasteries are situated in Lhasa itself, amongst them the two famous colleges where tantrism, magic, ritual and occult sciences are taught.

The three great lamaseries whose fame attracts thousands of pilgrims and where young lamas come to study from even the farthest regions of Mongolia and Manchuria, are not in Lhasa, but in its vicinity. Sera, already mentioned, stands about four miles behind the Potala; Depung is about six miles away, on the road to India; and Galden is hidden in a circle of mountains twenty miles distant.

These three, even if they are the largest and the most powerful, being state lamaseries, are not the only ones which Thibetans hold in high esteen. Amongst others, one can name Tashilhumpo, the monastery of the Penchen rinpoche.[1] It is located at Shigatze, in the Tsang province, and is considered to be the highest seat of learning in all Thibet. Several days' march from it stands the old historical monastery of Sakya, where lives the head of an important "Red Cap" sect. It contains an unique library of old Sanskrit and Thibetan manuscripts. Besides these, there exist many others, such as Lhabrang Tashikyil in Amdo, Kum-Bum in the same province, Zogchen in the solitudes of northeastern Thibet, and countless others.

Thibet is essentially a monastic country. While in the West our important buildings are generally schools, hospitals, factories and other products of worldly activities, in Thibet the gompas[2] are the only edifices offered to the attention of the traveller. Standing on the summits, silhouetted against the azure sky, or else concealed in the recesses of the mountains, all over the country, they symbolize a lofty ideal but one little understood nowadays even by their inmates.

The religious communities of Thibet form little states within the state, of which they are almost entirely independent. All are possessed of lands and cattle. As a rule, they carry on commerce of some kind. The larger gompas rule over a considerable territory peopled by tenants whose condition resembles that of the serfs of Europe in the Middle Ages. They cultivate, for their own profit, the land belonging to the monasteries and in return they pay each year a definite quantity of cereals, forage, and so forth. The families who devote them-

---

[1] "Penchen rinpoche," known to the foreigners as "Tashi lama," is the equal and even the superior from the religious point of view of the Dalai lama, but he has no temporal power.

[2] *Gompa*, monastery.

selves to rearing cattle pay their debt in butter, cheese, wool, and dried cow dung for fuel, and the surplus produce of the *doks* [1] also goes to them. All these serfs are obliged to undertake certain statute labours, such as the transport of the baggage of the lamas when they travel, and of the goods sent for sale to other regions by the managers of the monastery's temporal affairs, also the repair of the monastic buildings and various other menial offices. They are also forbidden to leave the country without obtaining permission, but this is rarely refused to anyone who wishes to absent himself for the purpose of trading, studying, making a pilgrimage, or any other good reason.

However restricted the liberty of these tenants may be, their situation is infinitely preferable to that of their compatriots established upon the domain of some great lay lord, and especially of those who are directly dependent upon the central government. It is rare for the heads of the monasteries to be hard upon their subjects, and, in return for the tax they pay, the peasants are really and effectively protected by the high religious dignitaries upon whom they depend. They also escape official civil jurisdiction. The misdemeanours and even crimes they may commit are judged by dignitaries of the *gompa* to which they belong.

Latterly, the Lhasa government, although ecclesiastical in character, is seeking to encroach upon the privileges of the monasteries, and especially to reduce their rights of jurisdiction, a fact which arouses vehement protestations, not only from the lamas, but from those under their rule.

The inhabitants of the *gompas* do not live in communities, although a kind of community of wealth exists among them by virtue of the fact that each receives a share of the income of the monastery. Part of these shares are delivered in kind— corn, butter, tea, etc. They differ considerably in importance, first of all, according to the wealth of the monasteries, and then according to the hierarchical standing of each monk. The

[1] Places where cattle are raised in the solitary pasture lands. Literally, *dok* means solitude, desert.

monks have yet other sources of revenue: a portion of the gifts given to their *gompa*, the performance of religious ceremonies, the presents offered by the relatives of the young men they instruct, etc. Lack of space makes it impossible for me to mention all of them in detail.

In spite of all the criticism that may justly be directed against the *gompas*, they afford an excellent retreat for the student, the thinker, and anyone else who desires an intellectual or spiritual life. Almost entirely free from material cares, the humblest lama may give himself up to a leisurely study of the religious and philosophical literature of his country, and if he succeeds in learning Chinese or Sanskrit and thus extending the field of his researches, he is greatly admired by his colleagues.

It is very true that many lamas do not seem to possess any of the qualities which a religious vocation demands, but the way in which they have been brought into the monasteries often affords sufficient excuse. Every Thibetan family esteems it an honour for one or more of its sons to adopt the religious habit; and, to this end, the boys destined to the priestly state are taken to the *gompa* at the age of eight or nine, and handed over to a master charged with their education.

Life vows do not exist among the Buddhists, who believe in the fundamental impermanence of all things, and these children may, therefore, return later on to the world and live as laymen without incurring the disesteem of their compatriots. Some of them do so; but many, not feeling sufficiently courageous to apprentice themselves to any other career, maintain the habit of the Order without respecting it as they should. As a rule, these drones of lamaism, somewhat lazy and gossiping, a trifle too gluttonous and especially too greedy of gain, are charitable and hospitable folks in spite of their faults. We may add to their credit, moreover, that however feeble their morals or limited their intelligence, they do maintain a reverence for learning and saintliness, being always ready to venerate those of their companions who rise above them by virtue of erudition or loftiness of character.

A large monastery in Thibet is a veritable town, the population of which sometimes amounts to as many as ten thousand persons. It is composed of a network of streets and alleys, squares and gardens. Temples in larger or smaller numbers, the assembly halls of the different colleges, and the palaces of the dignitaries rise above the common dwellings, their gilded roofs and terraces surmounted by banners and divers ornaments. In the *gompa* every lama lives by himself in a house of which he is sole proprietor, whether he has had it built at his own cost or bought or inherited it. This dwelling may be bequeathed by the lama to one of his pupils or to a relative, but the legatee must himself belong to the religious Order. No layman is allowed to possess a house in a monastery.

Certain high monastic palaces are veritable museums, full of artistic treasures. In them have been accumulated gifts received by a long line of Grand Lamas, or precious things acquired by themselves, over a period of several centuries. Enamel, lacquer, rare porcelain, marvellous embroideries, and the paintings of Chinese or Thibetan artists are to be seen there. To find such manors isolated in the midst of the vast steppes, or hidden in immense virgin forests, seems like a fairy tale. But is not everything a fairy tale in this extraordinary country, even to the name it gives itself, that of *Khang Yul*, "the land of snows"?

I have had the privilege, unique in these days, of living in several monasteries. After what I have said of them, and of their separate houses, one can understand how it was possible for a woman to live there. Nevertheless, there is a rule against such admission, and only very special reasons—my age, the studies I was pursuing, and, above all, powerful protection—procured me this privilege.

For more than two years I translated Thibetan books in the celebrated monastery of Kum-Bum in Amdo, in the northeast of Thibet, beyond the great Desert of Grass. There, seated on my balcony, on certain evenings, I could hear the lamas' orchestra playing on the roof terrace of the great assembly hall. The concert was being given to the gods. It was they, the Invisible Ones, whom it was desired to charm, attract, cause for a moment to rest, and smile among their younger brothers, the humans! What was asked of them? Nothing . . . nothing but to take pleasure in the music of our world. This was charming in its infantile poetry, and what miscreant would have dared to doubt that the light-footed goddesses did not brush over our dwellings, hastening toward the sweet strains that called them.

Meanwhile, in the vast edifice scarcely lighted by the lamps placed before the magnificent tombs and gilded statues of defunct lamas, the monks were seated motionless, attired in dark-crimson togas. They were chanting in deep tones solemn sentences of mystic import or transcendental philosophy, which raised the mind above captivating illusions.

Above them, the last notes of the bewitching melodies melted away, and soon the recitation of the sacred writings itself came to an end. A rapid gesture, symbolising the void, brought the vesper service to its close, and each lama returned to his own abode.

However great the charms of the studious life I led at Kum-Dum, and of the romantic surroundings in which I dwelt, they could not efface or lessen the impression made upon me by certain simple *gompas*, offering none of the splendours of the wealthy monastic city of Amdo. One of these was perched like an aerie, upon a mountain spur surrounded by forests. The villages, planted in the depths of the valleys, remained invisible from the monastery, and all around it was silence and solitude. There one could behold no princely palace, no temple crammed with ancient treasures. Some whitewashed cabins made of branches and clay served as dwellings for the humble lamas of this rustic hermitage.

The configuration of the surrounding mountain ranges arrested the passage of the clouds, and forced them to turn around the rocky summit which supported the *gompa*, forming a sea of white mist, with its waves beating silently against the cells of the monks, wreathing the wooded slopes and creating a thousand fanciful landscapes as they rolled by. Terrible hailstorms would often break over the monastery, due, said the countryfolk, to the malignity of the demons who sought to disturb the peace of the saintly monks.

The site lent itself admirably to the fearful imaginings of occult forces, and of those singular encounters with beings of other worlds. According to old traditions, gods and devils haunted the neighbouring forests, and for this reason *gompchens* [1] buried themselves in their depths, in pursuit of ends known only to themselves. I had my hut there, a tiny dwelling under the giant trees. The lamas built it for me, partly out of respect, but partly also, doubtless, from a spice of mischief, desiring to test my courage and see whether I dared to rival their mystics by living there alone, in the company of the phantoms. One night a storm of unusual violence overthrew my cell of branches and scattered its covering to the winds of heaven. Knowing the superstitious credulity of my friends the lamas, I insisted that it should be put up again in the same place. If I had left it, they would have been sure to conclude that the incensed deities had driven away the stranger who had been rash enough to establish herself in their district, and for me all chance of further study would have been lost.

The hut having been rebuilt, I had brought there a store of provisions to last a month, and expressly forbade anybody to visit my quarters for that length of time. My days passed peacefully, in company with the birds, which did not appear at all disturbed by my presence. Some roes came to look at me, and one day a big bear appeared, seemingly much surprised to find me there. Thus, in reading, musing, and cooking my sole daily repast, I awaited the end of my retreat. Spring was at hand. When the lamas came back to seek me, they found flowers growing around my dwelling, and I myself was flourishing. They thought I had overcome the dread forces, and the respect they manifested for me was enormously enhanced. Later on, I lived in another more remote hermitage close to the everlasting snows, and that time a prolonged stay of several years acquainted me with the secrets and the bliss of the Thibetan *gompchens'* life.

[1] Ascetics given up to meditation.

How many of these desert monasteries I could describe! I am thinking of one of them, a nunnery, isolated in the midst of rocks and glaciers, access to which is possible only during the four months from June to September.[1] After this short summer, the barrier of snow is raised once more and the recluses are immured for the rest of the year. Yet the *gompa*, however far it may be from the bustle and activity of the village, fails to satisfy the exacting mysticism of Thibetan thinkers. Farther in the deserts, higher still on their giant peaks, they seek caves and almost inaccessible shelters, where they may meditate and be ever alone, face to face with the Infinite and the Eternal.

The holiest temple of Thibet, which I went to see after my visit at the Potala, is called Jo Khang (the House of the Lord). It was built to shelter an ancient image of Siddharta Gautama as a youth, before he became a Buddha. That image was made in India and is supposed to have been carried to China about the first century B.C. The Chinese emperor, Thaijung T'aitsung, gave it as a dowry to his daughter when she married the Thibetan king, Srong Tsan Gampo. Amongst the credulous Thibetans many legends circulate about the image and its origin. Many say that it was self-created, and it is firmly believed to have spoken on several occasions.

Beside the Jowo (Lord) altar in front of which burn thousands of lamps, there are, in the temple, a large number of rooms that contain images of deities and of holy men.

A strange sight is the crowd of pilgrims perambulating silently in the dark, windowless edifice between these motionless personages, many of which are life size. The yellowish light of the butter lamps adds to the strangeness of the spectacle. From a distance it is sometimes difficult to distinguish the living beings from the host of dummies who receive their homage.

---

[1] The path leading to the hermitage where I stayed was also blocked from the middle of December to April. This is a common thing with anchorites' dwellings in Thibet.

Although the statues are of no artistic interest whatever, one receives a deep impression from those many faces, immutably serene, whose gaze seems fixed on some inward object and which tell of a mystic method that establishes the mind in an everlasting calm.

I felt saddened at beholding the procession of worshippers, lost in superstition and exactly following the path that was condemned by the very one whose memory they worship. "Beings led by ignorance, who tramp for fathomless ages the sorrowful road to renewed births and deaths," as the Buddhist Scriptures say.

However, the many sacristans and sextons, who, wrapped in their dark-red togas, are conspicuous everywhere in the temple, do not find any cause for sadness in the affluence of pilgrims. It is all profit to them, for they allow themselves a large share in the offerings of the faithful. They can be seen watching the crowd, ready to seize upon those who appear the richest or the most devout, from whom the biggest gratuities may be expected. As soon as the little group of pilgrims or the lone devotee is in their power, there is no end to the wonders they are led to witness, the holy relics that are placed for a second on their heads, the holy water that they are made to drink from various gold and silver pots, the stories that they must hear. And invariably an offering is requested by the comrades of the guide in charge of the various shrines.

I humbly confess that, as it could not have been my wealthy appearance which attracted these cunning fellows, it must have been my air of profound stupidity, for I was quickly provided with several uncalled-for guides, who took me into the most remote corners of the edifice, exhibiting a lot of articles of piety. I might have thought I was back in European Rome with its greedy sacristans.

I was again mistaken for a Ladaki. As I walked around a shrine, trying to avoid tasting of holy water once more (I had been sufficiently refreshed by previous draughts), I heard behind me a compassionate voice:

"Oh!" said some one, "give holy water to that poor woman

who has come from Ladak . . . so far away. How great is
her faith! . . ."

This time it was not the desire for money, but kind feelings,
which prompted the lamas. I saw young and smiling faces
around me. A man took hold of my arm and guided me to
the proper place, while others pushed away the pilgrims in
front of us. I could now admire, close to, more gems, more
golden and silver ornaments. A jewelled pot was bent toward
my hands, which I extended in the orthodox fashion. "Let
me drink and wet my head." I thought, "This is my baptism
as a Ladaki."

I had a happy inspiration when I chose the beginning of the
year for my stay at Lhasa, for at any other time it would not
have been possible for me to see so many strange festivals
and interesting ceremonies. Mingling with the crowds of holi-
day-makers, I saw cavalcades of gentlemen richly attired in the
style of past ages: and cavalry and the infantry of the ancient
kings, in their coats of mail, bearing shields and bucklers,
recalling the Thibet of former days. There was a certain
amount of horse-racing. It was disorderly, mad, joyous, and
amusing, but not to be compared, from the point of view of
horsemanship, with that of the *dokpas* in the Desert of Grass.

On several occasions I saw the man who is recognised as
the most learned in all the country, and who occupies the
throne of Tsong-Khapa.[1] Throughout the first month of the
year he preaches in the open air, under a canopy erected for
this purpose, close to the Jo-Khang. His audience is not
recruited from the crowd, as one might think from the fact that
he speaks outside the temple. The monks alone have the right
to sit crosslegged on the pavement at his feet, and those who
hear the preaching have been chosen by their superiors. They
are there by command. Woe to anyone who spoke to
his neighbour, and who did not maintain an absolutely motion-

---

[1] The founder of the Geluk pa sect. Literally, the sect of those who
have "virtuous customs," that known by the Westerners as "Yellow Cap"
sect.

less attitude. Woe also to the unfortunate layman whose religious zeal led him hither to listen to the discourses of the Supreme Master. The clerics acting as police officers for the assembly would soon lash him roughly with the long bundle of ropes they flourish continually in a martial fashion.

The great philosopher of Thibet is a spare old man with a thin, angular countenance and the appearance of an aristocratic and haughty ascetic. He walks with short, quick steps beneath the yellow-brocaded umbrella of honour which a friar holds over him, as if he were anxious to have done quickly with an annoying duty. The expression stamped on his intelligent face is that of the suppressed boredom of one to whom crowds and public ceremonies are distasteful.

Seated upon his throne, he does not preach in the way we understand the word in the West. He speaks without gestures, without raising his voice, with an air of detachment, such as the theories he is explaining demand. The striking contrast afforded by the doctrines expounded by the doctor, together with his refined appearance, and the ignorant, listless crowd, watched by the brutal clerical policemen surrounding him, are well calculated to surprise a stranger. As to *Ser ti rimpoche*,[1] being born, brought up and having grown old in such an environment, he probably does not notice it.

The first penetration of Western civilization into Lhasa may be traced in the uniforms of the khaki-clad soldiers. I really enjoyed seeing them, headed by a band which played English tunes not too badly, marching with a swaggering step out of time with the music. They are armed, as has been said before, with old English rifles that are still up-to-date in most parts of central Asia, and even possess a few pieces of mountain artillery that are carried by mules. They are immensely proud of the latter and air these short, fat, toad-like weapons in and out of season. One of them burst, killing several men, but the

---

[1] *Ser ti rimpoche*, "the precious golden throne," is the familiar appellation which the people of Lhasa give this high lamaist dignitary. His real title is *Galden Tipa*, "he who occupies the throne of Galden." That is to say, the throne of Tsong Khapa, founder of the Galden monastery.

accident did not lessen the admiration that the Lhasapas have for those which remain. In that blessed country, occurrences of that kind are even sometimes believed to be auspicious. In this connection, I can relate an incident which happened during my stay at Lhasa.

It is the custom, during the first month of the year, to make *mos* and to look in many ways for omens regarding the prosperity or ill luck that is to come to the state and especially to the person of the Dalai lama.

One of the omens is obtained in a rather strange way. Three tents are erected, and in each of them an animal is shut—a cock, a goat, and a hare. These beasts have, hung around their necks, charms which have been blessed by the Dalai lama. A number of men must fire at the tents, and if any of the animals are wounded or killed it means that calamities are awaiting Thibet and its ruler. If this happens, the monks of the three great monasteries, Sera, Galden, and Depung, must assemble and read the sacred Scriptures for twenty days and perform several ceremonies to counteract the ill will of the deities.

The year I was at Lhasa about twenty-five shots were fired at the tents, instead of fifteen, which is the usual number. English, Chinese, and Thibetan rifles were used. One of the last burst, and the man who fired it was severely wounded and died the next day. The fact that no tent had been hit, even after that prolonged test, was considered as most auspicious, and the accident that caused the death of the man added greatly to the confidence of the Thibetans regarding the welfare of the Lama-King! The unfortunate commoner, they thought, had been taken by some angry demon as a substitute for the most precious existence of the ruler.

During the many years I had spent among Thibetans I had exceptional opportunities of seeing at first hand the life of the different classes of people; but never before had I penetrated so deeply into the intimacy of the common folk as I did during my stay in Lhasa. The hovel in which I had found shelter was the centre of a small caravanserai where the strangest specimens of humanity were to be met. The wealthiest guests only slept under a roof, the others remaining in the open. Every act, even every thought, was public. I really lived in a novel whose plot was slum life, but what amusing and exotic slums! They had nothing of the lugubrious physical and mental aspect of those of the West. All were dirty and ragged, food was coarse and often scarce, but everybody enjoyed the great luminous blue sky, and the bright life-giving sun, and waves of joy swept through the minds of these unlucky ones devoid of worldly wealth. No one practiced any trade or craft. They lived, as birds do, on what they could pick up daily.

Apart from the acute lack of any comfort, I did not suffer among my strange neighbours. They never suspected who I was, and they treated me with simplicity and kindness as one of themselves.

Some had known better days. One was the youngest son of a man who possessed a little wealth. He had married a well-to-do widow much older than himself, and might have prospered, but idleness, drinking, and gambling had ruined him. When his wife had become aged he had taken a mistress, and after a time the legitimate spouse, who realised that she would end in poverty if she kept her unworthy husband, managed to get rid of him in a rather clever way. She called together his and her relatives, and declared her intention of retiring by herself to consecrate her last years to devotion. Her husband, she said, was in love with his mistress; she did not object to their marriage (polygamy as well as polyandry is legal in Thibet), but they would have to leave her house, to assume all debts that the man had made, and to agree that she was free from any obligation toward her husband. In fact, it was divorce. The man consented, a deed of marriage was drafted, and he went with his new wife.

The life of the former lovers was far from being smooth when I happened to make their acquaintance. The husband was a good-hearted, weak fellow, but an inveterate drunkard,

285

who was generally unconscious soon after noon, and so remained until the next morning. The wife, more than once, kept him company. Nevertheless, she was the more active of the pair and of a cleverer turn of mind. Indeed, her cleverness was the subject of tremendous quarrels. The husband asserted that during his prolonged sleep the woman stole his remaining properties—household utensils, blankets, etc. . . . The wife complained that her consort had sold her jewels and gambled with the product. When she raised her voice to a pitch high enough to arouse the drunkard from his stupor— and that feat required strong lungs—a picturesque dialogue followed. Often the man took a heavy stick that he had always at hand, being somewhat crippled by gout, and the lady then received a first-rate bastinado that left her weeping and bruised before anyone had time to come to her help. The room was very small, with only one door on the outside, and the cunning husband, who was a very stout man, always managed to block it with his fat body, a position from which he could reach his old sweetheart with his long stick in whichever corner she ran.

The miserable house was divided in three. The entrance room was occupied by the quarrelling couple I have just mentioned. I had a narrow cell at one side of it, and a dark room at the back sheltered another most remarkable pair.

They also had lived golden days. The housewife's manners were those of a woman of good family. Her husband, who owned some property at the time of their marriage, had been appointed an officer in the Thibetan army during the war with China. Then, as had been the case with his neighbour, gambling and drinking had ruined him.

Complete poverty did not, however, abate his pride. He was a very tall, rather handsome man, full of contempt for work, and he assumed the dignified mien of a knight bearing undeserved misfortune. Everybody addressed him with a Thibetan title somewhat corresponding to our "captain." To accept a humble job seemed repugnant to the aristocratic feelings of the "Captain," and as the government did not offer him a ministerial seat, he nobly took to the independent profession of begging. Each morning, after drinking his tea, my neighbour went out, a courier bag slung over his shoulder and a wallet thrown on it the way the hidalgos of yore carried their cape. Staff in hand, he walked, head erect, too conscious of his superiority even to condescend to be arrogant.

The "Captain" did not come back home before sunset. He lunched somewhere, taking nobody into his confidence as to the invitations he received. He was witty enough to be pleasant, and enjoyed a kind of celebrity all over Lhasa. People, amused by his manners, gave him what he requested casually, as if the aim of his daily outing was only to call as one gentleman on other gentlemen. He succeeded with that method, and his wife and his two children were regularly fed with the contents of the bags he brought back duly filled each evening.

The trouble in the drunkard's home grew worse when a turquoise ornament belonging to the housewife disappeared. At first the *nemo* accused her husband. But innocence prevailed, and the culprit was discovered in the person of the maidservant—for the lady of the small entrance room had a maid! Now a strange question was raised. The girl pretended she was entitled to an indemnity for having been called a thief. That term of abuse, she said, did not apply to her, because she had not stolen the jewel; she had found it lying on the ground in the room and had picked it up. Men acting as arbiters, as pleaders, as counsels and witnesses, soon filled the house. Some of them had never seen the turquoise locket or the girl, or heard anything connected with the case. They came early in the morning, ate, drank, and stayed late into the evening. From my small quarters I got the full fun of these strange proceedings, and of the peculiar arguments which were put forward, especially at the end of the afternoon, when spirits had infused original ideas into the brains of the assembly.

Once, when the discussion had been specially heated, the girl and her former lady began to exchange abuse, and then flew at each other. The men present got up to separate them—a rather hard task, for the infuriated females turned their nails against those who dared to meddle in their duel. Anyhow, they succeeded in pushing the maid out of the house, and, to prevent her from coming back, followed her to the street door across the courtyard.

One of those inexplicable thoughts that take possession of drunkards suddenly made the master of the house fix the responsibility of the incident upon his wife. He declared that she had brought shame on him before his guests, and he tried to play his usual trick of standing in the doorway and beating her. But this time, excited by her previous struggle, she flung herself at him and tore his long earring [1] from his ear, which bled. He retaliated by knocking her on the head, and she shrieked loudly. The "Captain's" wife ran out of the room to intervene between them. She had not taken two steps on this lilliputian battlefield when she received on the cheek a stroke that was not meant for her, and fell on a bench, calling for help. Yongden being away, I thought it was my duty to prevent the man from seriously hurting his wife, so I walked in with the intention of sheltering the now terrified woman in my room. But people were coming, and escape became possible. "Run away quickly," I urged the woman, protecting her retreat. She passed behind me and I never saw her again.

When the "Captain" came home that evening he found his lady with a swollen cheek that had already begun to turn black. To relate the scene that was then enacted with the flame of a brasero for footlights, exceeds my powers of description. The "Captain" had all the manner of a gifted actor. He declaimed half the night, in turn ferocious, clamoring for revenge, then full of pathos, telling of the suffering of his dame. Again, drawn up to his full height, his head nearly touching the low roof, he would speak of the insult done to his honour. The man to whom that rhetoric was addressed lay on a broken couch, more than half unconscious, and the "Captain," who was himself far from being sober, ended his soliloquy by denouncing the degrading habit of drink.

Next day the "Captain" took Yongden aside and declared

---

[1] Thibetan men, who can afford it, wear a more or less costly earring in the left ear and a small knob in the right one.

his intention of calling me as witness in a suit he meant to bring to obtain damages for his wife's bruised cheek. The young lama tried to persuade him to give up his idea, and offered him a little present. He took the money, but remained obstinate. His wrong was to be avenged, and I ought to help!

When Yongden reported this conversation to me I felt very annoyed. I would have to appear before several people eager to hear about the journey of pilgrims who, like us, had visited a large number of holy places. This would mean long talks, and Yongden and I would of course be questioned about our native land. It might turn out badly for our disguises.

We were drinking tea silently, wondering how we could avoid these dangerous meetings, when the door opened. In Thibet, especially among common folk, one does not knock at the door or ask any permission to enter a room or a house. A man stepped in. After the usual polite greetings, he told us that my neighbour, whom I had helped to escape the day before, intended to divorce her husband and wished me to appear as a witness to testify to her husband's brutality. As in the previous case, I endeavoured to induce the man to allow me to remain neutral, for both husband and wife had been obliging, and I did not want to say anything against either of them. But persuasion was useless, and he retired saying that he would insist upon my evidence being heard.

We thus decided to leave Lhasa for a week, ostensibly for the sake of visiting the great monastery of Galden, where reposes the massive gold and silver be-jewelled tomb of Tsong Khapa, the founder of the "Yellow Hat" sect, and many other interesting sights. That journey was far from being uneventful. Among other incidents, Yongden, when wandering alone through the monastic city, met a man who had known us well for a long time. He of course enquired about me, and the lama told him that I was still in China and that when his pilgrimage was over he would go back to me. Our old acquaintance then invited him to drink tea, but Yongden declined, saying that he did not feel very well and would call on another occasion. He quickly rejoined me, and as, happily, we had finished visiting the various shrines and the country around the monastery, we made haste to leave the place.

At Lhasa much tea and spirits had been drunk, but the two cases were still pending. A new period of festivities was soon to begin, and the judges had postponed the case until after these were over. This completely dispelled my fear, for I had decided to leave the day after the great *Ser Pang* pageant.

But I had not yet finished with the comedies and dramas enacted by my curious neighbours. One night I was awakened by one of the open-air lodgers of the courtyard, an old woman who asked help for her daughter, who seemed to be about to die. Yongden and I and the "Captain" and his wife ran hastily outside. We found the girl seated; she appeared to breathe with difficulty and uttered strange sounds a little like the noise of an engine letting off steam. "I understand now," the mother told us. "The god rides her." [1]

The girl was a *pamo.* I had seen a number of these people in trances, including this young woman herself a few weeks before, but that night she looked particularly excited. Her mother and sister hastened to fasten on her the symbolic ornaments of the *pamo,* amongst others the hat called *rigs nga*— because it bears five (nga) pictures of *Dhyani* Buddhas, each of them, according to lamaism, the spiritual father of a lineage (*rigs*).

She began to shake her head and to dance. Her chanting, which had at first been no more than a murmur, became louder and louder until she shrieked. Two dogs were tied up in the courtyard. The good beasts did not appreciate this nocturnal performance, which no doubt troubled their sleep. They began to bark, to howl, and finally, one of them succeeded in breaking his chain and jumping toward the *pamo.* Several of those present, who, like myself, occasionally fed the animal, went after it, pushing the *pamo* out of its reach. Like many mastiffs, this one was very mild with the people he knew, so we held him without great difficulty, and tied him up again. The

---

[1] Thibetan expression denoting a medium in a trance.

moon was shining brightly now, and Yongden noticed that the dog had carried something away in its mouth. On looking closer, he saw that it was the *rigs nga*, the *pamo* headgear, that had fallen down in the scramble. The dog kept it between its paws, after the fashion of its race when they begin to rend a piece of cloth.

The *pamo* had stopped her dance. She stood stiff and motionless as a statue. Her mother asked her if she had been hurt, but the girl seemed unconscious and did not answer. Then the old woman noticed that the *rigs nga* was no more on the *pamo's* head.

"Where is my daughter's *rigs nga?*" she lamented immediately. "Where has it fallen? Oh, what a bad omen!"

"The dog has it," I said. "Do not be so sorry; it was an old one. The lama, my son, knows a kind trader in the town. He will beg a new one from him."

I thought that, knowing I would give her another hat, the old beggar would feel consoled, but before I had even finished speaking she screamed loudly:

"Take it away from that dog. . . . It is the god. . . . The god is in it. The dog will kill the god and my daughter will die!"

"Has the dog really got it?" enquired the "Captain."

"Yes," answered Yongden.

"Then the *pamo* will die if he tears it," declared the gentleman mendicant, oracularly. It was not the time to reason with these fools.

At the noise the old mother was making with her: "The dog will kill the god, my daughter will die!" all the guests of our caravanserai had awakened and gathered around us—a picturesque assemblage, moving in confusion under the round and peaceful moon. None of them raised any doubt about the perilous situation of the god and of his medium, but none dared to affront the terrible black animal, the only sensible-looking creature amongst them, who regarded this unusual nocturnal agitation with the utmost astonishment and thus forgot to play with the *rigs nga*. The old woman was growing hysterical, her daughter remained lifeless as a dummy.

"A magic *phurba* is needed," a dishevelled orator said at last, and he began to explain how it was to be used by a duly initiated lama, in order to overpower the demon who had entered the dog and made him seize the *rigs nga* and devour the vital principles of the god and of his medium, which no doubt dwelt in the symbolic hat. But no magic *dague* was available. The "Captain" cut short the discourse.

"I will fetch my sword," he announced, "and stab the animal from behind."

I felt indignant that the stupid coward should murder the poor innocent dog. I could not bear the thought of it.

"Let me do it," I said. "I shall get the *rigs nga!*" Turning to Yongden, I ordered: "Make quickly a big ball of *tsampa.*"

He ran into the house and I went to the dog. It was a little risky. These Thibetan watchdogs do not like even their masters to take things away from them. Anyhow, the big animal got up when I spoke to it, and while I patted its head I quickly gave the witch's crown a kick and sent it flying some distance away. The mastiff did not notice it, or it did not care. Its attention was attracted toward Yongden, who came out with the ball of flour. "Eat that, my friend," I said. "It will be more tasty and nourishing than a god."

The afflicted mother immediately replaced the dirty hat upon the head of her *pamo,* and the latter suddenly recovered from her seeming insensibility and began to gyrate like a top. "The god has come back," shouted the ragged listeners. Then they began to tell one another strange stories about cases of the same kind that had ended badly for *pawos* or *pamos.* Each one had a miracle a wonder to relate but I had quite enough of the affair and hurried back to my cell.

The day had come when the annual ceremony of driving the "scapegoat" out of the town was to take place. The Thibetan scapegoat, unlike that mentioned in the Bible, is not an animal, but a man conscious of the part he is playing. It is supposed by the Thibetans that lamas expert in magic can divert to him the causes which would deliver others into the hands of the evil spirits, bringing upon them poverty, illness, death, and misfortunes of all kinds. So each year a voluntary victim called *Lus kong kyi gyalpo* (the King of Impurity) charged with the iniquities of the ruler and of his subjects is sent to sandy Samye, which is a Sahara in miniature. The lure of a considerable profit always induces some poor fellows to risk the adventure. There may be a certain amount of skepticism in their minds about the demons and the danger of becoming their prey; but more likely the *Lus kong kyi gyalpos* expect to be able to secure for a large fee some lama—still cleverer than those who charge him with the people's sins—who will cleanse and protect them. However, either on account of the atavistic credulity that they are incapable of shaking off entirely, or for some other reason, these human "scapegoats" often die prematurely, suddenly or in mysterious circumstances, or are afflicted with strange diseases. A former *Lus kong kyi gyalpo* died during my stay at Lhasa, the day before his successor was to be driven away to Samye!

I did not fail to wander through the town during the week that preceded the sending away of the "scapegoat," and watch him collecting the tax to which he is lawfully entitled by the government. He was dressed in a good Thibetan robe and would not have been recognisable but for the tail of a black yak which he held in his hand. He entered the shops and passed through the market, requesting money or offerings in kind. If any one tried to escape at too little cost, *Lus kong kyi gyalpo* remonstrated briefly with him. Had he not obtained what he wanted, he would have waved the yak tail above the head of the miser or on the threshold of his house, a gesture of malediction producing the most terrible consequences. All were giving liberally, it appeared, for I did not see *Lus kong kyi gyalpo* flourish the enormous hairy yak tail. A discussion arose on one occasion, and though I was too far away to hear the words, I had no doubt about the subject. The future "scapegoat" grew impatient and half raised his hand holding the strange weapon, but then several men intervened, and all ended satisfactorily, for I heard them laughing.

Lus kong kyi gyalpo collects his tax at the doors of the

wealthiest and highest in rank, as well as at those of the poor. The result is a veritable fortune for a man of a low station in life, as he always is.

I wondered if he would visit my hostelry; but he must have thought it really not worth his while to trouble the beggars who lived there for the few copper coins he might have gathered. Anyway, he did not appear. Fate caused us to meet once in the street, and the strange personage extended his hand toward me. Out of fun, I wished to see him use the black tail, so I said: "I am a pilgrim who has come from far away. I have no money." He only looked at me, sternly replying: "Give." "But I have nothing," I replied. Then he slowly lifted his arm, as I had seen him do in the market, and I should certainly have enjoyed the sight of the waving of the yak tail over my head but for two well-dressed ladies who stopped him, saying, hastily: "We will give for her!" They put a few small coins into the hand of the man, who went his way. "Atsi! mother, you do not know," the two kind women explained. "Had he waved that tail over your head you would never have seen your country again!"

On the day when *Lus kong kyi gyalpo* was to be driven away a dense crowd assembled along the road that the Dalai lama would follow to go to the Jo Khang, where he was to preside over the ceremony in which the "scapegoat" would be charged with the impurities of the people. This year, according to his horoscope, was a critical period of his life. A supplementary protection had therefore been arranged. Perhaps he thought, in all humility, that the weight of his own errors was sufficient for one man, and had consequently secured a private "scapegoat." The official *Lus kong kyi gyalpo* was to run to Samye as usual, while his colleague would turn northward and reach the first pass on the Mongolian road.

Soon the representatives of the clerical police, armed with saplings (readers must not think that my imperfect knowledge of the English language makes me write that word for another; they were really young thin trees, about ten feet long), began to maul the mob in order to clear the way for the kingly lama.

The scene was similar to that which I had witnessed on the evening of the butter *torma* festival, but on a much larger scale. I cannot relate all the comical incidents of the chase—men who dropped their belongings, fleeing women who fell down, children dragged along in tears. Nevertheless, everybody was merry, even those who were hit and must have felt their bones aching. People were penned like cattle in a large open place and allowed to breathe a little under the strict watch of various kinds of policemen armed with whips, enormous straps made of strings of plaited leather, and the saplings already mentioned.

At intervals, somebody ran along shouting orders. The arrival of the Dalai lama was announced. All, women included, had to take their hats off, and those who delayed were soon acquainted with one or another of the lamaist policemen's weapons. Thanks to my short stature, I escaped thumps and thrashings during the hours I stood there. When danger threatened, I always managed to find shelter among a group of tall Thibetans who acted as a protecting roof over my head.

The Dalai lama passed at last, riding a beautiful black mule, and accompanied by a few ecclesiastical dignitaries, all like himself dressed in religious robes—dark-red, yellow, and gold brocades, half covered by the dark-red toga. They wore Mongolian round hats of yellow brocade edged with fur. The Commander-in-chief rode before them, while some horse guards clad in khaki led the van and brought up the rear.

After *Lus kong kyi gyalpo* had gone through the ceremony at the Jo Khang I saw him hurried out of the city. He was clad in a coat of white goat fur, and wore one black yak tail as headgear, holding another one in his hand. His face was painted half white and half black. All along the way the crowd shouted and whistled.

More ceremonies were performed to bring back to the city the *yangku* (wealth and prosperity) that might have escaped in the train of the impurities carried off by the "scapegoat." The sun had set before all was over.

A town whose inhabitants had been cleansed in such way and

to which unlimited prosperity was promised, could not but be joyful. So was Lhasa that evening. Everybody was outdoors, chatting, laughing and, especially, drinking. The most hideous beggars, deaf and dumb, blind, eaten up by leprosy, rejoiced as heartily as the wealthiest and noblest citizens. I met acquaintances—I had made a few who did not suspect my origin—and willy-nilly was hurried into a restaurant, where I had to rise to the occasion by eating a great variety of Thibetan dishes. I must confess that I did not find it in the least difficult to submit to that ordeal, since Thibetan cooking is not to be despised.

The day following saw me perched, one among many, on the rocky spur of the Potala, to witness the great pageant called *Serpang*.

Never did I see a more original, more wonderful spectacle. Several thousand men marched in file around the Potala. They carried hundreds of huge multicoloured silk flags, hundreds of embroidered banners and state umbrellas. Dignitaries proceeded slowly under canopies, surrounded by clerics holding censers. Sometimes the procession stopped, and then boys danced. Couples composed of a man carrying a big drum on his back and another who beat the instrument from behind, went through graceful evolutions.

Elephants, also, walked gravely, escorted by fantastic paper monsters of the Chinese variety, performing all kinds of antics. Then, again, there were warriors of yore, clad in coats of mail, and finally, followed by the priestly servants of their temples, came the local deities whom I had already seen the day before.

Several bands marched with the procession, some of them with fifteen foot trumpets borne on the shoulders of several men. These huge musical instruments, sustaining the harmoniously wailing Thibetan hautboys, (*gyalings*) produced a solemn impressive music which filled the whole valley with deep sonorous voices. And when their vibrations had died away, Mongolian musicians delighted our ears with sweet pastoral tunes played on flutes, tinkling bells, and small drums.

The pageant moved in a fairy setting. Under the blue luminous sky and the powerful sun of central Asia the intensified colours of the yellow and red procession, the variegated bright hues of the crowd's dresses, the distant hills shining white, and Lhasa lying on the plain at the foot of the huge Potala capped with glittering gold—all these seemed filled with light and ready to burst into flames. Unforgettable spectacle which alone repaid me for my every fatigue and the myriad dangers that I had faced to behold it!

CHAPTER VIII

I LEFT Lhasa as quietly as I had entered, and no one suspected that a foreign woman had lived there for two months. I looked somewhat different from the beggar I was when I first entered the Forbidden City. I had promoted myself to a more respectable station in the social hierarchy. I was now a lower-middle-class woman, the owner of two horses and accompanied by a man servant whom Yongden had engaged at Lhasa. Official enquiries about travellers going from the capital to the frontiers are not very strict, so I could afford to make myself a little more comfortable. I had also purchased a quantity of books at Lhasa, and as the tour I was undertaking in the south of the country had, as its special object the hunt for old manuscripts to add to the excellent Thibetan library I had collected on my previous journeys and which was safely housed in China, horses were needed to carry the luggage.

As for myself, I had decided to continue to walk most of the time, finding it—now that I had no longer a load to carry—a most enjoyable sport.

One sunny morning in spring I followed once more the wide street leading to the Potala, across gardens where trees were now gay with the fresh pale green garb of new leaves.

I passed the gate of Norbu ling, smiling at the idea that the ruler of Thibet, who lived there, little imagined that I had been so near to him for so long a time. He knew me personally, since we had met more than once in the Himâlayas. He was indeed largely responsible both for my present journey and the previous ones, having pressed me to undertake a thorough study of the Thibetan language and literature. I had followed his advice, and the growing interest in Thibet which I had derived from my study had finally led me, after years of travel, to the Dalai lama's own capital. Had I given my name, and

298

had he been free, he might have liked to see me again, but his present Western suzerain does not allow him as much freedom as his Chinese master did. Whatever may be his own inclinations, he is no more at liberty to welcome a foreigner who is not sent to him, than he is to forbid his door to those who are recommended or delegated to him. So I went my way.

We crossed the river Kyi and ascended a small pass. There I looked back for a last vision of Lhasa. From that distance the Potala alone could be seen—a tiny castle suspended, it seemed, in the air like a mirage. I remained for a while gazing at the graceful vision, remembering the toils and troubles that my stay in Lhasa had cost me. I had had my reward. In a hearty *Mölam* I wished spiritual enlightenment and material welfare to all beings visible or invisible who lived in the Forbidden City that had been hospitable to me, and then, turning to the south, I began my descent. Lhasa had forever gone from my eyes and taken its place in my world of memories.

Quite near Lhasa, on the left bank of the Brahmaputra, one finds a miniature Sahara whose extensive white dunes are invading the whole country. One can observe there, though on a much smaller scale, a phenomenon like that witnessed in Northern Kansu and in Chinese Turkestan, where the Gobi[1] has swallowed up immense territories occupied, centuries ago, by flourishing estates.

In spite of a ridge which stood in their way, the sands have taken a firm footing in the Kyi Valley, and though still shallow on that side, their fine dust is beginning to accumulate along the hedges which border Norbu ling, the pleasure garden of the Dalai lama. It may possibly be that in a few generations Lhasa will be reached. Who knows whether, in a still more distant future, some savant, excavating the entirely submerged city, may not discover the Potala and the Jo Khang, just as

---

[1] *Gobi*, in Chinese—at least in the dialect spoken in Kansu and Turkestan—means a *desert*, so that to say the "desert of Gobi" is in fact a redundancy.

we now lay bare the palaces and temples which the sands of the great Gobi have overwhelmed.

On our way we passed the monastery of Dorjee Thag, most picturesquely situated against a rocky cliff on the river shore, with a small village at its foot. Farther off there were a few more villages whose fields are gradually disappearing beneath the mounting sands.

That snowy-white desert region through which the Brahmaputra, like a huge azure snake, winds its way serenely, imparts to the Samye monastery a peculiar air of mystery. Traces of miraculous events are pointed out all over the country. A high isolated rock, standing strangely in the bed of the river, bears witness to one of the most remarkable of these prodigies. Once upon a time this giant had removed from India toward the heights of Thibet. What was the goal of its adventurous journey? One cannot tell. Perhaps it felt impressed by the calm beauty of the wide Brahmaputra valley, its turquoise sky and its blue river, and, struck with admiration, its enormous bulk came to rest upon the sand. Since then, an unbroken trance has held it there, alone in the desert, its feet bathed in the stream. I envied it as I passed. Like it, why could not I seat myself on the shore of the blue river, and remain there forever, wrapped in solitude, sunken in unshaken rapture? . . .

Samye is an historical site. In the eighth century after Christ, the first Buddhist monastery of Thibet was built there. The legend tells that the demons, determined to prevent the erection of the building, pulled down each night the work done by the masons during the day. The famous magician Padmasambhava succeeded not only in conquering them, but in compelling them to become his obedient servants, and with their aid he built the monastery in a few nights!

The Samye monastery has long been the seat of powerful lamas; but since the establishment of the "Yellow Cap" sect and the superiority acquired by it over the "Red Cap," in becoming the official clergy of the state, Samye has lost its importance and is now an abandoned place where can be found hardly more than twenty *trapas*.

A number of houses inside the large enclosure of the monastery are now inhabited by the lay tenants of the *gompa* and have become small farms. Yet the few temples still remaining in the deserted monastery are kept in good condition. As successive fires have destroyed not only the original buildings, but those which have replaced them, the present edifices are not of great interest. Yet one of them deserves special mention, for it contains a most dreaded shrine and is the seat of one of the great official oracles of Thibet.

This shrine is called *U Khang* (House of the Vital Breath), because it is said that the breath of every being who dies on the earth is carried in it. There, in an inner room sealed with the seal of the Dalai lama, are placed a chopping-board and a knife of ritualistic shape. With these implements the devils each night cut up invisible corpses and—so say the Thibetans— one can hear from outside the noises of the chopping mingled with cries and laughter. The oracle of Samye alone is allowed to enter the shrine once a year to deposit a new chopping-board and knife. The old ones, which are removed, are then seen to be worn out by the use that has been made of them.

That "breath" which can be chopped seems a somewhat extravagant invention. It is but the popular gross interpretation of some esoteric beliefs and rites of the *nagspa*. Stories to make one's hair stand on end are told concerning the *U Khang*. Struggles of tortured "breath" against ferocious beings of another world, thrilling escapes of ghosts in search of the body which has been theirs, racing with infuriated female devils in pursuit of them! All the elements necessary to a first-rate nightmare may be gathered in the tales to which the *U Khang* has given birth.

Years ago, when the Lama Chöskyong[1] entered the shrine, he was allowed to be accompanied by a few members of his ecclesiastical household, but a dramatic incident put an end to that privilege. Once as he was on the point of leaving, the

[1] Chöskyong (Sanskrit: Dharmapala) or "protector of the Religion." Title of some deities in Mahâyâna and especially in Tankrit Buddhism, that is given to human beings amongst lamaists.

Changzöd [1] who followed the lama felt as if somebody was tugging at his *zen* [2] from behind.

"Kusho! Kusho!" he exclaimed, addressing the *Chöskyong,* "somebody is pulling my robe!"

Both men turned to look behind them. The room was empty! They then continued to proceed toward the door where, just as he was about to step out after the *Chöskyong,* the *Changzöd* fell dead!

Since then, the Lama alone enters the abode of the eaters of "breath," as he only is believed capable of protecting himself by the recitation of secret spells.

Outside the door of the shrine one can see a number of leather bags which represent the invisible wrappings in which the "breaths" are carried to the *U Khang.* There exist, say the people connected with the shrine, sorcerers who, while in a trance and unconscious of what they do, perform the peculiar function of seizing the "breaths" of the departed and bringing them to Samye.

But I must cut short this account. The field of the occult seems boundless in Thibet. Occult lore may there be studied at all stages and in all forms, from the most absurd, degraded, and repulsive, to those whose manifestations give cause for reflection and contravene all preconceived ideas.

Beginning with the ignorant quack who treats the villagers with words and gestures, the meaning of which is as unknown to him as to his clients, we may, before we arrive at the aristocracy of magic and witchcraft, make the acquaintance of many picturesque personages who roam about the country or remain rooted in retreats extremely difficult of access.

Incidentally, in the course of the preceding chapters, I have mentioned the *mopas,* who predict the future and discover hidden things; the vagrant *naljorpas* who, aping the true ascetics of that name, pretend that they can command the deities and the demons; and the *pawos* and their female col-

---

[1] Changzöd: Head steward.
[2] *Zen:* the monastic toga.

leagues the *pamos*, a variety of mediums who deliver oracular pronouncements in trances. The smallest fry of these last grovel miserably in the towns and villages, offering their services in exchange for food, while the greatest among them are highly honoured, lordly beings, living in sumptuous abodes and occupying, under the title of *Chöskyong*, high official positions.

There is also in Thibet a curious class, including persons of both sexes, but especially women, who are reputed to be hereditary keepers of "poison." What poison? Nobody knows. No one has ever seen a trace of it, but this very mystery adds to the terror it inspires. When the fatal times arrives, the one who is to administer it cannot escape the obligation. In default of a passerby who may afford him an opportunity, he must pour it out for one of his friends or relatives. One hears whispers of mothers who have poisoned their only sons, of husbands who have been obliged to hand the fatal cup to a dearly loved bride the day of their marriage; and if there is no one within reach, the "keeper" must drink the deadly potion himself.

I have seen a man who was said to be the hero of a strange poison story. He was travelling, and on his way through a village he entered a farm to obtain refreshment. The mistress of the house prepared him some beer by pouring hot water upon fermented grain placed in a wooden pot, according to the custom of the Himâlayan Thibetans. She then went upstairs. When left alone the traveller remarked, with some astonishment, that the beer placed before him, in the wooden vessel, was boiling in great bubbles. Near by water was also boiling in a cauldron, but in a natural way. The man took a large ladle of this, and emptied it over the suspicious-looking beer. At that moment he heard a fall on the floor above his head. The woman who had served him had fallen down dead.

This "poison" is a source of great worry to travellers in Thibet. There exist peculiar wooden bowls, which, it is maintained, are sensitive to the presence of poison in any beverage poured into them, and for that reason they are sold at very high prices.

Strange to say, in some households the family is convinced

that the mother possesses "poison." Where does she hide it? Nobody tries to find out, for all are convinced that there is no cure for such a fatality. They look askance at, spy upon the gestures and words of the unhappy woman, who in the end often comes to believes that this "poison" of hers really exists. Even the death of the tormented person does not put an end to the danger. The "poison" seems inexhaustible. It is transmitted, and the legatee has no power to refuse it. Willy-nilly, he is obliged to become a poisoner in his turn. It must be understood, however that when they administer the "poison," as well as when they bequeath it to a successor, these "keepers" are acting unconsciously, as the passive agents of another will. Nor do they remember their action afterward.

The *tantrik* rites, in the course of which the participants eat a piece of the flesh of a corpse, and others still more extraordinary—the art of prolonging life with all the energy of youth, by seizing upon the vitality of others; levitation and so forth—all these are practised, it is said, by small groups professing esoteric principles.[1]

There is an order of *nagspas* whose members are reputed to be experts in the science of killing, slowly or suddenly, from a distance. They are also said to be able to chase away evil spirits or to send them to attack some particular individual.

This gives rise to amusing comedies. A man who desires to harm another from jealousy or some other cause, sends for a *nagspa*, begging him to dispatch a devil to worry his enemy. The magician casts his spell, but the peasant, merchant, or noble lord against whom the rite is performed may learn what is going on. Then he has recourse to another *nagspa*, and the play begins. On his arrival the evil spirit finds an adversary whom he cannot conquer, and returns in anger whence he was summoned. His irritation makes him dangerous, and it is essential that he should promptly satisfy his ferocious instincts. For that reason he is sent back again, and once

---

[1] It is impossible to enter into the details of Thibetan mysticism and occultism, a subject greatly exceeding the compass of the present book. I intend to treat it separately, later on, giving the results of my special studies.

more finds himself overpowered. This game of ball, at the expense of the poor devil, may be prolonged, his fury becoming progressively stronger. Each of the *nagspas,* then, must look out for his own safety, for he who cannot master the invisible spirit will become its victim. It is rare, however, for things to take a tragic turn in performances of this kind, as in other more occult affairs which sometimes bring madness and death to those who attempt them.

Usually the peregrinations of the evil spirit only serve as a pretext for each of the wizards and his assistants to sojourn in the house of his credulous client and feast at his expense.

Certain objects, having being used for magic rites, must not, according to the popular belief, be kept in the houses of the laity or the non-initiate lamas, for fear that the beings who have been subjugated by means of them may revenge themselves upon their present owner, if he does not know the way to overpower them. To this belief I owe the possession of several interesting objects in my collection. People who received magic implements through inheritance have often entreated me to take these too dangerous legacies from them.

One day a gift came to me in a manner queer enough to be worth relating. In the course of a journey I fell in with a little caravan of lamas, and, conversing with them, as is customary on such travels, where encounters are rare, I learned that they were transporting a *phurba* (a magic dagger) which had become a cause of misfortune.

This ritualistic weapon had belonged to their head lama, recently deceased. It had begun its misdeeds in the monastery itself. Of three monks who had touched it, two were dead, and the third had broken his leg falling from his horse. The high pole of one of the large benediction banners suddenly fell, and this was an ominous portent. Terrified, yet not daring to destroy the *phurba,* for fear of yet greater misfortune, they had deposited it in a box, whence, soon afterwards, lugubrious and threatening sounds were heard to issue. Finally they had decided to lay the dread object in a lonely cavern dedicated to some divinity. But the cowmen living in the district had opposed this. They recalled the story of a *phurba*, which (though when and where nobody knew) had, under similar conditions, begun to wander through the air, wounding and killing many men and beasts.

The unhappy bearers of the magic dagger, which lay, wrapped up in papers with charms written upon them in a carefully sealed box, appeared very sad. Their discomfited countenances forbade my rallying them, and I was, moreover, very anxious to see the evil implement.

"Let me look at the *phurba*," I said. "I may be able to find a means of helping you."

They dared not break the seals and let it free, lest it escape; but finally, after a lengthy argument, they allowed me to take it out myself.

It was an ancient and very interesting specimen. Only the great monasteries own *phurbas* of this kind. Envy was aroused in my breast; I wanted it badly, but I knew that nothing in the world would induce the lamas to sell it. I must reflect a little and think out a way.

"Camp with us this evening," I said to the travellers, "and leave the *phurba* with me; I will look after it."

My words promised nothing, but the attraction of a good supper and a gossip with my people, who would distract them from their worries, decided them to accept.

When night fell I went some distance from the camp, openly carrying away the dagger, the presence of which, out of its case, while I was not amongst them, would have terrorized the credulous Thibetans. When I judged that I had gone far enough, I stuck the cause of the trouble upright in the ground and sat down on a blanket to think out how I could persuade them to give it up to me.

I had been there for several hours when it seemed to me as if the form of a lama arose near where I had fixed the magic dagger. I saw it advance, stooping cautiously. One hand came slowly forth from beneath the *zen* which enveloped him, and appeared in the indistinct light to grope for the *phurba*. With a single bound, quicker than the thief, I reached it and dragged it out of the ground. So I was not alone in desiring the mischievous implement! Among my chance companions there was some one, less simple than the rest, who knew its value and wanted to sell it secretly. He had believed me asleep. He thought I would perceive nothing, and next morning the disappearance of the dagger would be attributed to some occult influence, and a new story would be the result. It was really a pity that such a fine plan should not succeed. But I had secured the magic weapon, and held it so firmly in my closed hand that my excited nerves and the pressure of my flesh on the rough surface of its worked copper handle gave me the impression that it was moving slightly. And now for the thief?

All around me the immense tableland was empty. No doubt the marauder had been able to effect his escape whilst I was stooping to snatch the dagger from the earth.

I ran to the camp. It was quite simple. The one who was missing, or who came in after me, would be the thief. I found them all awake and chanting religious formulas to protect themselves against the powers of evil. I called Yongden to my tent. "Which of them has been absent?" I asked him. "No one," he replied. "They are half dead with fright, and I had to be angry with them because they would not go far away enough to perform certain acts!"

Strange indeed! I had been dim-sighted, deceived by an illusion. It was not common with me; but no matter, this perhaps would serve my purpose.

"Listen," I said to the men; "this is what has just happened. . . ." And I told them frankly of the vision I had had, and my doubts of their honesty.

"It is our Grand Lama. Undoubtedly it is our Grand Lama!" they exclaimed. "He wanted to take back his dagger and perhaps he would have killed you if he had been able to get it. Oh, Jetsunma, you are a true *gömchenma*, even though you are a *philing*. Our *Tsawai Lama* was a mighty magician, and yet he could not take his *phurba* away from you. Keep it now, keep it. It will no longer harm anybody!"

They were all talking at once, excited and terrified at the

thought that their lama-magician, more dreaded than ever, since he belonged to another world, had passed so close to them. Yet they were overjoyed at being rid of the enchanted dagger.

I shared their joy, but from another cause. The *phurba* was mine. Nevertheless, honesty forbade my taking advantage of their emotion to appropriate it. "Reflect," I said to them; "perhaps a shadow was responsible for the vision. . . . I may have been asleep and dreaming."

They would not hear of this. The lama had appeared. I had seen him. He had not been able to take back his *phurba*, and, by my superior power, I became its rightful owner. . . . I must own that I allowed myself to be easily convinced.

After leaving Samye I crossed the Brahmaputra near Tsetang, where the valleys of the Yanlung open out. This country is famous for the number of its places of pilgrimage. As to its physical aspect, it is pleasant and fertile, with nothing of the majesty of the forest of the Po *yul*, the Land of Grass, or the bleak tablelands near the Himâlayas. Its inhabitants take agriculture much more to heart than do those of the other provinces of Thibet. Well-built houses are to be seen in large numbers everywhere, and the people appear to be in a rather flourishing situation.

The charm of the mild climate and the fertile ground of the Yarlung valleys have been known for centuries, and the first kings of Thibet, long before Buddhism, under its lamaist disguise, spread through the country, had chosen it for their residence.

Like a conscientious pilgrim, I visited the celebrated *Nes sum, Ten sum*, six places of religious interest, amongst which is a cave—now enclosed in a monastery—where Reschungpa, one of the two foremost disciples of the great ascetic poet, Milarespa, lived for a time, practicing meditation. From there, I went to Tag chen Bumba, where there is a large *chörten* built over a smaller one. Two concentric apertures, one in each *chörten*, make it possible to see inside the smaller edifice, where, it is said, those whose minds are perfectly pure may discern countless lighted lamps, whilst, for ordinary mortals, there is but darkness.

I climbed the narrow staircase up to the opening and, gazing into it, began to reflect upon the symbol suggested by that inner *chörten,* yielding and refusing its radiance. I thought and thought and, somewhat forgetting where I was, remained longer than the average visitor, my forehead against the stone, as I gazed into the building. This was noticed, and the same evening, a *trapa* shyly asked me if I had seen many lamps!

Leaving Tag chen Bumba, I wandered in several directions across the country, in my hunt for books. Quite unexpected circumstances led me to discover, far out of the way, a lama who had inherited a fine library, and who, like many of his colleagues, did not care at all for literature or philosophy. I secured a good number of ancient and beautiful manuscripts from him.

The time had now come for me to decide upon my departure from Thibet. I looked toward China, whence I had come. I felt very tempted to turn eastward, and reach Yunnan by a new road. I could, had I so chosen, have left Thibet without anybody ever suspecting my arduous journey and my stay at Lhasa. But something made me feel that what I had done must be known. I obeyed this instinct and took the road to Gyantze, the town of southern Thibet which has become a British outpost.

On my way I saw the strangely shaped Yamdok Lake in which there is a peninsula with a small separate lake. Here I found the famous Sanding monastery, the residence of the high lady lama, *Dorjee Phagmo.* It was in a rather dilapidated condition.

Dorjee Phagmo (the diamond or most excellent sow) is considered a manifestation, under a human form, of a deity of the Buddhist Tantrik pantheon borrowed from India at a period when Buddhism had already completely degenerated, and primitive doctrine hardly existed any longer. Many are the legends about certain of the Sanding's abbesses, who in times of danger or in other peculiar circumstances show themselves in the form of a sow.

The reverend lady was not at Sanding when I was there. I had seen her at Lhasa and she had not yet returned from the capital.

I reached Gyantze at dusk and went straight to the bungalow. The first gentleman who saw me and heard a Thibetan woman addressing him in English was dumfounded. When he had recovered he explained to me that the bungalow's rooms were occupied and directed me to the fort, where the officials and a small garrison of Indian troops are quartered. My arrival there produced the same effect. When I said that I came from China, that for eight months I had wandered across unknown parts of Thibet, had spent two months at Lhasa and enjoyed in the Forbidden City all the New Year's festivities, no one could find a word to answer me. In any event, the gentlemen at the fort welcomed me most kindly and showed me the greatest hospitality, for which I shall ever remain thankful.

I had still before me the long, dreadfully cold road across the tablelands and blizzard-swept high passes, from Gyantze to the Thibeto-Indian border. But the adventure was ended, and alone in my room, I said to myself before closing my eyes in sleep:

"*Lha gyalo* [The gods have won]!"

The first white woman had entered forbidden Lhasa and shown the way. May others follow and open with loving hearts the gates of the wonderland, "*for the good, for the welfare of many,*" as the Buddhist Scriptures say.

THE END

Indomitable traveller, opera singer and anchorite, a onetime director of the Tunis Casino and the first Western woman to be granted an audience with the Dalai Lama — few women have shaped more fascinating lives for themselves than Alexandra David-Neel. She was born in Paris in 1868, the only child of an unhappy marriage, and constantly ran away from home. After studying eastern religions in Paris, she went to India and Ceylon, and thereafter toured the Far and Middle East and North Africa as an opera singer. In 1904 she married Philippe François Neel in Tunis: they separated almost immediately, but he financed many of her later travels and they wrote regularly to each other till his death in 1941.

In 1911, she left Paris for Northern India, where she subsequently graduated as a Lama, and spent a winter with her boy companion, Yongden, a Sikkimese lama, in a cave, dressed only in a cotton garment and studying Buddhist teaching. Later she spent three years in a Peking monastery. In 1923, having travelled with Yongden from Calcutta through Burma, Japan, Korea to Peking, covering nearly 5000 miles by mule, yak and horse across China into north-eastern Tibet, up into Mongolia and the Gobi, she arrived at the Mekong River. From here they set out, disguised as Tibetan pilgrims, for Lhasa. It is at this point that Alexandra David-Neel, in the liveliest of her many books, takes up her story, written in English and first published in 1927. It is one of the most remarkable of all travellers' tales.

In 1925, after fourteen years in Asia she returned to France, a celebrity. She was awarded many honours, including the *Grande Médaille d'Or* of *La Société de Géographie*. In 1936, with Yongden at her side, she went for the last time to Asia, staying eight years. A legend in her own time, she died just before her 101st birthday, in 1969.

DATE DUE

JA 4 '99			
ILL			
268042			
9/24/01			
ILL			
7504180			
7/4/02			
AP 6 '03			
JY 07 '03			
GAYLORD			PRINTED IN U.S.A